DESTRUCTION
AND
RESISTANCE

by Chaim Lazar

Second Printing

With a Preface by
Morris Chariton

Translated and Adapted from the Hebrew
by Galia Eden Barshop

Shengold Publishers, Inc.
in cooperation with
The Museum of Combatants and Partisans in Israel

By the same author

Destruction and Resistance / Hebrew, 1950
The Conquest of Jaffa / Hebrew, 1951
The Acre Fortress / Hebrew, 1953
The History of Aliyah Bet / Hebrew, 1958
Despite It All / Hebrew, 1959
                    English, 1985
Metzada Shel Varsha / Hebrew, 1963
Muranowska 7 / English, 1966
The Jewish Resistance / English, 1977
Testimony: From the Days of Destruction and Resistance /
    Hebrew, 1978

Second Printing

ISBN 0-88400-113-X
Library of Congress Catalog Card Number: 84-52354
Copyright © 1985 by Chaim Lazar

All rights reserved

Published by Shengold Publishers, Inc.
New York, N.Y.

Printed in the United States of America

Contents

Part One—The Ghetto

Part Two—The Forest

Preface

It is good to do a mitzva.

My lovely wife Carmie and I took our first trip to Israel in February 1970. At the suggestion of a close friend, perhaps my mentor, David Wdowinski, we stayed at a small hotel in Tel Aviv called The Savoy.

David Wdowinski was the co-founder, in 1925, of the Revisionist Movement in Poland. Later he was one of the leaders of the Z.Z.W., the Jewish Military Force, in the Warsaw Ghetto.

We chose this small hotel because it was one of the places Menachem Begin hid out during the Revolt.

Everything was new and exciting for us. My wife was amazed at how sociable and friendly I became in that environment, as if everyone was a potential friend with whom I shared something of interest.

Before leaving for Israel I had already decided that learning Hebrew was central for me, and I therefore registered at the main Ulpan on Park Avenue in New York City. Classes began on the Sunday after we returned, and were tremendously enjoyable, but I had fashioned myself a tough routine: run a business all week, study Hebrew almost every night, and four hours of classes every Sunday. The price was not long in manifesting itself: a strain on my relations with my wife and children.

Not long after this, Carmie and I planned our second trip to Israel for July 1970, and David Wdowinski made his arrangements for the end of April. It would be his seventh trip. He was 75 by this time, and had had a major heart attack some time previously. My wife and kids and I all went to the airport to see him off. El Al assembled all its passengers at the Orange terminal in Kennedy Airport, which is hard to find, and we arrived late. David was already on his way to the plane, and we missed him. But we thought we would see him on his return in three weeks' time, and laugh at our late arrival.

It was not to be. David suffered a heart attack in Tel Aviv and died there—as a matter of fact, on the shoulder of Chaim Lazar after giving a speech about the Holocaust at a reception in his honor. He was buried on the Mount of Olives in Jerusalem.

Before leaving for our July trip, a friend, Lottie Dannenberg, asked us to do a mitzva and deliver a radio to Chaim Lazar, a close friend of David's in Tel Aviv.

My enthusiasm for this trip had waned considerably after David's death. As my mother herself said, he was like a father to me. My own father, Leo Chariton, had suffered a major heart attack shortly after I entered the army in September 1944, and died in January 1956, six months after the birth of my eldest son, Lawrence.

Staying this time at the Ami Hotel in Tel Aviv, I called the Lazars to arrange to deliver the radio. The radio didn't seem to interest them particularly. People did.

We had a memorable evening that lasted until 2 am, when my wife insisted we return to our hotel, feeling that we were imposing. The next morning we drove to Jerusalem with Chaim Lazar, the author of this book. I call Chaim, fondly and in jest, "my one-arm bandit."

A few words about the loss of that arm. While blowing up a German troop-train making its way to the Russian front, one of Chaim's men pulled the cord too soon, and Chaim was seriously injured in his arm. The circumstances of the operation to remove the arm after their return to their base about forty-five miles away, must be read to be believed. A rusty saw was the instrument, which two doctors had tried to sterilize, and while the operation was taking place, there was sand constantly trickling in on them through the ceiling of the bunker. It's a miracle he survived.

When Chaim took us to the Mount of Olives to visit David's grave, I discovered that he had been buried back-to-back with Jabotinsky's biographer, Joseph B. Schechtman. They were both very close to Jabotinsky, both leading figures in Polish Revisionism.

In his biography, Schechtman describes Jabotinsky's early years in the Zionist movement. In 1906 he wrote an article called "Your New Year," in which he describes his new-found love for the Jewish people and Zionism. He talks of the Jewish custom in which a woman, upon her marriage, cuts off her hair, a symbol of her complete devotion to her husband, and draws an analogy with his own new-found devotion to the Jewish people—complete, all-consuming.

During the twenty years that I have known Chaim Lazar, I have found in him the same selfless devotion to the welfare of the Jewish people, their dignity, their meaningful survival. For me, this is the best of his ten or more books. This is him. . . He was there. . .

Our relationship began in July 1970, the result of a mitzva. For four years I did not see him again. Then Chaim came to New York in 1974 and we resumed our friendship, which has since deepened and broadened immeasurably. And it is getting stronger all the time.

Chaim's outstanding sense of humor has carried him through difficult times. One incident in 1974 comes to mind: on a visit to our home, his first request, made as he entered with a smile on his lips, was "Do you mind if I take my arm off?" He unscrewed it and put it in the closet.

I believe there is a vital message in this book, if only one is attuned to it. The vile things suffered by the Jews during that period must be made to serve some useful purpose: it must inspire us never to be a helpless minority again, dependent on the so-called mercy and good-will of other nations. Supporting Israel with our hearts and souls is in keeping with that aim.

Morris Chariton

At the Knesset (right to left): Dov Shilansky, Mr. and Mrs. Morris Chariton, Chaim Lazar.

At the opening of The Museum of Combatants and Partisans, Tel Aviv, April 4, 1976. Standing in front of the plan of the Warsaw Ghetto are Larry Chariton, formerly Natziv Betar in the United States, and Chaim Lazar.

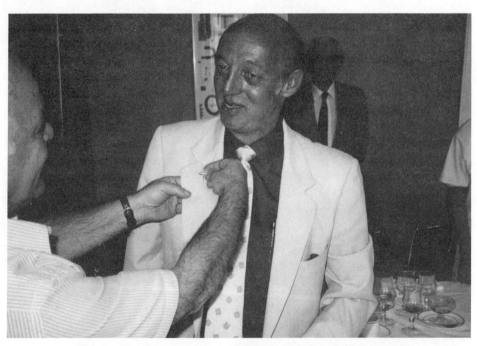

Morris Chariton receiving a pin of the Knesset from Dov Shilansky, Speaker of the Knesset, September 1989.

Introduction

This book chronicles the destruction of Jewish Vilna. Many readers, particularly those born after the Second World War, may be unfamiliar with Vilna's glorious past and, therefore, cannot fully appreciate the extent of the loss. Hence, this book properly begins with a glimpse of Vilna as it was.

Vilna was in many ways the quintessential Jewish Diaspora city, earning its title "Jerusalem of Lithuania." In terms of scope and depth of Jewish life, Vilna has never been surpassed.

Jewish settlement in Vilna dates from the 16th century. First known mention of a Jewish community in Vilna was in 1568. In 1573 the first synagogue was built, and in 1633 Jews were given a charter allowing them to live in the city and work in all fields of trade and craft.

In the middle of the 17th century Vilna became a center for Torah learning. In the 18th century the illustrious Gaon of Vilna, Rabbi Eliahu Ben Shlomo Zalman, became the symbol and pride of Vilna. His disciples developed a form of study stressing discipline and accuracy. From this tradition grew what has come to be known as the "Litvak" personality: a combination of will-power and devotion to principle.

After the "Haskala" (Enlightenment), this energy began to be channelled in new directions. Printing houses were established, which published books on all kinds of subjects, secular as well as religious. The famous Straszun Library was built, the richest public collection of Jewish books in possession of Eastern European Jews. Schools, seminaries, and yeshivas were set up throughout the city.

Zionism took strong root in Vilna. The first conference of the "Hovevei Zion" movement was held there in 1889; in 1902 the religious Zionist movement "Hamizrachi" held its founding conference in Vilna; and in 1903 Herzl, himself, visited the city. So prominent was Vilna in the Zionist world that in 1905 it became the seat of the Central Office of Russian Zionists.

Vilna was the birthplace of the Russian labor movement. Its first labor leaders, Aaron Liberman and Aaron Zundelevich devoted themselves to the general Russian cause, but in 1897 an organization arose that addressed itself to the specific problems of the Jewish working masses, the "Bund." One of its mem-

7

bers, Hirsh Lekert, attempted to assassinate the Vilna governor for flogging Jewish and Polish workers in a May Day demonstration and was hanged—a martyr to the Revolution.

Awareness of the dignity and needs of the Jewish masses led to the development of Yiddish secular culture and education. The YIVO Institute for Jewish Research was established, the PEN Club, and the "Young Vilna" writers group. Vilna was the home of writer Chaim Grade, sculptor Mark Antokolski, violin virtuoso Jascha Heifetz, and many other luminaries.

But the very core of Vilna was the poor Jewish worker—the tailor, shoemaker, drayman, furrier, etc., struggling to make ends meet. Many emigrated to America, South Africa, Israel and other places, where under favorable conditions they could exercise their initiative and make new lives for themselves. However, thousands remained and dreamed of Redemption—until Hitler's soldiers put an end to their dreams.

It is to the memory of these people that I dedicate the English edition of my book *Destruction and Resistance*. Blessed be their memory.

Part One
The Ghetto

Dawn of Disaster

Early spring 1941. The winter was dying, fighting for its life. Banks of clouds vied with the rays of the springtime sun, and these, in turn, strove to pierce the gray cover blanketing the heavens and outline the whitening mountain ridges in gold. Along the Cross and Fort foothills, one could already see strips of green, the handiwork of spring as it wove its colorful carpet over the earth. The trees in the Bernardine and Telatnik parks were awakening from their winter sleep, and their branches, their tips held high, met the caressing sun before bursting into bloom. The brisk Vilenka River, always on the move, was swollen with the melting snows, carrying them swiftly to the Viliya River. The scent of the forests fringing the city permeated every lane and filled every house, arousing the muted senses and inviting the universe to come alive.

The people of Vilna celebrated the coming of spring. The guest houses and entertainment spots were crowded. The streets and public parks teemed with men, women, and children, young and old, dressed in their holiday best. The city squares remained lively past midnight.

The Red Army band filled the air with lusty melody. People attended rallies staged by the working class. Workers and Communist youths marched jauntily in parades.

This atmosphere of celebration belied the underlying fear and unrest.

The residents of Vilna were as if in the grips of a fever. Their way of life had been drastically altered a year before, when the Communists took control of Lithuania and instituted their regime. Age-old traditions had crumbled.

Now war was at their doorsteps. The Soviet Communists were openly talking about the outbreak of hostilities, but the people chose not to believe them.

No one wished to think about the morrow. Everyone grasped at the immediate pleasures of life in an atmosphere of "eat, drink, and be merry, for tomorrow we may die."

A sudden epidemic hit the city. Rumor had it that German agents had poisoned the wells. The hospitals were filled with thousands of the stricken; the doctors were at a loss. Scores of coffins wended their way to the cemetery every day.

On June 12, fear became a reality: the local police and their secret agents in the NKVD arrested property owners, Zionist stalwarts, and anyone else slightly tainted with counterrevolutionary inclinations. The arrested were taken out of the city. People were ordered out of their beds at night or yanked off their jobs. They were taken in cars to the railroad station, put aboard in large contingents, and shipped out eastward.

Jewish homes went into mourning for the arrested, as if they were already dead. The roundup lasted three days. Rumor had it that the roundups would be resumed in a week, after the NKVD had sufficient time to draw up fresh lists.

Despite all the indications of pending doom, disaster struck unexpectedly, like a thunderclap. People simply could not believe that behind their doors lurked the Angel of Death, scythe poised.

Vilna got its first taste of bombardment on Sunday, June 22. The city went berserk. People ran about without reason or purpose. All eyes bulged with fear. The rumors grew wilder: Green Bridge was littered with corpses, and no one gave them more than a fleeting glance . . . the railroad station was in shambles . . . a large bomb had scored a direct hit on an apartment house on Poholenka Street, demolishing it and burying its occupants . . . an incendiary bomb had ignited one end of Ponarska Street, and the flames quickly spread to the other end . . . the Red Army had crossed the border and was moving swiftly into enemy territory . . . many Nazi planes had been shot down . . . Hitler was promising that in less than two weeks' time he would address his people from Moscow's Red Square . . . Vilna's mayor had fled the city.

The rumors set everyone's nerves on edge. No one was capable of clear thought. The people lived in a nightmare, eager for morning just to see what the next day would bring.

Jews did make an effort to think. They stood on the corners and talked about what might be done. Stories about assaults kept mounting: a Jew had been beaten to death. Jewish women standing in line at food stores had been pushed out by the others. Jewish stores were being pillaged. A Jewish child had disappeared.

On the fighting front, the Germans were already in Kovno (Kaunas). Grodno had fallen. Nazi planes bombed Minsk. A train carrying hundreds of fleeing Jews had been blown up. The Lithuanians were putting together a new, pro-Nazi government. The Poles were threatening to "square accounts" with the Jews.

Everyone was stricken with fear. Mothers bewailed their missing sons; they had either been aboard a blasted train or had fallen into Lithuanian or Polish hands.

During the night there was heavy shooting by the Lithuanians at the retreating Russians. Eleven Russian corpses were counted on Troki Street. The Russians put up a strong fight, until they were finally overcome. The civilians sat in their homes, waiting. No one had the slightest idea of what would happen next.

On Monday night Lithuanian students wearing swastika armbands staged a parade. Their faces were distorted with savage hatred as they scoured the streets for stray Jews.

Hundreds of young Jews headed for the outskirts of the city, intending to press on eastward. The trains were no longer running. Most of the refugees were forced to go back. The roads were blocked by the disorderly retreat of the Red Army. Vehicles and discarded arms lined the roads. The soldiers, their faces streaked with dust, were utterly exhausted.

The first column of German tanks rolled into Vilna on Tuesday morning, from the direction of conquered Grodno. Their arrival was cheered by the Lithuanians, particularly the students. Flowers were showered on the steel monsters. The swastika was flown along with the Lithuanian colors.

Next came the decrees. The Jews were ordered to surrender their vehicles, bicycles included. They were not to walk on the sidewalks. Eighteen main streets were closed to them. They could buy food only during specified hours and stand in separate lines. They were under curfew from 3:00 in the afternoon until 10:00 the next morning. They were to keep away from the non-Jews. They were to report daily for forced labor.

The penalty for any violation of these decrees was death.

The Germans took hostages: the leaders of the community, headed by Dr. Wygodzki. They were put into Lukiszki prison. At that time, no one imagined that they would never return.

The Kidnappers

From the day that the Jews had to surrender their radios to the authorities, contact was virtually severed with the outside world. The only channel was the daily press, which kept announcing, in bold print, the brilliant victories of the Wehrmacht. The inside pages were devoted to venomous diatribes against the Jews, the Russians, and the Western powers.

A Jew living in my courtyard, Eliezer Schuster, did not turn his radio in. Every night we gathered in his home to listen to news from abroad. We listened but drew no comfort from what we heard; it only depressed us.

The Judenrat, approved by the German Military Governor, was located on Straszun Street. Early each morning hundreds of Jews gathered there. The Germans looked them over and took them away to forced labor. If the employer was a "good" German, the laborer could bless his good fortune; he might yet come home after work with a crust of bread or a tin of preserves, which the German threw at him as he would to his dog. But pity those who worked for a "bad" German.

At night the workers came back with stories: "Today the Germans ordered us to race each other while we carried sacks weighing a hundred kilos each. Anyone tripping and falling was brutally beaten unconscious as he lay on the ground." Or, "today the Germans made us climb a steep hill while we carried large stones. When we fell to the ground, they unleashed their dogs at us. The dogs lacerated our arms, yet we weren't allowed to defend ourselves, even if we had the strength for it." The speaker opened his shirt and showed us the clawed, raw flesh.

"Today we unloaded railway cars. The German overseer thought he saw one of us, a young fellow, make a suspicious move. The German drew out his pistol and shot him dead. We were ordered to throw the corpse on a pile of garbage and then go one with our work. Later the overseer told us to bury the body. All this was witnessed by the victim's father."

"Today the Germans brought to our work site several pretty Jewish girls and ordered them to clean the latrines with their hands. One of them asked for work tools. The Germans gave her a plate and a spoon, and ordered her to eat the feces. After this degrading act, they made it clear that any girl 'acting up' in this manner would be punished in the same fashion."

Jews working for the Germans were given a corroborating document, the *Schein*, intended to shield the bearer from calamity. Everyone was bent on getting one. Since there were several kinds of *Schein*s—square, round, or rectangular—people argued as to their relative merits. Also, some were issued by the military and others by the civilian authorities. Each worker was convinced that his *Schein* had the most miraculous powers of salvation.

The abductions began. The kidnappers, known as *hapuness* (grabbers), were mainly Lithuanian policemen or plain Gentile folks who rounded up the Jews they caught and dragged them off to unknown destinations.

These abductions, once confined to the streets, were now conducted inside the homes of the victims. A sharp rap on the door, and the invaders would break into the house and take away the males, removing also any of the household furnishings that pleased their fancy. The women and children were thrust into the courtyard, and the home was "sealed."

The brutality of the Lithuanian police was beyond description. Their Jew-hatred had become good business. Reportedly they received bounty for every Jew they turned in. There was no risk involved; it was common knowledge that the Jews would not fight back. Easy money. As for the *Schein*s, they were torn up on the spot.

A day in July. Hundreds of Jews were milling about the yard of the Judenrat building, waiting for the Germans to come and take them to work. Suddenly the yard was encircled by Lithuanian policemen. The waiting men were hauled off to Lukiszki. Once there, they were grouped in two or three hundred and marched along Legionowa Street and out of the city, in the direction of Ponar Forest. The men were sure that the Germans had a large labor camp in that area. The women who tried to accompany their kin were stopped at the city limits and forced to return.

But something bothered the men. The Germans were known for their thoroughness. Why then were they taking along the elderly and the invalids, men of whom no employer would be proud? What did the Germans expect to achieve with such manpower?

Yellow patches had to be sewn on to the clothes, one in front and the other in back. The patch was searing to the touch. You'd think that people would stay home rather than wear the yellow stigma in public. The patch was a blot on the human conscience, the tombstone on the grave of civilization. But let the world be ashamed, we thought. We shall wear it with pride.

Josef Glazman, commander of Betar in Vilna, leader of the F.P.O., chief-of-staff on the Jewish partisan camp "Vengeance" in the Narocz Forest.

Josef Glazman

One day I ran into Shimon Rosenfeld, a young man who had escaped from Wohlynia to Lithuania in 1939. I hadn't seen him for more than a year. His trousers were torn, and his shirt was ragged. Hunger marked his face.

Several weeks earlier, he told me, the Russians had arrested him on charges of being a Betarist*. He was held in Lukiszki and interrogated for hours on end.

*Betar—the youth organization of the Zionist Revisionist movement, organized in 1925 by Ze'ev Jabotinsky.

The day before the outbreak of the war, he was taken from the prison to the railway station and put into a boxcar together with scores of other men, to be deported to Siberia, but the Russians were not geared for the operation. The boxcar remained on the siding, heavily guarded. When the Luftwaffe flew over Vilna, one of its first targets was the railway station. Bombs were coming down on all sides, and the men in the car were sure that death would cheat the Russians of their prey.

Two days later the area fell silent. Suddenly the men had a feeling that they were no longer under guard. They broke the door open and fled. Shimon went to stay with a man he had met in the boxcar, on the Street of the Glaziers. He now mentioned to me that Josef Glazman was in Vilna. I was surprised. I hadn't seen Josef for a long time, nor had I received any word from or about him. I decided to visit him at once.

Josef was staying with the Daichess family on Rudnicka Street. There I met, for the first time, Paula Daichess, pretty and vivacious with her round face, golden hair, and sparkling eyes. She was optimistic about the future. How was she to know that she would not only miss the Redemption but would not even live long enough to see her people being liquidated?

I found Josef in a dark, introspective mood. He had dedicated the past years to

Paula Daichess, leader in the Betar youth.

the rescue of Jews, helping many of them find their way to the Land of Israel. But he did not save himself. Now, as a leading figure in the Betar movement, he was constantly being sought by the Lithuanian police. The approaching Holocaust was doing away with all his plans. He had no thought of escape—not when his comrades were in danger. Right now, he was formulating new plans, which he would not disclose until the situation would become stable enough to indicate which way the winds were blowing.

One day Shimon Rosenfeld came to me. His body was covered with welts and bruises. Two days earlier, he and other Jews were rounded up by the Lithuanians and taken to Lukiszki. At the entrance to the prison, they were forced to run the gauntlet of two rows of Lithuanians armed with iron bars and rubber truncheons. They beat the Jews passing through mercilessly. Any Jew who fell was finished off on the spot. This was repeated at various points through the prison compound to the cells. The congestion was such that moving about was impossible. The men's animal needs had to be attended to right then and there. The air was suffocating.

From time to time the Lithuanians came in, demanding money and gold. When the loot was insufficient, they beat those closest to the door. The victims tried to move out of range, but succeeded only in crowding the others even more. Men actually trampled one another.

At dawn the prisoners were taken out to a spacious courtyard and ordered to mount trucks waiting to take them away. Suddenly a luxurious car drew up. A German came out and proceeded to read names from a list in his hand. Those who responded were set aside in a separate group. When one of those called did not reply, Shimon instinctively responded in his stead. Several minutes later the German rounded up all "his" Jews in Lukiszki to work for him.

Shimon was glad to evade the fate in store for him. Little did he realize that the respite would be short.

The Rise of Violence

I visited Paula and Josef daily. She was always smiling, eyes bright. It was comforting to be in her presence in those calamitous days. Somehow her smile made one forget the grief and the insults.

This time I found Josef lost in thought. "Jews are going to Rzesza to work," he finally said. "I think I'll go there. It makes no sense to risk your life foolishly before we do something practical and see how it develops. In Rzesza the chances for weathering the first period should be better. Before we take action we must know more about the intentions of the Germans. *Then* we can act."

He urged me to accompany him to Rzesza. "Go ahead, fellows," said Paula. "I will come to visit you."

A period of murder and violence began.

On Nowogrodzka Street a German shot a young Jew to death. He ordered the body buried in the patch of earth in front of his house. When he learned that the murdered man had a wife and a child, he went in and apologized to the widow. Later he brought her cigarettes and preserves. The Jews, forgetting what he had done, said he was a good German.

In Sznipiszki the Germans staged a pogrom. All the Torah scrolls and sacred vessels were taken from the synagogue, thrown on a pile in the central square, and set afire. The rabbi and scores of lay scholars were forced to dance around the bonfire and sing Soviet songs.

The violence centered on Nowogrodzka Street. Pillage and murder were rampant. Usually there was no trouble in this quarter, for here and in the adjacent alleys lived the "tough" Jews: draymen, porters, meat dealers, abattoir workers. The Polish Endeks never dared anger them, having felt their muscle. Now the Germans broke in and devastated the area. Blood covered the floors and walks, and no attempt was made to resist!

One morning a tumult was heard in the neighborhood. The men at once hid themselves, and the women stood where they could warn their husbands. Cars and German soldiers entered the area. It turned out that the Germans were on a "culture spree": they broke into the famous Straszun Library, removing thousands of books, manuscripts, and rare editions—the literary and cultural wealth accumulated over the centuries. The rest was set afire.

The episode gave the Jews a brief respite, even the hope that the Germans might vent their vindictiveness on the library. The hearts of the people were heavy at the sight of the catastrophe, but they reasoned that if the Jews survived, their cultural treasures would not be lost. No one seemed to think that the destruction of the library was but a prelude. By reducing the Jew to the mental status of cattle in the field, the Nazis hoped to lead the Jews to slaughter, submissive and beaten.

Rumor now had it that the Germans were about to round up Vilna's Jews and place them in a ghetto. No one had a clear idea what ghetto life was like, but everyone talked about the new decree in a tone of fear and trepidation. There was speculation as to the location of the new entity. Streets were mentioned: Sznipiszki, Nowogrodzka, Stefanska. It was reported that in the Gentile district, the Germans and Lithuanians were clearing the houses of their non-Jewish occupants to prepare the area for the ghetto. No one imagined that the ghetto would be resurrected in the same congested alleys of the medieval Jewish Pale. Certainly all the Jews in Vilna could not be contained in the few streets and alleys. How would the Germans manage the situation?

In the courtyard of the Judenrat building, Jews were milling around one young man, a refugee from Poland, who had arrived in Vilna in 1939. He said that several days before the outbreak of the war, he had received a letter from his parents, who lived in the Warsaw ghetto, and they had written that the living conditions in the ghetto were not so bad. They were working for the Germans and were earning enough to live on. The young man displayed a picture of his family which accompanied the letter. They looked well. They were smiling and well dressed. The only thing in the picture which bore evidence of the ghetto was the white band with the Jewish star, which each of them wore on his sleeve. "If only I could get to them," said the lad, "I would be safe."

The Jews listened and consoled themselves. "So one can get along in the ghetto after all." They were filled with hope and each went his own way.

One day I met T. Lutkiewicz, a Polish fellow-worker of mine before the war. The meeting made us both very happy. The next day he came to visit me. He brought brandy and began relating the following story: During the first few days after the outbreak of the war, he came across a group of German officers. At midnight, after they had drunk themselves to oblivion, a German colonel declared that Germany would lose the war since Hitler had made a serious mistake by entering into war against Russia. If Hitler had invaded Britain, he would have been victorious, but the attack on Russia had sealed his fate. That, added the German, was the opinion of high-ranking officials in Germany, but because of the terror of the Gestapo, no one dared to say so aloud.

Lutkiewicz, too, was of this opinion. But he did not think that the Jews would live to see Hitler's downfall. The war would continue for many years, and meanwhile the Germans would be able to annihilate all the Jews. He could not give me any practical advice, but he said that I must be very careful, for there were hard times ahead of us.

He described the awful slaughters perpetrated by the Lithuanians against the Jews in the cities and the towns. Already, he said, there were dozens of towns without a single Jew left. And we were only in the first month of the war. . . .

I met a young woman from Deutscheshe (Niemiecka) Street. She told me that the previous day she had listened to Radio Moscow. The German forces were being routed along the whole front and the Red Army was making rapid advances.

She was filled with hope. She had a brother in Moscow, an officer in the Red Army. Her second brother left Vilna the day the war broke out, and he, too, was no doubt serving in the Red Army. She had to remain behind to take care of her sick mother, but she was not worried. Soon her brothers would return, crowned with victory, and then the Germans would pay for their cruelty toward the Jews. . . .

She was burning with the desire for vengeance. Was the flame still burning when she stood on the edge of the pit at Ponar?

"The Great Provocation"

On August 5 I heard that a group of fifty Jews was about to leave for agricultural work on the estate of Count Tyszkiewicz, fifteen kilometers from Vilna. I decided to join them. The people gathered in the courtyard of the Judenrat building and made preparations to leave.

Suddenly there was a big commotion. One of the members of the Judenrat, Langbert, entered excitedly and announced that the Germans were demanding a sum of five million rubles by the following morning. If the money was not delivered on time, a calamity would befall the Vilna community.

Everyone was seized with fear. It was obvious that, despite all efforts, it would be impossible to collect the sum demanded. From 3:00 P.M. on, Jews were not allowed on the streets.

The task was, nevertheless, immediately undertaken. The members of the group which was about to leave for the estate were the first to go around collecting. The next day the members of the Judenrat appeared before the Germans with only three million rubles and this sum already included jewelry and silverware. As punishment for the nonfulfillment of the order, the Germans executed several prominent Jews who had been held hostage.

We set out for the estate accompanied by a peasant who came to fetch us. The road passed through Ponar Forest. Jews working in the outskirts of the city could not believe their eyes. They were used to seeing hundreds of beaten and downtrodden Jews along this route every day, dragging their feet with the last of their strength, accompanied by a large guard of Germans and Lithuanians. Now they saw several dozen healthy Jews walking with powerful strides along the same route, without a guard. . . .

For the first time since the outbreak of the war, we found ourselves in the heart of nature. We filled our lungs with the air of the fields and forests. Our eyes devoured the beautiful landscape of the Vilna environs. It seemed as if we had not enjoyed the splendor of a Lithuanian summer for ages. Nature, too, seemed happy to see us. The world was so beautiful and good; the sun was so bright and caressing. If only there were no human corruption!

Echoes of shots reached us from the depths of the forest. We did not pay any

attention. Near the estate we met a non-Jew. He told us that that day the Lithuanians had killed four hundred Jews in the forest. "Don't you hear the shots? They
murder people like this everyday." We looked at him incredulously. Was he
mocking us or did he want to scare us? He was probably a madman or a mere
chatterbox.

The non-Jew saw that we did not believe him. He shook his head at us and
continued on his way. We worked in the fields bordering Ponar. Every day we
heard shots from within the forest. The peasants said that Jews brought from Vilna
were being killed there, but none of us believed them. News reaching us from the
city reported that occasional messages were received from the abducted people and
everyone was convinced that they were employed somewhere.

German army units sometimes camped on the Tyszkiewicz estate on their
way to the front. One middle-aged German told us that before the war he was a
Social-Democrat, but that he was forced to register as a member of the Nazi Party
to receive a business permit, since he had a wife and two children to support.
Hitler, he said dejectedly, promised that they would be in Moscow within two
weeks, but more than two months had gone by. Now, they were told, the German
Army was 40 kilometers from Moscow and was preparing to give the Russians the
knock-out blow and return home. He asked us if we knew anything about the
situation on the fronts and whether it was true that he would return home soon.

September 2. This was the second day that continuous shooting was heard
from Ponar. The peasants were saying that thousands of Jews were brought there,
including women and children, and were being shot. Naturally, we did not believe
them. It was just like anti-Semitic peasants to try to bring our spirits down!

That same day, three of us went into the woods to chop down trees for posts.
Near a brook we encountered several Gypsy families. The oldest Gypsy, whose
face was deeply lined and whose beard was flecked with gray, sat near a campfire
while the family members prepared the meal.

We started a conversation with him. Hearing that we were Jews, his face
became sad and he shook his head slowly. He said: "You are going through hard
times. Don't you hear the shots? They are shooting your parents, brothers, and
sisters. You are mistaken if you think that the work you are doing will save you.
The Germans will find you everywhere. There is no escaping them. I do not envy
the non-Jewish city-dwellers either. They are forced to witness the horrible acts
done to you and are powerless to help. They, too, groan under the heavy yoke of
the Germans. Only we, the Gypsies, have it good. All the earth is ours. If we do not
like one place, we go to another. Nothing binds us to one particular place. I do not
know how people can spend their whole lives in one place. We Gypsies are the
only ones who really enjoy life. By wandering we have the possibility of getting to

know God's creation and enjoying the beauty of the world. We have no property and do not need it. This is the secret of our freedom. We are not slaves of property. We are happy in our lot and are free as the birds in the sky.''

He continued to elaborate on the world-view of the Gypsy, not knowing that the cup would overflow and that his people, too, would be hunted down by the Germans and annihilated.

The shots continued for three days. At dawn of September 4, we still heard solitary shots from the direction of Ponar.

We heard that the Germans had spread rumors that a German soldier had been murdered in the Jewish streets. The army and police forces surrounded the narrow streets and took away more than 4,000 people. For the first time, women and children were also taken to Ponar.

The Vilna Jews were convinced that they were going to be taken outside the city to a detention camp or a labor camp. They called this "action" the "great provocation."

Several days later, they learned the objective of the "action": the Germans wanted to clear out the narrow streets to set up a Jewish ghetto.

"Days of Awe"

Saturday, September 6. From the early morning hours, the sounds of engines filled the streets. Dozens of cars of the German Army, Gestapo, and Lithuanian Police streamed towards the mainly Jewish-inhabited lanes and streets. Every house was surrounded by strong guards.

An order was given. Within thirty minutes all the Jews had to leave their homes and go to the ghetto set up in the narrow streets, the same area where Jews were confined during the Middle Ages. It was forbidden to bring into the ghetto any gold or silver objects. One could take only packages that could be carried by hand or on the shoulders. It was forbidden to take more than 300 rubles.

The labor of generations was abandoned to the Polish and Lithuanian looters who stood ready to carry off the booty. Giddy with victory and craving for blood, they accompanied the pathetic procession of thousands of Jews groaning under their burdens and under the blows of the oppressors. When the caravan reached the gate of the ghetto, a great and bitter outcry was heard: an old, gray-haired Jew slumped to his knees and died. He was a symbol of what awaited the Jews in the ghetto.

Four kilometers from the estate where we worked was the town of Landwarowa. Every day several dozens of Landwarowa Jews came to the estate to work. They said that in their town, life was going on as usual. Though the situation couldn't be compared with what it had been before, not one incident of robbery or murder had occurred.

A young woman said that one night a Lithuanian policeman entered one of their homes and, cursing and threatening, took clothes and other household possessions. The next day she went to the German commandant of the town and complained to him. Two hours later all the pillaged goods were returned.

"We have good Germans in the town," the Jews said complacently. One day the Landwarowa Jews stopped coming to work. Several days passed until we learned that on the first day of Rosh Hashana, the Germans collected all the Jews of the town and brought them to an island in a lake near the town of Trakai. That same day they murdered all the Jews from the two towns. During the "action," two Jewish girls jumped into the lake and began swimming towards the forest on the bank. The Lithuanians let them get away a bit and then took bets among themselves as to who would score the best hit. They opened fire and two big red spots floated to the surface of the lake.

On the eve of Rosh Hashana we received permission to go to the bathhouse in the Vilna Ghetto. We were ten Jews, among the workers on the estate. This was the first time that we were in the ghetto. The narrow streets were humming with people—tortured Jews, struggling to survive. One had to wait in a long line until one's turn came to enter the bathhouse. By the time our turn came, there was no more water left.

During the long hours of waiting, the Jews told us about their life. Most of them had but one concern: making a living. The majority were without means, as they had not had the time to take many of their possessions with them into the ghetto. Everything was abandoned to the non-Jews, who continued to pillage Jewish property day and night. Winter was approaching and there was no shelter. The congestion in the ghetto was terrible. There was no air to breathe. Everyone was very worried about the fate of relatives who were abducted and imprisoned in Lukiszki or taken to Ponar. Their situation was, no doubt, much worse than that of the Jews in the ghetto, they sighed, because in Lukiszki and Ponar they lacked even the bare necessities the ghetto dwellers had.

They were not worried about their own lives. No one believed that they were in any danger.

We told them that we worked near Ponar and that all the Jews taken from Vilna were being shot. We did not even finish telling them our story and they were ready to lynch us. "How can Jews dare to spread such tales and create panic? As if there were not enough misfortune and worry, they had to come and add salt to our wounds. Well, we'll teach them good manners."

We felt ourselves in danger. With difficulty we managed to get away from them and get lost in the large crowd. For more than an hour, they searched for the "sowers of fear" to teach them a lesson.

I visited Emma, an acquaintance of mine from before the war. She was happy to see me. She had thought that I had been dead for some time. She was living in one room with several other families. Despite the tight quarters, the room had a festive air. The floor was clean, the table was covered with a white cloth, and two candles stood ready for lighting. The children were washed and groomed and were eagerly awaiting the Sabbath meal.

Emma was mourning her husband, who had been abducted by the Lithuanians. It was not easy to bear up alone with children, when it was so hard to make ends meet or obtain a *Schein*. She had heard that all the Jews would be taken from the ghetto and transferred to another place. Emma wanted to stay in Vilna, but she did not know what to do. If her mother in America only knew of her situation, she would, no doubt, move mountains in order to help her. She parted from me, in mute sadness. Did she know in her heart that we would never meet again?

Yom Kippur eve at the estate. Several people were going to the city again. They wanted to be among Jews to pray together. We remained on the estate.

At dusk we gathered in our attic room. An old Vilna Jew, a baker named Reznik, recited the *Kol Nidrei*. Before my eyes arose visions from the recent past.

Yom Kippur eve at home. Father, wearing a white *kittel** and wrapped in a prayer shawl, the prayer book under his arm, blesses the children before going to the synagogue. He calls us one by one into a side room, places his hands on our heads and says, "May the Lord bless thee and keep thee. May the Lord make thee as Efraim and Menashe" and ends his blessing with "Happy New Year." I already knew that my family was no longer alive, and a stream of tears ran down my cheeks. For hours the tears flowed. All the grief, depression, humiliation, and bitterness which weighed on my heart during the last few months found release in tears. But there was no comfort.

The day after Yom Kippur, Levin the tailor and his son returned from the city, the only two from the whole group who survived. Their appearance was frightening. They were shattered; their clothes were torn and they were utterly exhausted. They said that the synagogues were overflowing with people and that the Jews had entreated their Father in Heaven to redeem them from the cruel murderers and to inscribe them in the Book of Life. (Oh, how the Jews needed mercy then!) But as the time approached for the concluding prayer and it seemed that the heartrending

---

*A *kittel* is a white garment worn by Orthodox Jewish men on the High Holy Days and the first two days of Passover at the *seder*.—TRANS.

cries would annul the harsh sentence, the ghetto was surrounded by soldiers and policemen. Germans and Lithuanians broke in and began snatching Jews, loading them onto trucks and carrying them off to Ponar. There was terrible panic in the ghetto. Jews looked for hiding places. Parents ran around searching for their children whom they had lost during the uproar. For hours the rioters ran amok, cursing and carrying off thousands of Jews. So related the tailor and his son. That same day we also heard the thunder of shots from Ponar Forest.

Serenity

The rainy season had begun. The number of workers on the estate was diminishing. Several families had returned to the city, to the ghetto. They were sick of the loneliness and the hard work. They heard that people were ''getting along somehow'' in the ghetto and decided to return. Close to thirty people remained with us: men, women, and three children. After the work in the field was finished, we were worried about our fate, but the manager of the estate announced that we would continue to work there on internal jobs.

All the women and most of the men began working in the basements on potatoes. Once again we were spared the pain of hunger. Leaving work, we would filch some potatoes to cook in our rooms later.

Yehoshua Katz, a Jew who spent his whole life near Ponar, and I were selected to help the chief herdsman. The work in the cowshed was difficult, but had side benefits: we had a sufficient quantity of milk and a supplement to the bread ration. It was good to be with the mute animals when the whole world around was corrupt and bloodthirsty. There one could dream about a bright future. One could pour out one's bitterness before the cows, and it seemed as if they understood. I must admit that those months when I formed a friendship with the cows were the happiest period in my life since the outbreak of the war.

Our connection with the ghetto had been completely severed. From time to time came vague, insubstantial rumors which, however, could not update us on the real situation. Yet they were substantial enough to fill our hearts with fear for the fate of the Vilna Jews. After each bad rumor which reached us, more shots resounded from the direction of Ponar, and their echoes filled the void during long days and nights.

March 14, 1942. A clear frosty day. The road leading to Vilna was upholstered with pure snow which squeaked under foot. The brilliance of the sun's rays blended with the shining whiteness of the snow, spread over the earth like a beautiful mantle.

The day was so lovely, but my heart was filled with shadows. I never felt so lonely, so superfluous. I had no one left in the world. No relatives and no friends. I was wearing rags and my hair was long and wild. The small crust of bread which I carried was my only possession.

For several days and nights I hid on the estate, after escaping from the Lithuanians who carried off part of the Jewish workers. The past was bitter and the future was hazy and it seemed that the present did not exist at all. If I were killed, no one would shed a tear.

But it was impossible to remain on the estate. I would have died of hunger or fallen into the hands of the murderers lying in ambush for me. At daybreak I left the estate unnoticed. I walked unhurriedly, since no one awaited me in the ghetto.

On Sunday afternoon I arrived in the ghetto. It was a day of rest, and the Jews had not left for work. The narrow streets were buzzing with people discussing and arguing politics.

It was the third month since life in the ghetto had returned to "normal." There were no more "actions." The constant fear of being taken out of the ghetto to the terrifying unknown had passed. The main concern now was to hold on until better days.

Everyone was sure that better days would come and that they would live to see them. After all, hadn't the Germans promised that there would be no more "actions" and had the ghetto leaders not repeatedly reassured the Vilna Jews that they were in no danger? Had they not constantly preached work and patience?

That was the mood I found upon my return to Vilna. Many of my friends in the ghetto were surprised to see me.

Within days I became acclimatized, in no way different from a veteran resident of the ghetto.

*Yaakov Gens, chief of the
Vilna Judenrat.*

Underground

Once life in the ghetto took a definite course and the Jews began to reconcile themselves to their situation, the young people set about organizing themselves, according to their leanings. Anyone able to elude the roundups, but who was the sole survivor among his family and friends, felt the strong need to make contact with his comrades in the movement. These now became his family. It was easier to bear the cruel blows of fate when there were partners-in-suffering and companions with whom to consult to avoid misfortune.

Only a few gave serious thought to armed resistance. The reality was so stark that such daring plans were inconceivable. All that the ghetto inmates were concerned with was how to assure their survival, how to get hold of a *Schein* and protect themselves against abduction, to obtain housing and work and find bread or potatoes to keep body and soul together. Hence, the meetings were initially for the purpose of formulating action of mutual aid.

Young Betarists gathered in the home of Borka Schneider, 4 Rudnicka Street. They decided to organize the surviving youths. These remnants could be easily organized. After all, the Movement had been underground from the day the Red Army entered Vilna, and its activity had gone on, uninterrupted, during the entire year of the Russian occupation. The strong ties which kept the comrades together that year were now being put to the test.

Josef Glazman was in a labor camp in Rzesza, near Vilna, waiting for an opportune moment to launch rescue action, or, if such was the will of the Almighty, to avenge the bloodshed. He kept in close touch with his comrades in Vilna all the time he was in Rzesza. Paula Daichess met with him twice a week to bring him news from his comrades, and she returned much encouraged by what Josef had to tell her. She traveled the fourteen kilometers between Rzesza and Vilna on foot—to all intents, a Polish girl with blond braids, which gave her features a distinctly Aryan look. Always energetic, she never lost her merry mood. She never gave up the thought that, some day, she and the others would get to the Land of Israel, where she would visit the grave of her brother, Shloyme, tragically killed in an outbreak of internecine fighting in Herzliah. All these dreams perished when Polish women acquaintances came upon her on one of her journeys and denounced her to the Gestapo. The Germans executed her in short order.

When this contact was broken, Josef visited the ghetto; many of the Rzesza laborers went to their quarters in the ghetto after work. He met with his friends and assured them that soon he would be one among them in the ghetto. In the period between the actions against the "yellow *Schein*s", Josef settled in the ghetto and immediately began to implement his plans.

Following the "yellow *Schein*" roundups, during late October and early November 1941, Gens, the commander of the Jewish Ghetto Police, looked for ways to maintain order among the inmates, whose respect for the ghetto police was rather thin, to the point where orders were being ignored.

The head of the supplies department in the ghetto was Chaim Trapido, former manager of the Kovno *Jewish Voice*. He was one of the few senior members of the Ghetto Administration who did not have Jewish blood on his hands. He was to be of great help in the formation of the Underground inside the ghetto.

Trapido told Gens about Josef Glazman, describing him as a former Betar Commissioner for Lithuania, an extraordinarily talented young man with tremendous influence on the young. He urged Gens to summon Josef and entrust him with one of the more important roles in the administration of the ghetto. Gens agreed and offered Glazman the post of Deputy Commander of the Jewish Ghetto Police.

Josef was not enthused. He had other more urgent duties to perform. At that point, he was engulfed in reorganizing Betar along a regular program of activity—first and foremost, maintaining the physical well-being of the comrades, obtaining work for them, and providing hiding places for comrades without a *Schein*. Some groups formed a collective; they set out to work together, pooled their meager resources, and shared the food they bought. An exemplary group of ten was the "Decima Betaris," who found a place of work in the vegetable patches of Saltaniszki, outside the city. They returned to the ghetto late at night, their pants pockets crammed with vegetables. If they managed to elude the guards at the main gate, they distributed the vegetables among their hungry comrades.

One night, the group was caught by the Gestapo and searched. A few managed to break away and escape in the darkness. Four girls were taken to the Lukiszki prison. The comrades were stunned; any attempt to smuggle even a potato into the ghetto could end in death. After great effort and by dint of bribery, they were able to free the prisoners and return them to the ghetto—one of the few miracles that took place in those dark, gloomy days.

With Josef's arrival, the situation changed: thought was now being given to feeding the spirit as well. Basic principles were laid down for the organization of the Movement, according to the existing circumstances. There was practically no possibility for carrying on regular activity in the Underground. With twenty-five thousand Jews crowded into the narrow streets and twenty to thirty people living in one room, it was almost impossible to avoid overhearing their conversation. The activities of the Movement stood in sharp contradiction to the official policy of the leaders of the ghetto.

The first meetings took place in the street; after a while they were transferred to public institutions. Some of the comrades who were employed in these institutions would stay later at work, so that they would be the last ones out, which enabled them to take the keys. In the evening, they would return to open the door for their comrades.

At first, they organized in groups of three. After a while, they enlarged each cell to include five persons. Josef was in charge of the command which carried out this work; Borka Schneider was the secretary and all matters were concentrated in his hands. The command prepared detailed work programs in all areas, including the arranging of cultural and propaganda activities among the youth. They also saw to the organizing of a system of mutual aid and the stockpiling of weapons.

At the time, it was still alleged that Jews who were taken out of the ghetto were transported to work camps or to another ghetto, outside of Vilna. Rumors began spreading that someone even received regards from a relative who was snatched in one "action" or another. They even told of the Polish railroad worker who one day came to a woman, bringing with him a note from her husband, who was in a labor camp outside of Minsk, together with some thousands of Jews from Vilna. All of them were alive and well, the note read.

They started to look for the woman. Everyone wished to see the note with his own eyes, but, alas, no one knew who the fortunate woman was or where she lived. But this did not detract from the people's blind optimism; they simply refused to come to grips with the fact that Ponar had long since become one huge cemetery. And yet, there were a few who would not delude themselves. The first order of business, therefore, was to spread the bitter truth about Ponar among the youth so as to prepare them for what must be done.

Truth from Ponar

By that time, there were already several people who had managed to flee from the blood-soaked forest but their return was kept secret. The administrators ordered them not to tell anyone about their experiences, so as not to spread panic; they felt they could manage the masses better if the story remained unknown.

The testimonies of the survivors were noted down by Efroymchik, a worker in the legal department of the Judenrat. He was there when the survivors rendered their testimony. He later gave the notes to us. What follows is one of the many testimonies we have, given by a Vilna schoolteacher, Tema Katz, who was taken out of the ghetto in the first few days.

Late Saturday night, we finally entered the ghetto, and with our remaining strength, we reached the courtyard of 14 Straszun Street. The yard was full of people. It was drizzling, and everyone sought shelter for himself, his children, and relatives. I, my husband, son, and two daughters pushed into a crowded cellar and dozed off. We were awakened by a sudden noise. We went out, to see everyone packing his belongings, ready to leave. The Lithuanians were prodding them on. We took our bundles and joined the others, but were turned back at the city limits. As we crossed Deutscheshe Street, we were sure that they were taking us in the direction of Lukiszki. Along this street we saw groups of Jews under police escort. The streets were strewn with bundles and valises, discarded by refugees, which blocked the sidewalks. The gutters were clogged with pillows and bedding, thermos bottles, linens, and shoes. We saw figures huddled in the doorways; why, we didn't know. We saw their frightened eyes, but it was clear that they decided to remain and resist.

At the break of dawn, we saw groups of Jews coming from the

opposite direction and being driven into the ghetto. In Lukiszki, we were separated: my husband and son were sent to join the men. I and my daughters (Feiga, aged seventeen, and Minna, aged ten) remained with the women. The prison yard was full of Jews brought from Lidska, Makowa, and other streets. We had no idea what was awaiting us. We thought we would be taken back to the ghetto. We were kept outside for two days and then put into cells. We learned that the previous inmates had been sent to Ponar, but no one thought that all of them had been killed.

We remained there until Thursday. At 2:00 A.M. the prison square was suddenly illuminated with floodlights. We were put aboard trucks, fifty to sixty women in a truck. In each vehicle there were armed Lithuanian sentries. The trucks headed for Ponar.

We came to an area of wooded hillocks and were dumped among them. Still, the mind would not keep pace with reality. We were arranged in rows of ten and prodded toward some spot, from which came the sound of shooting. The Lithuanians then went back for more batches of people.

Suddenly, the truth hit us, like an electric shock. The women broke out in piteous pleas to the sentries, offering them rings and watches. Some fell to the ground and kissed the sentries' boots, others tore their hair and clothes—to no avail. The Lithuanians pushed one group after another to the site of the slaughter. By noon, when it became clear that there was no escaping this fate, the women fell into a kind of stupor, without any pleading or resistance. When their turn came, they went, hopelessly, to their death.

Suddenly, we saw a group of men. At their head was an aged rabbi, wrapped in his prayer shawl; passing us he called out "Comfort Ye, Comfort Ye, My People." We were seized with trembling. The women broke into moans, and even the Lithuanians took notice. One of the guards ran up and hit the rabbi with the butt of his rifle. My daughters and I were on the ground. Other women did not wait to be led away, but broke from the rows and went on. The rows were broken. The women sat down and waited for a miracle to halt the massacre. I had one thought in mind: to be among the last.

Our turn came at 5:30. The guards rounded up the remaining women. I felt my older daughter's hand in my own. . . . When I came to, I felt myself crushed by many bodies. Feet were treading on me, and the acrid smell of some chemical filled the air. I opened my eyes; a young man was sprinkling us with lime. I was lying in a huge common grave. I held my breath and strained my ears. Moans and sounds of dying people, and from above came the amused laughter of the Lithuanians. I wished myself dead, only not to hear the sounds. Nothing mattered. It did not dawn on me that I was unhurt.

A child was whimpering a short distance away. Nothing came from above. The Lithuanians were gone. The whimper aroused me from my stupor. I crawled toward the sound. I found a three-year-old girl, un-harmed. I knew that if I survived, it would be thanks to her.

I waited for darkness to fall; then, holding the child in my arms, I wriggled up to the surface and headed for the forest. Not far in the interior, I came upon five other women who had managed to survive. Our clothes were smeared with blood and burnt from the lime. Some of us had nothing but our underclothes on our skin.

We hid for two days, in the forest. A peasant came by and was frightened out of his senses. He let out a weird shriek and fled. But he was not decent enough to come back and help us. He was sure that we were ghosts from another world, bent on punishing the evil-doers.

Lyova Ziskovich, a Betar leader, member of the Headquarters of the F.P.O. after Glazman left the ghetto.

F.P.O.

One day, a book reached us, the single copy in the ghetto of Uri Zvi Greenberg's *Book of Indictment and Faith*. This book was a font of inspiration to us at our gatherings. The words of indictment seemed to have been penned, beforehand, against the ghetto leaders. From it we drew strength, faith, and confidence. Everything that was transpiring seemed to have association with some passage. We quoted it constantly in our call to the masses for revolt and resistance.

We were also inspired by Saul Tchernichovsky's *Baruch of Mayence* and Yaakov Cohen's *Songs of the Zealots*. These spurred the young people towards daring deeds.

> *The enemy increases the horror.*
> *We haven't the strength to endure*
> *Vicious murder by aliens,*
> *Ravaging our people's honor.*

Death is bitter, but less so
When the enemy dies.
Death is cold, but less so
When warmed by the blood of the foe.

The frequent gatherings helped the people overcome their abject living conditions. After a day of hard labor, insults, and beatings, half-starved we entered another world, far from harsh reality, from the yellow patch and the sword suspended overhead. We established a family relationship, a filial attachment, united by a common purpose: resistance and revenge.

The education program was conducted by Rivka Karpinkes, Niussa Lubotski, Yehudit Solonoitz, Borka Schneider, Molka Hazan, Mordechai Goldman, Moshe Brause, Lyova Ziskovich, and me. Each of us had several cells which convened twice weekly. We met with Josef every week.

We kept busy and had reason to be gratified. Our ideology was gaining support. New cells were being formed. The Organization was striking ever-deeper roots. We were happy not to be part of the "golden youth"—young people who refused to believe that evil would ever overtake them.

The first mass convention in the ghetto was held on Chanukka, 1941. For the first time, Josef met with scores of Betarists. For the first time, these young people heard an intense call not to yield to fate, not to accept annihilation. For the first time, they heard Hebrew songs in the Hebrew language resounding in their ears. At first, they seemed like echoes of a bygone age. But the song of rebellion was slowly replacing the lamentations and sighs which, thus far, had filled the void in the ghetto.

Every festival was used for meetings and get-togethers. Betar celebrated

Niussa Lubotski, Betarist
member of the F.P.O. Head-
quarters, fighter and liaison.

Nissan Reznik, member of the
F.P.O. and Zionist Youth.

Passover with more than a hundred in attendance at the *seder*. We still remembered the *seder* in our parents' homes. But our nostalgia was interrupted by Josef's words as he spoke about the Moses of our generation—Ze'ev Jabotinsky, who had sought to redeem our people from bondage and lead it forth from its exile, but the people did not respond and was now paying the price. We felt the day would come when we would leave the ghetto in triumph.

By the end of 1941 several youth groups were already functioning in the ghetto. The largest was a Communist organization, headed by Itzik Wittenberg, Hienna Borowska, and Berl Sherezhnevski. The second in size and quality was Betar, followed by Zionist Youth led by Nissan Reznik and Shlomo Entin and, last, Hashomer Hatsair under Abba Kovner. All of these movements operated independently. They maintained contacts, of sorts, amongst themselves, but had not as yet reached the stage of cooperation.

Josef Glazman was striving for a single force that would unify young people of all movements. Disunity in time of danger was clearly intolerable. The foe was making no distinction between one Jew and another and was not checking party membership cards. The foe had to be confronted by a strong Jewish force, ranks closed.

Glazman's persuasive arguments won out. The contacts were strengthened. In January 1942, a gathering was held of the representatives of all the movements, in Josef's room at 6 Rudnicka Street: Itzik Wittenberg and Hienna Borowska for the Communists, Glazman and Major Frucht for Betar, Nissan Reznik for Zionist Youth, and Abba Kovner for Hashomer Hatsair. The following resolutions were reached at the gathering:

1. To establish an armed combat organization to function underground in the Vilna Ghetto. The organization will include all the movements represented at the meeting, for the purpose of organizing all the forces in the ghetto.
2. The Organization's primary objective is to prepare mass armed resistance against any attempt to liquidate the ghetto.
3. The Organization will carry out acts of sabotage behind enemy lines.
4. The Organization will propagate the idea of resistance in other ghettos, and will form bonds with fighting forces outside the ghetto.
5. The Fighting Organization in the Vilna Ghetto will actively join the ranks of the partisans fighting behind enemy lines, and will help the Red Army in the common war against the Nazi invader.
6. Resistance is a nationalistic act, a people's struggle for its honor.
7. The Organization's activities will be centralized in one Command,

under a Commander in Chief. The Command will consist of three members: Wittenberg as the chief, Josef Glazman, and Abba Kovner.

Thus the F.P.O. (*Fereinikte Partisaner Organizatsia*, United Partisan Organization) came into existence. At one of the meetings of its leaders, it was decided that Josef should accept Gens's proposal to become Deputy Commander of the Ghetto Police Force. It was felt that, in his highly placed post, he could do much to build up the new Organization.

Josef accepted the decision. He would, at least, try to persuade the police to mend its ways. Gens summoned the entire police force and formally introduced Josef as its Deputy Commander. Josef responded with a delineation of the role of the police. He summarized the losses of Jewish Vilna during the half-year since the outbreak of the Russo-German fighting: 50,000 men, women, and children had been massacred in Ponar. Tomorrow, he said, the fate of the parents and friends might descend on the survivors. The massacre would continue as long as the Germans were in control. He warned against illusions. The role of the police was to help their suffering brethren, not to lord over the oppressed. He pleaded with the police not to stain its hands with Jewish blood. His keyword was "vengeance."

The news from ghettos in Poland and White Russia was that things were quiet. To date, no roundups were reported, and the Jews felt that they would outlive the enemy and enjoy a better life after the war. The representatives of the movements decided to dispatch emissaries to acquaint them with the realities of the annihilation, to warn them of the impending doom, and to urge them to organize for armed resistance.

In December 1941, shortly before the establishment of the F.P.O., a delegation from the Vilna Ghetto went to the Warsaw Ghetto: Israel Kempner and Yehuda Finchevski for Betar, Shlomo Entin for Zionist Youth, and Adek Buraks for Hashomer Hatsair. The mission to Bialystok included the Betarist Tusia Lichtenstein. Betarist Yaakov Leizerovich went to Grodno.

Abrasha Hvoinik, member of
the F.P.O. and the Bund.

I. Kowalski, member of the
F.P.O., organizer of the
underground press in Vilna.

Iron and Dynamite

The historic session which founded the F.P.O. was followed by feverish efforts to rally people and secure weapons, and to begin lessons and drills. Under the conditions in the ghetto, this called for intensive work. Trusting virtual strangers was risky, and arms acquisition even more so. Any Jew making his way along the city streets outside the ghetto took his life into his own hands. Many Jews were put to death because their knapsacks were found to contain bread, potatoes, or cereal. A Jew caught with a weapon was not only slated for death; under interrogation, he might endanger the lives of other ghetto residents. The Germans instituted collective retribution in all the countries they occupied. On the other hand, it was clear to all of us that the risk had to be taken. An organization proclaiming slogans of revolt obviously could not justify its existence unless it had arms to back it up.

It was decided that only known individuals would be admitted who would prove equal to the test. Every recruit had to undergo rigorous examination. In time, the F.P.O. Command was joined by Nissan Reznik of Zionist Youth and Abrasha Hvoinik of the Bund; after extensive negotiations, the Bund decided to join the F.P.O., even though this meant working together with Zionists.

The Organization grew quickly. The fighters threw themselves zealously into the cause and devoted all their energy to the task. First came the 3-man cells—all of one political coloration, but the next step already involved cooperation. The boundaries began to disappear with the formation of the 5-man mixed units. The atmosphere was of complete trust, despite divergence in other areas. It was already understood that the hour of trial would find the people united.

The 5-man unit was the military nucleus. Four such cells formed a department, and several cells together formed a battalion.

The cell meetings took up educational and ideological issues, but the main subject was the doctrine of conspiracy, spiritual stability, and instruction in the use of weapons. The Betarists were outstanding in all of these areas; spiritually, they were ready to fight, unlike the members of the other groups, who had only recently abandoned the doctrines of pacifism they had espoused for many years.

Josef organized a course for instructors. Of the ten participants, six were Betarists: Josef, Molka Hazan, Moshe Brause, Moshe Szymeliski, Lyova Ziskovich, and myself. Drilling without respite, the instructors became expert in the use of arms and combat tactics, which they passed on to the others.

At one of the sessions, Josef explained to us the use of the Russian Diktiarov machine-gun. With what love we handled this marvelous tool, and how happy we were when we mastered its operation! Already we ventured guesses as to how many Germans it would kill in a single burst. Vengeance.

Of the thirteen arms smugglers in the ghetto, eight were Betarists. The Pilovski brothers bought up arms from the farmers in the Vilna area. One night, when one of the brothers—Israel—was in the home of a farmer, in a suburb of the city, laden with pistols and ammunition, the house was surrounded by the Gestapo. The Germans broke in, but Israel, jumping out through the rear window, scurried through the farmyard, shot it out with the Germans, and disappeared in the nearby woods, in the end managing to bring his precious load into the ghetto.

The brothers Nionka and Iza Talarent lived in the "Keilis," a special block inhabited by about a thousand Jews who worked in the fur factories near the city. They made contact with the Lithuanians guarding the block and acquired weapons through them. The guards also provided a hiding place for the weapons whenever they had difficulty bringing them into the ghetto.

The ghetto had been subject for some time to roving gangs of homeless and orphaned boys, fourteen to seventeen years of age, who lived off thefts. The ghetto residents grew tired of the nuisance and organized them into Youth Transport Brigades. The boys earned money by delivering items in pushcarts and doing various jobs for the ghetto dwellers. Molka Hazan was the most popular youth counselor, and they readily hauled concealed weapons for him.

Miriam Bernstein, active in
the espionage division of the
F.P.O., member of Betar.

Miriam Ganionska, active in
the espionage division of the
F.P.O., member the F.P.O.,
member of Betar.

Zundel Leizerson served in the *Arbeitsamt* Police. His job was to accompany Jews to work, find new sources of work for them, etc. Since he often left the ghetto, he had the possibility of forming ties with non-Jews. He became one of the leading arms smugglers in the ghetto.

Moshe Brause was a former lieutenant in the Lithuanian Army and had studied at the university in Vilna; he used his many connections with Lithuanians to purchase arms. He was also one of the best instructors in the Organization.

Through Miss Olka Rafalovich I came into contact with a Lithuanian, Rutkauskas, and bought large quantities of arms from him. Three policemen stationed at the ghetto entrance were members of the Organization: Yulek, Chaim, and Gamka. They were very helpful in smuggling arms into the ghetto. Without their active aid, it would have been almost impossible to smuggle in arms. Chaim Luski and Gamka Sturman were members of Betar.

Under the leadership of Josef Glazman, the F.P.O. set up a special espionage division. The division had to obtain information concerning the extermination plans of the Germans and the designs of the ghetto leaders against the Fighting Organization. Among the most active people in this division were Betarists Miriam Bernstein and Miriam Ganionska. Following Josef's orders, Ganionska succeeded in gaining the confidence of the Lithuanian Gestapo leader Burakas,

Major Marošas, and the commander of the Jewish Police Force in the ghetto, a collaborator named Dessler. Miriam Bernstein worked in the criminal-political division of the police. The important information they supplied enabled the Organization to prepare itself for every calamity and to make emergency plans. It is unnecessary to dwell on the importance of this division. Without it, it would have been impossible to conduct any underground work.

One day the Betarist Itzhak Kowalski came to the Organization's Headquarters with a bold proposal. Being a printing expert, he was willing to set up a secret printing press. With the Headquarter's approval, he found work in one of the large printing houses in the city where the Lithuanian daily paper was printed. Every afternoon, when the workers finished their work, Itzhak took out of the printing house large quantities of type and gave them to a non-Jew waiting outside. This went on for a month without any hitches.

One day Itzhak arranged with the same man that the latter meet him at dusk to receive important equipment for the establishment of the secret press. In the evening Itzhak left his job, loaded with equipment and tools. Some of them he concealed under his clothes, but he also carried a package in his hand. While leaving the yard, he came across the Lithuanian manager, Škemas. The latter asked him what was in the package in his hand and Itzhak coolly replied that it contained old papers, which the manager had permitted him to take home for heating since he did not have any wood.

Itzhak did not find his friend at the designated meeting place. (The next day it was learned that he could not come to the meeting because the Gestapo was following him.) Itzhak, therefore, was in a very precarious situation. He had no alternative but to take the equipment with him into the ghetto. From the weight of the burden, the belt of his pants tore apart and his pants fell down. With great difficulty, he arrived at the entrance of the ghetto, one hand holding his pants and the other, the valuable package. But events took yet another unexpected turn; that same evening the Gestapo was conducting searches among Jews returning from work. He calmly waited until an opportune moment, and when the Gestapo men were busy flogging a woman, he slipped inside. Several days later, the city was flooded with manifestos and leaflets in Lithuanian and Polish, calling on the population to rebel. The manifestos were signed "The Polish Patriots Organization" and "The Free Lithuania Organization." A paper, too, began to appear in the underground, named *Standard Wolnosci* (*The Flag of Freedom*). At Itzhak's suggestion, even fake food tickets were printed. The commodities received through the tickets were sold in the ghetto and the income went towards the purchase of arms.

Thanks to Itzhak Kowalski, for the first time since the outbreak of the war anti-German propaganda appeared. Thus, the Gestapo learned that they faced a serious opponent.

Eventually secret workshops were set up to repair weapons. Betarist Moshe Szymeliski, an expert locksmith, worked day and night assembling arms, preparing spare parts, and making repairs. Betarist Mordechai Goldman was the manager of the ghetto workshops. He put them at the disposal of the organization. Borka Schneider, who worked in the Social Aid Society of the Judenrat, gave the Organization the use of the Society's halls. Betarist Niussa Lubotski, the most active and loyal of the women fighters in the Organization and a clerk in the Housing Department of the Judenrat, placed the department's offices at the Organization's disposal.

The ghetto Jews were cut off from the outside world. The only news we received came from German sources, and it was impossible to verify them. However, our lives depended on what was happening on the fronts. The Organization bought a radio receiver and every day, a bulletin appeared with a summary of the news. The fighters "devoured" them and afterwards publicized these documented reports throughout the ghetto.

The radio was in Josef's room. This room also served as a meeting place for the Headquarters, as well as an arms cache.

In the summer of 1942, the Organization's Command decided upon the first sabotage operation near Vilna. A mine was assembled and the site of the sabotage action was determined. Witka Kempner, Itzhak Mackiewicz, and Moshe Brause were the executors of the plan. It was not easy to take the mine out of the ghetto and carry it to its destination. Moshe Brause implemented and was responsible for this difficult mission. Witka and Itzhak, equipped with Aryan papers, waited for him at the designated place. With extraordinary courage, Moshe passed through the entrance and the city streets, laden with large quantities of explosives.

The action was successful. A German military train, full of soldiers and ammunition, ran over the mine and was blown up. The first act of sabotage in one of the areas in which the Germans felt safest! In honor of this achievement, the Headquarters organized a celebration for a small circle of the Organization's activists. The commander of the Organization, Itzik Wittenberg, praised the operation as follows: "This was an act of partisan sabotage in the rear, causing the enemy considerable losses. The Germans, who felt safe in a place so far away from the front, have learned that the rear is not particularly safe and that an organized fighting power is operating underground. We heard that they have reinforced their guards along the railroad. Every soldier whom they have to keep here instead of sending to the front reduces their fighting manpower. And the German soldier on his way to the front witnesses an act of sabotage at the beginning of his journey, which demoralizes him and shakes his confidence in victory. For us, the F.P.O. fighters, this action of ours has great significance. It proves to us that we are a force. And the awareness that the enemy has not succeeded in breaking our spirit will make our work easier in the difficult days to come."

Ideology of Appeasement

Summer 1942. The calm in the ghetto had already lasted for several months. The Jews were adjusting to their situation. New hopes stirred in their hearts. The ghetto leaders were promising that no ill would befall the Vilna Ghetto. One only had to fulfill the work quota imposed by the Germans. A day would come when all of the ghetto inhabitants would be counted among the "useful Jews" and, naturally, the Germans would not kill workers helping their war effort. This was the ideology of the leaders and it was gaining adherents.

Josef Glazman never stopped taking advantage of his official position to help strengthen the underground. He found appropriate employment for the fighters to ease their burden and enable them to devote all their strength to the work of the Organization. He provided exit permits to the city when needed and secured passes for free movement in the ghetto during curfew hours so that people could attend training sessions. He obtained money to purchase arms. In short, Josef was involved in everything. His intimates were amazed at his energy. He was both an ideologue and a man of action. He was an army instructor, head of the "Fifth Column," battalion commander, member of the Headquarters, Betar commander, and instructor in a course for Betar leaders. He also found the time to be active in the public life of the ghetto. At every literary meeting, at the weekly literary soirées offered by the Association of Artists and Writers, he was among the organizers and speakers. Outside his office, there was always a long line of people seeking his help. From morning to evening, he would listen to their complaints and look for ways to help them. Josef's name was mentioned by all with affection and admiration.

Meanwhile, while the ghetto leaders were promising peace and quiet, the Gestapo was making plans for the next stage of extermination. First and foremost, they wanted the Jews themselves to help them in this. Their wish was granted. Salik Dessler, the chief of the Second Police Station of the ghetto, became the chief collaborator, and since he was close to those in power, he began to adopt an overbearing attitude. He spread a network of agents and detectives throughout the ghetto streets. These people would listen to every conversation and slip of the tongue. In this way Dessler hoped to have unlimited power over the unfortunate Jews.

But Josef thwarted him. Therefore, he had to be discredited in the eyes of the commander of the Jewish Ghetto Police, Gens, and in the eyes of the ghetto masses. Gens's attitude towards Josef did, indeed, change. For some time, he had not been pleased with Glazman. The young man was too stubborn, too self-righteous for the head of the ghetto. He did not agree with the political line adopted by Gens, and once Gens found a supporter in Dessler, he was ready to begin acting over Josef's head. But the masses were with Glazman. They saw him as one of the few who felt their own pain and sacrificed himself for the people.

Josef realized that he had no chance of changing the situation in the police. He saw that, instead of helping the unfortunate Jews, the police was oppressing them. For some time he had wanted to leave the police and devote all his time to the work of the Organization, but he was bound by the decision of the Headquarters, which hoped to derive more benefit from Josef's position. However, now that the Organization was firmly based, Josef saw no point in continuing in office. He wanted no responsibility for the actions done against his will and conscience, and he submitted his resignation.

An official announcement was published in the ghetto stating that henceforth Gens would be head of the ghetto and Dessler would be his chief-of-police and second-in-command. This caused quite a flurry. The better-informed ghetto inhabitants saw the change of leadership as a bad omen. From now on, sinister forces would rule unchecked and there would be no ray of light to illuminate the darkness.

The ghetto leaders, who feared for their positions, did not want to remove Josef from the scene altogether for fear that this might infuriate the masses. They asked him to head the Housing Department of the Judenrat. In such an administrative job, they thought, he would be unable to endanger their positions. Josef was disinclined to accept the new proposal, but the Organization's Headquarters once again decided that he should accept the appointment.

Living conditions in the ghetto were terrible, with twenty-five thousand to thirty-thousand Jews occupying several hundred apartments. On the average, twenty to thirty people lived in one room. The narrow rooms were used by the tenants for all purposes. They peeled their rotten potatoes and prepared their meager meals there. There, they ate, heard the news, and rested from a hard day's work. The walls of the rooms were lined with shelves up to the ceilings, piled with the ghetto residents' remaining possessions. One who has not seen these "palaces" in all their "grandeur" has not seen poverty or congestion. But there were also apartments whose owners lived in relative comfort. When the ghetto was set up, these people were the first to take rooms and vehemently defended their ownership rights, allowing no new tenants to disturb their peace.

Josef threw himself into his new job. He went from house to house to see how the situation could be improved. Afterwards, he determined the minimum space for each ghetto resident and began moving the tenants, despite the anger of those who lived comfortably. During the transfer Josef kept several rooms in reserve, where he housed the Organization's members. These rooms served as places for meetings and training lessons. He placed at the Headquarters' disposal two rooms with a separate entrance where the Headquarter members could work without being disturbed. Naturally, these rooms were ostensibly occupied by tenants.

Josef also installed secret arms caches, which were almost impossible to find in the event of searches and yet were easily accessible in times of need. One of Josef's most daring projects was to build passages connecting the buildings, thus allowing Jews to circumvent the 9:00 P.M. curfew on movement in the streets. This restriction had interfered with the Organization's nocturnal activities. Moreover, there was the danger that one day the Germans would come to destroy the ghetto and, as a first step, they would stop movement in the streets. In such a case, it would be impossible to gather the fighters for defensive war. Josef therefore ordered fences to be destroyed and passages built between the yards. After feverish work, everything was ready. All the Organization's members received detailed plans of the passages and spent evenings examining them. It was virtually possible to cross the entire ghetto without setting foot on the streets and without being detected by the police.

Josef knew that a day would come when it would be impossible to bring arms through the ghetto gates, owing to the increasingly strict guard. Once the day of armed resistance arrived, the war would certainly end with the retreat of the Organization's members and the surviving Jews, who would continue the war elsewhere. A retreat route must, therefore, be prepared. Josef began to build a secret exit to the city. This required great caution and absolute secrecy. It was also difficult to obtain the needed building materials. But this work, too, was successfully completed.

Martin Weiss, S.S. officer
charged with the liquidation
of the Vilna Ghetto.

Bloodied Hands

Gens rose in status: the Germans appointed him the official representative of all the ghettos in the Vilna area. There were several thousand more Jews in the neighboring towns. Gens sent policemen and clerks to these towns to organize life there along the same lines as the main ghetto in Vilna.

One day Miriam Ganionska brought news that an "action" was about to take place in the Oszmiana (Oshmyany) Ghetto, inhabited by over 4,000 Jews. She said that Gens and Dessler had negotiated with the head of the Lithuanian branch of the Gestapo, the German murderer Martin Weiss, over the number of Jews to be executed. Weiss demanded 1,500, while Gens and Dessler were willing to "give" no more than 500. They finally reached a compromise, but the Germans set one condition: the Jewish police was to carry out the "action."

Miriam was told to go with the police to Oszmiana to warn the Jews there and to save whomever she could. Several days later the police returned from Oszmiana to the Vilna Ghetto. No one in Vilna was aware of what had happened in

Oszmiana. But Miriam gave the Headquarters a copy of the report on the action, written by Dessler. The report read as follows:

On Wednesday at 10 A.M. I summoned the officers and discussed with them how to conduct the "action." There were many technical questions, such as what would happen if they were unable to control the crowd or if the people refused to gather in the square. It was suggested to round up the old people in the synagogue. There are two synagogues in Oszmiana, an old one and a new one. Even though I am not Orthodox, I did not want to gather those who were about to die in the synagogue. I gathered there those who would remain alive. I ordered all the Jews to assemble in the square, according to their towns, with each group headed by its council and rabbi. The action went smoothly. Everyone left their homes and went to the synagogue in groups of fifty. We did not want the last groups to know what happened to the first. When one group approached, my police made a selection, since we wanted to save the young people and the intelligentsia, who are our future.

Before the action, we inquired every few hours about the mood of the Jews. One of the members of the Jewish council told me: "They are ready to make a sacrifice as long as the matter ends with that."

We faced another problem: Were we entitled to take upon ourselves a selection of people? Perhaps it would be better to bring in Lithuanians? On Friday Mr. Gens sent me six Lithuanian policemen from among Weiss's men and expressed his wish that they stand near the entrance of the synagogue and do everything asked of them, as if it were the Lithuanians making the selection. But I left the Lithuanians at home— first of all, for fear that the Jews would panic; and secondly, one should not trust murderers. They could open fire, and we would be held responsible.

We did everything ourselves. We selected people according to the instructions of the Jewish council. We gathered the people together in the square and began looking for those hiding in their homes. Wagons arrived in the square and we put the people inside and sent them away.

This happened at 1:00 P.M. and I kept the masses in the synagogue until they calmed down. At 3:00 P.M. I stopped the action. I gathered the policemen in one place and opened the doors of the synagogue. An order was given for everyone to go home and not to congregate in the streets. That night people avoided us, but the next day they began to realize that we had saved them."

Miriam went on to say that the police pillaged the property and jewelry of the Jews. While talking, she pulled out of her pocket a little bag full of gold and pearls and laid it on the table in front of Headquarters and said: "On the way back I was able to filch this bag from them. With the arms we will buy in exchange for the value of the jewelry, we can perhaps atone for the sin of Jews who stain their hands with the blood of their brethren."

The rumor that the Jewish police had carried out the action in Oszmiana spread throughout the ghetto and caused great bitterness. From now on, the people were openly hostile towards the leaders and regarded the policemen as out-and-out enemies. The Underground grew from day to day.

To placate the people, Gens called a meeting of public activists and tried to justify his behavior. He addressed them in these terms:

"Seven days ago Weiss came to me and, in the name of the Gestapo, ordered us to go to Oszmiana. He said that 4,000 Jews live there and it is impossible to feed them all. Therefore, their numbers must be reduced and people who are useless to the Germans selected out and shot. He ordered us to remove 1,500 people from the ghetto. I replied that we could not fill such a high quota. We started to bargain. When Dessler reached Oszmiana, the quota had been reduced to 800. By the time I arrived in Oszmiana with Weiss, he had agreed to reduce the number to 600.

"Actually, only 400 old people were taken from Oszmiana and handed over to the Germans. When Weiss came and demanded women and children, I told him to take the old people. He replied that the old people would die in any case during the winter, and that we had to reduce the ghetto immediately.

"The Jewish police saved all those who should have been saved. Those who went did not have much longer to live anyway and forgave us. We had no choice but to make a sacrifice for the sake of our future. I regret that we could not have been present during the "actions" in Kiemieliszki and Bystrzyca. Last week all the Jews there were shot indiscriminately. Today I received a visit from two Jews from Swieciany [Sventsyan] who asked us for help. Jews from Swieciany as well as Vidzy and other places are concentrated in their town.

"I stand before a dilemma: What will happen if we are asked to repeat such an action? I do not want to soil my hands and send my police out to carry out this dirty business, but I say that it is my duty to soil my hands. We have to save the young people and not be ruled by our sentiments. I do not know if all of you understand me and will justify my actions now or even when we are freed from the ghetto. But this is the position of the police: to save all those who can be saved, without regard to personal feelings.

"Rosenberg recently said that the Germans have to destroy all the Jews. If he ever came here, our ghetto would tremble. We, a persecuted people, murdered in

Ponar, hiding in bunkers and separated from our relatives, have in one year succeeded in building new lives for ourselves. We have been more successful in this than the non-Jews. This is the strength of the Jews! If you do not want Rosenberg's threat to become a reality, let us use all means possible in our struggle against the Nazi enemy.

"I assume responsibility for all past and future acts. I wanted to inform you of the situation, to explain the naked truth, so that you would understand why Jews stain their hands with the blood of their brethren. And I ask for your moral support of my actions."

The meeting did not produce the desired results. However, the people calmed down somewhat. Fresh disasters caused the old ones to be forgotten. The dark present overshadowed events of the past. Yet, the prestige of the leaders had been irreparably damaged.

Josef Under Arrest

One day Gens and Dessler invited Josef to meet with them and asked him to go to Swiecany to handle housing matters there. Josef refused and even excoriated them for their treacherous behavior. He told them that they were sorely mistaken if they thought that they could save their own lives in this way.

This was the first time that they had heard such sharp criticism. They were sure that Josef would accept their authority, since so far no one had openly opposed them.

Gens summoned the police and invited Josef as well. He made a long speech about his difficult tasks. He proudly pointed out that, thanks to the leaders and the police, the ghetto enjoyed ideal security, but it would not last long unless everyone chose to work loyally and trust in the leadership. However, if there were people who, through criminal conduct and stubbornness, tried to destroy the public order and undermine the important work accomplished since the establishment of the ghetto, he, Gens, had the power to destroy them.

Having issued this warning, Gens selected the policemen who would go to Swiecany and once again ordered Josef to help him. But Josef took advantage of the roll call to voice criticism of the leaders and the policemen, who had stooped to spilling Jewish blood. He attacked their collaboration with the Germans and denounced them. He called upon the youth to rebel against the Gestapo and its Jewish agents, and announced that he personally would disobey the order and not go.

Gens ordered Josef to be arrested and held in the ghetto jail on Lidski Street.

The Organization's Headquarters decided to send a delegation to Gens to demand that Josef be freed. Itzik Wittenberg, the Organization's leader, and Borowska, both Communist leaders, placed this demand before Gens.

The ghetto leader saw this as proof of the existence of a united underground force in the ghetto. For what connection would the Communist leaders have with the Betar leader, Glazman? He and Dessler decided to destroy this force, once and for all. Escorted by a large guard, Josef was taken to Sorok-Tatar, about 25 kilometers from Vilna. There in the forest was a labor camp which prepared lumber for the Germans.

The ghetto was in an uproar. Josef's arrest and proud remarks were the talk of the day. Everyone spoke of him with respect and sympathy. But the police suppressed all free speech and intensified a program of internal terror. Jews were beaten up without cause. Dessler's spy network increased its intimidation of the ghetto inhabitants.

Miriam Ganionska and Miriam Bernstein announced that searches and arrests were being planned mainly against Josef's comrades and fellow Betar members. The Betar Command called an urgent meeting to discuss the situation and decided to send someone to Sorok-Tatar to talk with Josef about it and ask him for instructions.

With German permission, several cars left every Sunday for the forests of Sorok-Tatar to bring back lumber for the ghetto inhabitants. On November 15, as an emissary from the Betar Headquarters, I went out with the workers, found Josef, and discussed the situation with him. Upon my return I found a large guard at the gate waiting to arrest me. At the same time other policemen from the political-criminal division made a search of my room.

At 10:00 P.M. I was taken to Gens for interrogation. In the waiting room I met Niussa Lubotski and Borka Schneider, who had already been interrogated. Niussa said that she knew nothing, and since she was a young woman, Gens let her off with a strong rebuke. Borka was beaten badly during the interrogation, but Gens was unable to get a word out of him.

Now came my turn. Entering the room, I greeted Gens with a "good evening" and was shocked to be answered with a strong slap. Gens began the interrogation: "Why did you go to Josef? What did you tell him? What message did he send back to his comrades?" Each question was accompanied by a slap. But I remained silent. Gens lost his temper. He took a rubber truncheon and said: "Now you will talk." He began to strike me with all his might. I felt weak; my head was spinning and I was covered with perspiration. One thought went through my brain: "How easy it would be if I did not know what I do know." But I remained silent. When Gens tired, he began to try to move me by words. He spoke softly, like a father teaching his son. "Tell us the truth. Don't think that you are better Jews than we are. We are concerned with the existence of the ghetto and the safety of the Jews in it. We constantly sacrifice ourselves to achieve this aim. We want to prevent the destruction of the ghetto. In Minsk Ghetto the Germans found one Jew with a radio receiver and immediately destroyed the whole ghetto. In another place they found a gun and destroyed the whole ghetto. In a third place they found a Jew in touch with the partisans and killed all the Jews. Do you think that we won't fight against the Germans when the time comes? I was an officer in the Lithuanian Army. I have thousands of friends among the Lithuanians, and when I need it, I will receive enough arms from them for all the ghetto people. When the final liquidation comes, I will gather all the youth and declare war against the enemy. But it is too early now. You, with your separate activities and irresponsibility, will bring ruin upon us."

Dessler entered and he, too, began to try gentle persuasion. He wanted details on the organization of the Underground, the number of people, and the quantity of arms.

My blood was boiling. In my anger I forgot my vow of silence and began to shout at them: "Bastards! Traitors!" Gens immediately changed his tone and attacked me, shouting and beating me repeatedly. He threatened to turn me over to the Gestapo, to send me to Ponar. . . . All in vain! The interrogation went on for two and one-quarter hours, but I did not utter one word. Gens finally said: "Go home and treat your wounds with cold water. Tomorrow morning we will continue the interrogation."

I lay in a sick-bed for three weeks. Many weeks later my body was still covered with bruises.

Meanwhile, the police squad went to Sorok-Tatar to bring Josef back to the ghetto for interrogation. Josef was sent to Lidski again. Every day he was taken for interrogation before the chief investigator of the ghetto, Dr. Nussbaum, but with no results. They did not dare use the rubber truncheon on Josef.

Two weeks after his second arrest, Josef asked to be allowed to meet with Gens. The meeting was held several days later. For four hours Josef spoke to Gens, and at the end of the conversation he was set free. Gens's intimates could not understand this development but the ghetto was happy.

The year 1943 arrived. On New Year's Eve, the Jewish police held a gala party. Hundreds of people envied those who were able to buy tickets in time. The "golden youth" of the ghetto filled the hall to capacity and spent a pleasant evening, just like in the "good old days," as if nothing had happened in the meantime.

At exactly midnight a shot was heard in the hall and a police officer entered excitedly and rushed towards Gens. The people were seized with fear. Everyone wondered: "Germans in the ghetto? An action? Has the enemy decided to put an end to the New Year's Eve merriment?"

Gens got on the stage. Everyone waited breathlessly for him to speak. He smiled—a good omen—and began to speak: "Just now one of the officers on duty told me that there is complete quiet in the ghetto." A sigh of relief escaped the lips of the celebrants. Gens summarized the events of the past year, eulogized the dead, and spoke at length of the great achievements of the ghetto leadership. If the Jews only knew how to behave properly, he promised, the ghetto would be in no danger. He ended by saying: "Let us celebrate this night next year as free people."

The public received his speech with prolonged applause. No one even imagined that they were on the threshold of a year in which the ghetto would be destroyed and Vilna Jewry annihilated.

Arms Searches

The Underground was not secretive about its planned revolt. The Head-quarters announced a collection among the members to buy arms. They hoped to collect 500,000 rubles. Everyone understood the importance of the matter and not only contributed their last coins, but also their valuables: watches, rings, and clothes. Within a short time, the total reached 1,000,000 rubles.

New arms were bought with the money. The Organization's stockpiles became highly variegated; they seemed like museums or exhibitions of various kinds of arms. Each newly acquired weapon was a source of joy and celebration.

Mordechai Goldman, in charge of the ghetto workshops, went every so often to Oszmiana and to other towns which still had ghettos, ostensibly to organize the workshops there along the same lines as those in Vilna. In fact, he was organizing the youth for armed resistance. During the destruction of the Oszmiana Ghetto, thirty armed young people went into the forest. Their other fellow-members of the Organization went to Vilna and joined our organization. Units from other towns also left for the forest.

One day Irena Adamowicz, a Polish nun and righteous non-Jew, appeared in the ghetto. She was very devout in her religion and spent most of her waking hours in prayer. She had become close to the Jews even before the war. She had kept in contact with members of Hashomer Hatsair and only after her arrival in Vilna did she meet Josef and come into contact with Betar. Since the outbreak of the war, she had been concerned with saving Jews. She succeeded in placing many of them in convents, and afterwards put herself at the service of the underground organizations in the ghettos. Several times she crossed the whole Nazi-occupied territory in eastern Europe, passed information from ghetto to ghetto, and carried out various missions for the underground organizations. On one mission for our Headquarters, she went to the Shavli (Siauliai) and Kovno (Kaunas) ghettos and brought back the first news from there. She also brought back letters from various activists and a letter from a Betar group. Irena also served as a liaison between us and the Polish underground in Vilna. She tried to persuade the Poles to cooperate with us and supply us with arms.

After long negotiation and unkept promises, we realized that the Poles would not help us at all. One evening we were sitting with Josef and he told us at length all the details of the talks with the Poles. It seemed that even the moderate and enlightened ones wanted no contact with the Jews, though the danger of annihilation threatened them as well. Actually, it would have been no risk for them. All they had to do was put at our disposal their arms, which were growing rusty from being buried underground. But they could not set aside their hatred of the Jews even for one moment.

The ghetto leaders now knew that they had to treat the underground organization with caution, since it was composed of people from all parties and was both strong and influential. They decided to wait for the right time to renew their attack upon it and destroy it. For the time being, they found it expedient to pretend to have accepted the Organization's existence and to seek peaceful relations with it. Every now and then, they met with the Communist leaders, one of whom knew Gens even before the war. Afterwards they would invite the Organization's leaders and discuss ghetto affairs to coordinate activity. Sometimes Gens contributed considerable sums from the Judenrat fund which was, ostensibly, to be used for social purposes, but, in fact, was used to buy arms. On the surface, relations between the Organization and the ghetto leadership were correct but, in reality, the latter was constantly plotting how to get rid of the former.

A period of mass searches began. Every night the police held sudden searches of people suspected of belonging to the Organization. The searches were very thorough and, again, the main targets were Betar members. The police claimed that it was looking for gold and valuables, strictly forbidden by German order. However, the purpose of the searches was obvious. The police wanted to uncover arms caches to make it easier for them afterwards to destroy the Organization. The searches revealed nothing. Sometimes the police found a little gold and jewelry and confiscated them, but they did not find arms.

Eventually the police did not bother concealing the object of its searches. Once they held a search in my room, directed by Taubin, the head of the

Arbeitsamt police and one of Dessler's main agents. After a two-hour search he turned to me and said: "I must admit that you are clever fellows. You know how to hide your weapons."

When the house searches did not yield the expected results, the police began to search pedestrians in the streets. Anyone who went out into the street with a package in his hand or something bulging in his pocket could become a victim of these searches, which were generally accompanied by blows. The Organization's Headquarters ordered tighter conspiracy. Arms caches were guarded with increased vigilance.

One morning the police was sent to the room of Kravchinski, who had tried to commit suicide. Kravchinski was one of the first instructors of the Organization. He was one of those interrogated after Josef's arrest, where he admitted that he once had a gun but that he had given it to a man whose name he did not recall. From that day on, Kravchinski was very depressed and could not forgive himself for his slip of the tongue during the interrogation. He thought that it was only through his statements that the police came to know of the Organization's existence. This thought gave him no rest. The Headquarters people tried to calm him down and convince him that his statements had caused no harm to anyone and certainly not to the Organization. But Kravchinski remained unconsoled.

When the police arrived in his room they found him hanging from a rope, but he was still alive and they saved him. They found a letter to Josef, in which he had written that he could not rid himself of a feeling of guilt towards the Organization and, hence, decided to atone for his sin by taking his life. (Afterwards, it was learned in the ghetto that, before the war, Kravchinski had undergone treatment in a mental hospital. He later repeated his attempt at suicide and succeeded in snuffing out his life.) The discovery of Kravchinski's letter was used by Gens and Dessler as a pretext to disgrace Josef in the eyes of the masses and to destroy the Fighting Organization. The Jews would finally realize Josef's pernicious effect on the ghetto!

One night they sent the police to arrest Josef, Niussa Lubotski, Borka Schneider, Isaiah Lubotski and myself. They put us in the ghetto jail on Lidski Street and intended to transfer us to the labor camp on 4 Zawalna Street.

Several weeks before, the Germans had liquidated several labor camps around Vilna, in which the remaining Jews from various towns worked. The official pretext for the liquidation of the camps was the recent increase of partisan activity and the Nazis' wish to protect the Jews from the "bandits." The workers in these camps were taken to Vilna by the Germans and, as there was not enough place in the ghetto, they were put in a special block on 4 Zawalna Street. Naturally, the Germans' "generosity" aroused suspicion regarding the fate of these Jews.

Gens and Dessler found no better place for Josef and his comrades than this camp. First of all, the Germans could destroy it any day and, thus, they could be rid of Josef. Secondly, the Jews at 4 Zawalna Street did not know Josef and would not protest if he were taken out and handed over to the Gestapo. In this way Gens and Dessler hoped to destroy the main forces of the Organization.

The ghetto was in an uproar again. The Headquarters gave an order to the fighters to be ready for action and warned the leaders not to dare remove the prisoners from the ghetto. It demanded they be freed immediately. Well-known activists knocked repeatedly at Gens's door, demanding he release Josef and his comrades or else an end would be put to the ghetto leadership. Its prestige had plummeted, in any case. The activists claimed that the masses were with Josef, and that Gens's action could have unforeseeable results.

Police guard was increased on Lidski Street but members of the Organization succeeded in contacting the prisoners. Their mood was high, for they knew they had on whom to rely. People congregated in the streets and discussed the recent events. Meanwhile, negotiations were going on between the activists and Gens, and the two sides remained adamant in their positions. In the late afternoon, Gens gave way, mainly due to the influence of Trapido, the head of the Supplies Department of the Judenrat. The prisoners were freed, to the joy of the fighters and the ghetto Jews.

Once again the Organization had the upper hand. But the incident served as a warning. It was clear that the leaders had decided to destroy the Organization and would stop at nothing.

An "Action" in Kovno

At the end of March 1943, the Germans had ordered the Jews in all the towns near Vilna to move to Kovno Ghetto, as there was a shortage of workers in Kovno and, moreover, the Jews in the towns were not safe from partisans. If anyone of the Vilna Jews wanted to join the transport to Kovno, said the order, he was free to do so. Naturally, the ghetto Jews regarded this invitation with great suspicion. They had long ago stopped believing the Germans. But after several days, they convinced themselves that this time the oppressor was not lying. In the Kovno Ghetto, place was being made for 5,000 people and, besides, no one was forced to go to Kovno. The choice was up to the individual. The ghetto leaders promised that the transport would reach its destination safely.

This transport became the main topic for discussion in the ghetto. Jews consulted with one another, interpreted the matter each in his own way, sought compelling reasons—and found them. Many saw the proposal as an indication of the improved attitude of the Germans towards the Jews. Every unusual event gave rise to speculation, commentary, and guesswork, and engaged people's attention—until a new event eclipsed the former impression. In fact, the ghetto was in a constant state of tension and ferment. People were always debating whether things would improve or deteriorate. The eternal Jewish optimism made the ghetto-dwellers see "good signs" everywhere around them and draw encouraging conclusions. The Jews were consoled by the belief in their own cleverness. Clearly, the stupid Germans would be unable to deceive the Jews and eventually would fail. This disparaging attitude towards the "goy" and the exaggerated self-confidence of the Jews made the Jews allies and accomplices of their destroyers.

Josef pointed out the fact that the Jews lacked a sense of collective responsibility. They did not understand that the fate of the individual depended on the fate of the whole community. Everyone thought that no ill would befall him and he would be saved. This one had a non-Jewish friend who would save him; that one hoped that his money would take care of everything; a third was preparing a hideout for himself; and a fourth simply believed that he was invulnerable to death. If these Jews had only understood that all Jews are responsible for one another; if they had only understood that salvation of the individual is linked to salvation of the community, they would have concluded that only mass resistance could save the masses. Had the ghettos resisted, the Germans would not have pulled out forces from the front to carry out their extermination plans. Had the Jews invested in the purchase of arms the same sums they spent on arranging hiding-places or other private means of survival, their chances of survival would have been much greater.

The Jews had convinced themselves that there was really going to be a transport to Kovno. Several hundred people signed up, particularly those who had relatives in the Kovno Ghetto and had not seen them since the outbreak of the war. Jews from the neighboring towns, who had gotten stuck in the Vilna Ghetto, but had no connection to the city, also signed up. They were ready to try their luck in another place.

Among those who signed up were also many from the camp on 4 Zawalna Street, who heard that relatives or acquaintances were going on the transport to Kovno. Run-of-the-mill Jews signed up as well.

At the train station in Vilna, train cars stood which were to take part in the transport to Kovno. Every day technicians would leave the ghetto to repair the cars in preparation for the journey. The ghetto Jews did not understand why they were sealing all the cracks and openings in the cars and why they were covering the doors and windows with barbed wire. The news that the transport would be carried out by Jewish policemen and that they would accompany the convoy all the way to Kovno eased the apprehension.

In the morning of April 4, a transport of Jews arrived from Swieciany, Mikhailishki, Oszmiana, and other places near Vilna. The Germans announced that the train would wait until evening so that the Vilna Jews could take their belongings with them and find place in the cars. By the afternoon the people were ready to leave the ghetto. The passengers finished their preparations and packed their belongings, mainly kitchen utensils and broken furniture, and went their way. Each possession had cost them dearly and they did not want to leave anything behind. They passed through the ghetto gate, laden with large packages. In the first row walked Eliashkevich, a young woman from Kovno. Smiling, she waved goodbye to her acquaintances and said: "May we meet again soon as free people." When the war had broken out, she had found herself stuck in Vilna. She was studying in the university and could not return to her city. She had received news that her mother was still alive and was in Kovno. Soon she would see her mother and tell her all the trials and tribulations she had undergone. . . .

That same morning, soothing news had come to Vilna. All the train cars were marked "Kovno" and the Polish mechanics and station managers had shown written orders to take the transport to Kovno. All the passengers had already received passes like those used in the Kovno Ghetto. They had all received free tickets which were stamped "Vilna–Kovno." There were almost no German soldiers or Lithuanian policemen in the station. The Jewish police were in charge of keeping order. The policemen accompanying the transport were in a separate car—the last one. Gens himself headed the guard of policemen. He also helped his "own" Jews with initial arrangements in the new ghetto.

Late that evening everything was ready for the journey. The wagons were sealed. Four thousand Jews occupied eighty cars. At midnight they came to a wooded area. The train turned off on a side track leading into the forest. It stopped, and the passengers found themselves surrounded by many German and Lithuanian Gestapo men, pointing their guns at them. They immediately understood that they had been cruelly deceived. They were in Ponar.

Gestapo officer Weiss, in charge of all the actions, went up to the policemen's car accompanied by several Gestapo men and told Gens: "Take your police and go back to the city. We warn you not to resist or try anything stupid." A car brought them to the Gestapo offices. There a feast awaited them and beds to spend the night. The Gestapo knew how to recompense their accomplices. In the early morning, Gens and his police reached the ghetto. Everyone who saw them, trembling, ashen-faced, and depressed, understood immediately what had happened.

That same morning several survivors of Ponar arrived, most of them wounded. They were fortunate enough to have broken through the cordon of murderers and to have escaped the torrent of bullets. They related what had befallen the passengers.

When the train pulled to a halt and the passengers understood what awaited them, they went into a panic. The forest reverberated with shouts, cries, and curses. The Jews, especially the young ones among them, began to break down the doors in an attempt to escape. But they found themselves surrounded by a tight cordon, and anyone who tried to escape was mowed down by bullets. Even the darkness of night did not help them.

The Germans ordered all the passengers to leave the cars and take their belongings with them. Those who did not obey were shot on the spot. Several meters away from where the train stood, they began to descend a slope which led into an enormous pit—50 meters long, 20 meters wide, and 3 meters deep. When they came to the pit, they were ordered to dance, and while they did so, the Germans opened fire on them from all directions. There were several Jews who put up strong resistance, seriously wounding several Germans and Lithuanians. The terrible slaughter lasted the whole night, and when morning came the bloody business had been completed.

The sun shone and sent its rays over the shattered bodies of 4,000 Jews who the day before had left on a trip, full of hope about the new life awaiting them in the Kovno Ghetto.

The news about the slaughter traveled through the ghetto with lightning speed. A terrible depression descended on all the inhabitants. For over a year, there had been no big "action" like this one. True, in the summer of 1942, several dozen old people had been taken from the ghetto, but this small "action" had almost no effect on ghetto life. There had also been killings in several towns, but the number of victims amounted to "only" several hundred and all these events took place far from Vilna. Now the sword of Damocles once again hung over the ghetto, and many saw this action as the beginning of the end for Vilna Jewry. Many were ready to go into hiding and stocked their bunkers with foodstuffs. Most of the Jews were helpless and panic-stricken. Their self-confidence had been undermined, together with their faith in the leadership.

That day Gens and Dessler did not appear in public. They, too, were very disappointed by the Germans, who had deceived them shamelessly. Perhaps they also feared the anger of the crowd. Everyone believed that Gens truly knew nothing of the German plot, but they suspected that Dessler did know and had helped the Nazis through his silence.

That morning Gestapo officer Weiss had come to the ghetto, demanding that a company of Jewish policemen be put at his disposal to go to Ponar and help bury the dead. He wanted precisely those twenty-five policemen who had accompanied the transport. Gens summoned the policemen near the gate and told them: "Last night 4,000 of our brethren were murdered by the Germans and now they have ordered you to help bury them. Each of you must regard this as a sacred and honorable duty." Dessler got into the car together with the squadron of policemen. However, before the car moved, Weiss went up to Dessler and whispered something in his ear, and the latter got out and returned to the ghetto. The policemen saw this as a bad omen. In the ghetto no one believed that these policemen would return. Everyone was sure that the final liquidation had commenced.

Late that evening the squeak of wagon wheels and the clomping of horses' hooves were heard, and the ghetto dwellers were astonished to see the squadron of policemen return. They immediately drew the conclusion that the Germans did not plan to destroy the ghetto. But there were some who saw precisely this as a bad omen: if the Germans were no longer hiding the secrets of Ponar, this meant that the days of the Jews were numbered.

One of the policemen who returned from Ponar, a member of the Fighters' Organization, came to see me. He sat on the bed with a frozen expression on his face. I tried to get him to tell me what he had undergone, but to no avail. He sat there for hours without saying a word. After midnight he broke out in a flood of tears and began to relate his experience:

"When we left the ghetto we thought that we were seeing it for the last time. We were sure that this was the end of the road for us. Several kilometers before Ponar, the car stopped and we were ordered to continue on foot. Around us we could see peasants hurrying home with booty on their backs: the abandoned possessions of the murdered victims. The closer we came to Ponar, the sharper the smell of fresh blood. We entered a large gate on which hung a sign: 'Entrance also forbidden to Wermacht soldiers. Trespassers will be punished by death.'

"When we entered among the trees, a frightening sight met our eyes. On the right stood Lithuanian soldiers, armed with automatic weapons. Around them lay many empty bottles. The whole area was strewn with corpses and pieces of human bodies. Human brain, fingers, fingernails, hair, and clotted blood stuck to the trees. Weiss led us to a huge pit that was full of half-naked bodies. The Lithuanians brought shovels, and we were ordered to cover the bodies with earth. As the pit was very large, Weiss told us to go inside it and spread the earth around to cover all the bodies.

"The Lithuanians walked around the edge of the pit with their guns cocked, and we were sure that Weiss had ordered us to go inside it so that the Lithuanians could easily kill us. Any moment we expected to hear the rat-tat-tat of their machine guns. One of our policemen stopped his work and said "Kaddish" for the victims which he trampled and for the souls of his comrades who were about to be killed. But after we had finished the work, Weiss led us to a second pit, even larger than the first. The same scene followed. Finally Weiss led us on a tour of the whole area. He gave explanations as if he were a tour guide at an exhibition. 'This is the grave of the Jews who were kidnapped in 1941. . . . This second grave is from the "provocation action". . . . And these are the graves from the "actions" of the "pink pass," "yellow pass," and Yom Kippur.' Over one grave Weiss said: 'This is *Jeszcze Polska Nie Zginela*' (the first words of the Polish national hymn. He meant that Poles were buried there.) He also pointed out the grave of Lithuanian priests and the graves of Russian POWs. With sadistic pleasure he spoke about the large pits full of human bones.

"At the end of the tour he ordered us to gather up the scattered and mutilated corpses and throw them into a third pit, smaller than the other two but not yet filled. We found a young woman, hugging her infant son. The baby's head and the woman's breast had been shattered by the same dum-dum bullet. Several steps away lay a young girl with long blond braids. She was dressed in a pretty silk dress. Obviously, she had adorned herself in honor of Kovno. Her left leg had been smashed above the knee by an exploding bullet. It remained attached to her body by a very thin strip of skin. Further on we found the corpse of an old man. While moving it, we could see the exposed skull. Not a bit of brain remained. Beyond the railroad tracks lay a boy and girl, both face-down, hands tightly linked. They were brother and sister, who had tried to escape their bitter fate. In death, as well as life, they were not parted. Who can believe all the horrible sights we saw? How can I begin to explain what we felt while we stood inside the pit and trampled the hundreds of corpses, while the sun shone from a blue sky and a nightingale twittered in the trees. . . .

"For hours we gathered up the bodies and limbs and brought them to the pit for burial. While working, one of our men tried to get a few words out of a Lithuanian policeman. Perhaps *he* could tell us our fate. The Lithuanian proudly explained that he and his comrades dug the pits and killed the people brought to Ponar. They had been doing this from the very beginning of the war. In response to a direct question as to why we had been brought there, the Lithuanian said: 'Apparently Weiss wants to fill the third pit as well. It would not bother us.' At dusk Weiss told us: 'You can choose from the train cars the most valuable belongings and the best food and tell the ghetto that I have sent a gift to the hungry Jews.' We filled up 14 wagons, which stood ready to take us back to the ghetto. While poking around the cars we heard groans. In one corner lay a young man whose body had been pierced by seven bullets. Carefully, so that Weiss would not detect anything, we placed him in one of the wagons and brought him to the ghetto, together with Weiss's 'gift.'

"Even if I live to a ripe old age," said the policeman in conclusion, "I shall never forget the horrors I saw today."

For several days, groups of Jews left the ghetto to transfer the belongings from Ponar to the Gestapo warehouse in the ghetto. Other groups sorted out the objects. While examining the clothes, they sometimes found wads of money, gold, or jewelry sewn inside the clothing. Among the sorters were also a number of members of the Fighting Organization. Despite German vigilance, they succeeded in bringing sums of money to the ghetto to use for the purchase of arms.

Several days later, dozens of wagons arrived in the ghetto, filled with blood-stained clothes. This was the present which the Gestapo had sent the ghetto Jews. Like a funeral procession, the wagons moved along the narrow streets on their way to the Judenrat warehouses. Tearful Jews led the way. Were they mourning those who had already gone to their death or those who were to follow them?

Unrest spread throughout the ghetto. The leaders tried to calm the public and called upon them to be disciplined. The Gestapo heads were promising once more that no ill would befall the Vilna Ghetto. Gens gathered together the leaders of the Workers' Brigade and told them: "True, the Germans deceived us this time, but we have clear proof that our ghetto is not in danger. We must buy time and, first and foremost, we must restore public order. Discipline, order, and confidence in the leaders are the foundations of our lives and the secret of our survival. Let us mourn the dead, but let us also concern ourselves with the living. This is possible only through hard work and fulfilling our tasks faithfully. Let us live in hope for better days, which must surely come soon."

Gradually, people calmed down, but ghetto life never returned to normal.

A New Spirit

In the spring of 1943 the Headquarters finished drawing up the bylaws of the Fighting Organization. The Organization was already so well based that the Headquarters decided to convene, for the first time, all the commanders and instructors. The assembly took place in the soup kitchen at 31 Deutscheshe Street, where Headquarters member Nissan Reznik was manager on behalf of the Judenrat.

For the first time, people who never suspected each other of belonging to the Organization met one another. The commander, Itzik Wittenberg, explained the bylaws. He spoke about the situation of the Jews in the German-occupied countries and his conclusions were pessimistic. In his opinion, the ghetto would not last long.

The bylaws were diligently studied in groups and in cells. They included instructions to fighters and set out all the rules for mobilization and behavior during battle. They warned that the fighting would begin in an atmosphere of panic and the Organization might suffer initial defeats. They defined the composition and structure of the Organization: two battalions, each of them consisting of six to eight groups. Each group contained three 5-member cells. The mobilization of fighting forces could take place in two ways: by order from Headquarters or spontaneously. A mobilization order given by Headquarters required every fighter to appear in Deutscheshe Street and to arrive under all conditions, even if this meant breaking a passage through with cold ammunition. Spontaneous mobilization would occur in the event of sudden danger to the ghetto when Jews would begin running to their hiding-places. In such an event, each F.P.O. fighter had to take up position immediately, without waiting for a call-up order. An Organization member who went into a shelter would be considered a traitor. The bylaws stated what a fighter must do if he is cut off from his comrades or is the last survivor in battle. He was required to fight with all kinds of ammunition and even without arms; save precious ammunition; and, in the absence of an order from his superiors, act on his own initiative. A wounded fighter was required to turn over his weapon to his comrade. The bylaws also had a contingency plan in case the Command was arrested; if this happened, a sub-Headquarters would be activated.

The bylaws were debated and the Organization commander answered various questions that arose during these debates. He said that in the case of a partial ''action'' against a few, the Organization would not act. It was not entitled to take risks, through premature action, which could bring about its own destruction. It could not leave the ghetto without a defense force. That would be a quixotic act, tantamount to suicide. But if a premature response was folly, delayed action was no less a crime. The Organization would begin operation during an ''action'' which, in its estimation, marked the beginning of the end for the ghetto.

The Organization did not demand an immediate exodus to the forest. The Organization's members would go to the forest only as a result of battle. After accomplishing its task in the ghetto, it would take as large a number of Jews as possible and make its way into the forest, there to continue its war against the enemies as an inalienable part of the general partisan movement.

Very hazy reports reached the ghetto about the Warsaw Ghetto Uprising, but they were enough to force the Vilna Jews to face reality. No one had imagined that the Germans would dare destroy a ghetto which contained hundreds of thousands of Jews. Now everyone understood that destruction was inevitable. They began to discuss ways of escape: going to the forests, building shelters, obtaining Aryan papers, and so forth. Yet at the same time, everyone talked with enthusiasm and pride about the resistance of the Warsaw Jews. Many Jews secretly vowed to do the same and not go as sheep to slaughter.

The ghetto also received news of the large partisan movement that arose in White Russia, headed by Markov. Upon hearing accounts of the courageous acts of the partisans in their war against the Germans, many imagined themselves among the fighters in the forest. There was whispering about arms being smuggled into the ghetto in preparation for armed resistance. No one could identify the arms smugglers or those preparing for revolt, but the rumors were persistent and were the main topic of conversation. Everyone was excited. Everyone wanted to buy arms, but how could one get them? Where would the money come from to pay for it?

People began building underground shelters. The Jewish power of invention wrought wonders in this field. All kinds of basements, tunnels, and secret passages were dug in places where no one would dream of looking for them. These bunkers were outfitted with all kinds of provisions for a prolonged stay. Those who could not afford a shelter made do with temporary arrangements. The main thing was that it gave them some sort of moral support.

The Fighters' Organization stepped up its propaganda campaign among the masses in their homes, in their places of work, and in the streets. Everywhere it gained new adherents to the idea of armed resistance. By now people were ready to listen. At times it seemed that if the Germans tried to destroy the ghetto, the whole ghetto would rise up in self-defense.

This change of mood was felt in the Organization. It recruited dozens of new fighters. The growing number of fighters required more arms. The Headquarters knew that in time of need, the weapons in the warehouses would not suffice and ordered that ''cold'' arms be prepared as well. The fighters gathered axes, clubs, iron rods, and other tools. They prepared them not only for themselves but also for the hundreds of Jews who, when the active resistance began, would be willing to risk their lives and join the fighting ranks.

The ghetto leaders sensed this new mood. They made desperate efforts to calm the public and prove that the Vilna Ghetto was different from all the other ghettos and would not be destroyed. When they discovered how powerless they were to restore calm among the masses, they increased their internal terror. Police Chief Dessler organized thugs to work for him, thus extending his espionage network. The police beat up Jews left and right. Lidski jail was always packed with prisoners.

The Jews feared one another and spoke guardedly. Who knew whether the things told to one's friends would not reach the ears of the police? Panic and constant fear were the lot of the ghetto Jews.

The Germans issued new orders. Every Jew must wear a metal tag around his neck with a number, like a dog. Everyone received a personal *Ausweis* (a kind of identity card bearing his picture and fingerprints). This card also recorded the number on the tag. Long lines formed in front of the Judenrat offices, which distributed the new documents, without which it was forbidden to be seen on the streets. Every German, Lithuanian, or Pole could check a Jew's document and tag, and Heaven help anyone caught without them!

One day the ghetto was shocked to hear a report that a German soldier had turned over to the Gestapo a young Jew who had wanted to buy a gun from him. The fellow was cruelly tortured and interrogated in order to force him to reveal the names of his friends. He was executed, and the ghetto authorities received a strict warning.

One evening the Jewish workers in the *Bautelager* (the German arms warehouses) did not return from their work at the regular time. A feeling of worry and concern spread throughout the ghetto. That same night it was learned that the Germans caught a Jewish fellow named Zalman Tiktin stealing arms. While he was being led under heavy guard from the warehouse to the quarters of the camp commander for interrogation, he broke loose and escaped. But he did not get far. Several dozen meters away he fell, wounded by bullets. When the Gestapo officers asked Zalman why he had wanted to steal arms, he shouted back: "Against you! To avenge the blood of my parents whom you murdered!" They put him in a German hospital to recover from his wounds so that they could force him to reveal the names of his comrades. Zalman knew what awaited him. He tore the bandages from his wounds, thus killing himself.

Tiktin was a member of the Organization. On the day of his death, a ceremony was held in his honor, and the company to which he belonged was named after him.

One morning the Jewish gate guard caught a young man named Levin, who came from one of the small towns around Vilna, carrying a gun. The latter refused to surrender the gun, so the guard arrested him. For several hours the police tried to persuade him to hand over his gun, promising him that no ill would befall him. But Levin stood his ground. Moreover, he began to threaten to use his weapon. Gens warned him for the last time, and when Levin still refused, Gens shot and killed him.

Glazmanists

The ghetto leaders exploited such incidents to claim that the Underground's activity could bring disaster upon the ghetto and only they could save it from catastrophe. They hoped in this way to reassert their power and restore their waning prestige. They decided to make another attempt to destroy the Fighting Organization. One day several policemen went to Josef Glazman's apartment with an order to arrest him and to take him to the Rzesza labor camp 15 kilometers from Vilna. Josef announced that he would not comply. The policemen attacked him with rubber truncheons, manacled him, and dragged him through the narrow ghetto streets to the police headquarters at 6 Rudnicka Street. Josef did not stop resisting and was beaten by the policemen along the entire way.

The news of his arrest and the way in which the police treated him spread quickly. The Jews were shocked. If the police dared to behave towards Josef in this way, the end of the ghetto was, no doubt, near. Everyone was panic-stricken. The Organization was also shocked. The command called up several companies and put them on the alert. Once again a delegation was sent to Gens. He claimed that the matter had come to the attention of the German authorities and it was necessary that Josef leave the ghetto, where he faced danger.

The command decided not to accept Josef's deportation and to use force, if necessary. Fighting detachments entered Rudnicka Street, where Josef was being held. F.P.O. people hid near the police station and waited for what would come.

At noon the policemen stopped all movement in the ghetto and ordered the Jews into their homes. All seven streets of the ghetto were now under supervision of the ghetto authorities. There was reinforced guard on Rudnicka Street. The building entrances were closed and no one could enter or exit. Every guard was responsible for one house, to see to it that there was no movement. In the yards, behind the locked gates, the F.P.O. members stood on the alert.

The street was empty of people. Suddenly a noise was heard outside. A wagon left 6 Rudnicka Street, with Josef inside, hands in irons, and surrounded by policemen. One policeman geed up the horses. The distance to the gate, on 18 Rudnicka Street, was not far. Suddenly, there was the sound of frantic running. The locked gates were flung open and the fighters jumped outside. In a flash they reached the wagon. The policeman continued to urge the horses on. Only five houses stood between him and the gate, but the fighters fell upon him with force. Someone jumped onto the wagon. Another held Josef while struggling with the policeman.

Time was precious. They had to get away as soon as possible from the dangerous area of Lithuanian gate guards. Josef was already on the ground, surrounded by fighters. He tried to snap his handcuffs but was unsuccessful. Having no alternative, they brought him handcuffed back to the center of the ghetto. Several policemen lay in the streets. Their comrades went to their aid, confused and irritated.

Now all the gates were opened and the people ran outside. They saw Josef, his hands bound, and several dozen youths around him, walking along Rudnicka, Shawelska, and Straszun Streets. Some of the crowd joined the group. There was great excitement and amazement. Several streets around the site of the Organization's Headquarters, where the situation was being discussed, were entirely in the hands of the fighters. There were no policemen to be seen. The ghetto inhabitants looked with wonder at the youths; they formed a cordon and would not let anyone through who did not know the password. Even top officials of the ghetto leadership were dependent on the goodwill of the young girls who barred their way.

Gens and Dessler called the Headquarters members to a meeting and pleaded with them: if Josef did not leave the ghetto, they would have to resign. They would be a laughingstock in the eyes of the masses and no one would continue to accept their authority. Moreover, if the matter became known to the Gestapo, the latter would begin an investigation and this could jeopardize the whole ghetto. For if they heard that the Jews had a Fighting Organization, they could begin the immediate destruction of the ghetto. It was mandatory, they said, to save their prestige. They asked Headquarters to agree that Josef be sent to Rzesza, only for a few days. And if not, there would be no alternative but to allow the Organization itself to assume leadership of the ghetto.

The Headquarters could not imagine undertaking the daily administrative affairs of the ghetto and did not want to be in any way close to the Gestapo. It, therefore, agreed to a compromise proposal, but gave serious warning to the ghetto leaders that if they did not keep their word and did not return Josef within a few days, the Organization would take strong reprisal measures.

Accompanied by Organization members and ghetto inhabitants, Josef returned to the police. But this time he was not shackled. He went as a victor. Now every Jew knew that there was an organized and armed force in the ghetto, much stronger than the forces of the official leaders, including the police itself. The ghetto called the Organization's people "Glazmanists." It now knew that the Jewish people were not helpless. There was a force ready to oppose the Germans. And many things which had hitherto been unclear now became evident to all.

Hiding from the Judenrat

During the first months of 1943, the Germans ordered that a Jewish work brigade be sent to the Kovno environs. The ghetto authorities issued an announcement to the Jews to sign up for the journey, promising good conditions in the work camps to which they would be sent. But the ghetto Jews were experienced. They did not believe the promises and they did not respond to the calls. The leaders ordered the *Arbeitsamt* to provide the number of people wanted by the Germans. The *Arbeitsamt* drew up lists as it saw fit, and its special police went from house to house and ordered the people whose names appeared on the lists to get ready to leave.

There was bargaining over human lives. Anyone who had "connections" or was able to bribe the policemen saved himself from deportation, and another name was written in his place. And, as always, the victims were the poor and the lonely, who had no one to protect them. Workers' detachments left the ghetto for Palmon, Paniemun, and other places near Kovno.

News reached the ghetto that the people had, indeed, reached their destination, but that the living conditions in the camps were unbearable. Palmon was a camp not for only Jews. There were workers of all the nations of Europe, including Russian POWs. It was the only international camp in Lithuania.

The life of the Jews in the mixed camp was very hard. Not only were they given smaller portions of food than the non-Jewish workers, but they also had to suffer the insults and maltreatment of their fellow prisoners. The latter wanted to find favor with the Germans by beating up the Jews, and perhaps they also got some consolation in this for their own fate. The Jews did not bother asking why the non-Jewish prisoners maltreated them. There was only one conclusion to be drawn: even on the brink of death, the non-Jews could not forget their hatred of the Jews.

Several days after Josef was sent to Rzesza, an order came from the Germans to send 50 people to work in Ponevezh (Panevezys), my native city. This city had been *judenrein* since the outbreak of the war. The annihilation of the Jews of Ponevezh had begun, in fact, with the outbreak of heavy fighting between the *Reichwehr* and the Red Army, before the Germans had even entered the city. Several days after the occupation of Ponevezh, all the Jews were taken to a ghetto on the edge of the city together with the Jews of Krakinava, Rogave (Raguva), Puzhelot (Puzele), Kupishok (Kupiskis), Shadove (Seduva), and other towns in the area. This was the first ghetto in Lithuania. Some time later the Lithuanians removed all the men from the ghetto, took them to Paiosti Forest, four kilometers from the city, and there killed them after unimaginable tortures. Several days later the Lithuanians returned to the ghetto and told the women that if they turned over all their money and jewelry, they could join their men and would be allowed to remain there. The women were grateful to the Lithuanians for their kindness, gave them all their possessions, and, in high spirits, were led from the ghetto. The Lithuanians kept their promise: they brought all the women to the huge pit in which lay the mutilated bodies of their men and cruelly murdered the women as well. In this mass grave, 16,000 Lithuanian Jews found their final rest.

That was in August 1941, before the establishment of the ghetto in Vilna. Now, two years later, the Germans were moving hundreds of Jews to Ponevezh from the Kovno Ghetto and forcing them to build an airfield in Paiosti, near the place of the slaughter. They demanded that Jewish workers from Vilna be sent there too.

The ghetto authorities saw this as another opportunity to weaken the Fighting Organization. One day they ordered Borka Schneider and me to join the transport which was to leave for Ponevezh in a few days. Miriam Ganionska told the Headquarters that she had heard that Dessler told his cronies, "I must shear this Samson. I hope that this time I shall succeed."

The Headquarters decided that we should not go. The whole organization was called up, and fighting units took up positions in various places throughout the ghetto. They were ready to act in the event that an attempt was made to remove the two of us by force. Day and night the Organization's fighters stood guard and followed the course of events. The Headquarters warned the ghetto leaders not to dare harm us.

But this time the leaders were unwilling to give way. They ordered the policemen to arrest us, come what may. As the police had begun thorough searches, the Headquarters decided that we should hide in a bunker to prevent a clash among Jews. The Organization's aim was to fight against the Germans so as to save Jewish lives; it must not use its arms against Jews. The relatives of one of the fighters were co-owners of a bunker under construction on 31 Deutscheshe Street. Under order of the Headquarters, we descended into the bunker and hid there.

In the yard of that same building was a toilet belonging to all the tenants. In one of the corners was a narrow opening covered by a metal lid. It had been used for cleaning and repair purposes and now served as an entrance to the bunker. Metal stairs led approximately two feet down. On the right was a kind of iron porthole which was hermetically sealed. When it was opened, one found the beginning of a narrow tunnel several meters long, which one could pass through only by crawling on one's stomach. At the end of the tunnel was another iron porthole, and beyond was the entrance to the bunker. When the second porthole was closed, an electric light switched on, and in the dim light one could discern a 4 × 4 square meter room. It contained a bathroom, faucet, and shower. The room behind it was wide and served as a bedroom. The double-decker cots were wooden and could accommodate over 100 people. A third room was for dining and cooking. It contained a table, dozens of cans of kerosene and cooking stoves, and assorted kitchen utensils. The fourth and last room was a storage room. Inside the walls were tin containers with dried biscuits and full sacks of groats, potatoes, sugar, and other foodstuffs. A tunnel connected this room to the central chimney of the building. One could go up the chimney with rope ladders and come out into open air. In the bunker were fans connected to the chimney. When everyone would be inside the bunker, the opening on the side of the bathroom would be flooded with water. Naturally, the Germans would not think of searching for a bunker two feet under water.

The bunker was very safe. It was one of the best and safest in all the ghetto. However, it did not save those who later used it. After sitting inside for several days, they became restless and wanted to know what was happening outside. One fellow went up the chimney by the rope-ladder, and when he reached the top he saw German and Lithuanian guards on the roofs around. He descended to report the fact.

But the Germans saw him as well. Before he could report the news, dynamite exploded and the bunker filled with smoke. The fans stopped working and it became increasingly difficult to breathe. Panic broke out. The women started to cry, the children screamed, and the men were helpless. They decided it was better to go out and surrender to the Germans than choke to death. The Germans, who could not have imagined that more than one person could hide inside a chimney, and who had thrown the grenades only to kill the one fellow, were very surprised when such a large group of Jews came out. They were still joking about it on the way to Ponar.

Borka and I hid inside this bunker for several days. Every night one of the Organization's members would come and bring us food and books to read. Sitting inside the "grave" made us very depressed. It was hard to come to terms with the idea that hundreds of people were planning a long stay in such bunkers.

After the transport had departed for Ponevezh, we left the bunker. I was immediately taken to the hospital, for after receiving the order to leave, I had come down with typhoid fever, and sitting in the cold and damp underground certainly did not make me any healthier. . . .

The ghetto received very distressing news about the fate of the Jews in the work camps around Vilna and there was fear for their future. A week had passed since Josef was taken to Rzesza, and there was still no indication that the authorities intended to send him back. When the Headquarters demanded that the promise be kept, it received evasive answers.

Hirsch Glick's Gift

Summer 1943. Gestapo officer Kittel came to Vilna as the new ghetto commander. The Jews were very worried about the change of command. Their experience over the last two years had taught them that every new commander brought with him new decrees.

It was said in the ghetto that Kittel was a native of Austria and that before the war he had been an actor and had even appeared in films. Now he worked in the Gestapo Division, carrying out the extermination of the Jews. Despite his young age, the officer had already proven himself. In many Jewish communities of eastern Europe, it was Kittel who had planned and carried out the extermination. When he came to the Vilna Ghetto for the first time, the narrow streets emptied of people. But some time later it was learned that he was not so terrible. He was seen standing in the street with a big smile on his face. He stood and talked with Dessler, waving his hands about like a real Jew.

Kittel had the reputation of being a music lover. He even promised to bring the ghetto symphony orchestra several instruments which it needed. The Jews were immediately hopeful: a person who loves art cannot be so bad. Perhaps good days will come under his rule. There was some basis for this optimism. In all his many visits to the ghetto, no one had ever seen him get angry or had heard him shout, curse, or even threaten. He was always pleasant and generously agreed to all the requests of the ghetto leaders.

Kittel visited the labor camps near Vilna and in the ghetto; he was reportedly very satisfied with the work of the Jews and the great benefit they brought to the Reich. One day, Kittel went to visit the work camp in Bezdany, 25 kilometers from Vilna. The work there was very hard, and all the workers were young and strong. Kittel was very satisfied with this camp and its productivity. He praised the young workers and promised that he would visit them again soon. He also increased their food portions and brought them presents.

The young men in Bezdany were all armed. They were all determined not to return to the ghetto and a life of subjugation and humiliation. If they discovered that extermination were near, they would all arise, escape into the forests, and join the partisans. They were sure that the time was not far off. And now, after Kittel's promises, it seemed that the time had not yet come. It was best to wait a bit.

Meanwhile, they could buy more arms, prepare clothing, and save money to hold out in the forest.

One morning several refugees arrived in the ghetto from Bezdany. They were frightful-looking; their clothes were ripped and their bodies were bruised and injured. They said that the day before, Kittel had come on his second visit with a truck full of soldiers. At his order, everyone gathered in the dining-room in one of the barracks. The soldiers unloaded several large jars of fine jam, a sack of sugar, and a crate of butter off the truck.

Kittel was in high spirits. He spoke to them for over an hour and told them it was because of their work that they remained alive. He promised them that if they continued to work diligently, the Germans would treat them well. He pointed to the large jars and said that only soldiers at the front got such food. He continued to raise their hopes and even said that at the end of the war they would live in the Third Reich under the auspices of National Socialism and its great leader, Hitler.

After the speech, Kittel asked the barber to shave him. He entered another room with him and ordered the man not to move until he returned. Meanwhile he said: "You can distribute the gifts I brought among yourselves." The workers began the distribution without imagining that it was a trap. After being shaved, Kittel gave the barber a cigarette and asked him if he wanted a light. When the latter said yes, Kittel took out his gun and said: "Here's your fire," and shot him. The shot was a signal to the soldiers. They opened heavy fire on the barracks where all the workers were concentrated and threw hand grenades and incendiary bombs inside. A few minutes later the barracks was up in flames. Those who tried to escape were shot and the others were burned alive. Thus ended the story of Bezdany, a story of strong lads, armed and ready to fight, who did not know when to seize the opportunity.

Panic broke out in the ghetto. Everyone saw the Bezdany affair as a clear sign that the end was near. The leaders were embarrassed and confused. Only recently they had been able to sway public opinion to their side against the Fighting Organization by pointing to the case of the labor camp in Biala Waka (Baltoji Voke), where the escape of a few Jews had led to mass retaliation. Now they were at a loss for words. But they recovered several days later. They had a tried remedy for pacifying the people: the Gestapo leaders had repeated their promise that the Vilna Ghetto would come to no harm. . . .

Within the Organization anger mounted against the leaders who had not kept their promise to return Josef. Clearly, what had happened in Bezdany yesterday could happen tomorrow in Rzesza and, therefore, there was much concern over Josef's fate. Discussions were held on how to bring Josef back and how to warn the Rzesza Jews not to fall into a Gestapo trap.

Meanwhile, Josef was spreading the idea of resistance in Rzesza. There were still many Jews there who believed the Germans and their promises. Josef spoke with each of them and tried to convince them that the Germans should not be trusted and that they were plotting to exterminate every last Jew. His words made an impression. The Jews waited for a signal to escape from the camp. Some of them hid in peasants' homes and prepared hiding-places. One urged Josef to go with him, promising him a safe bunker. But Josef rejected the offer. He did not think about saving himself; he thought about his friends in the ghetto. He knew that he had to be with them in battle. The day of destruction was not far off and the Organization's members would have to fight for their lives and honor.

When word came to Rzesza about what had happened in Bezdany, all the Jews escaped from the camp. Despite the beefed-up Lithuanian guard, everyone got away. Most of them, led by Josef, headed towards Vilna.

In the ghetto it was learned that many Jews from Rzesza were hiding in the new Jewish cemetery in Dabrowka, near the city. As always, panic broke out. No one knew what had happened in Rzesza, but it was assumed that it was a repetition of the Bezdany affair.

The Jews decided to hide in the bunkers. Any minute they expected the arrival of the Gestapo in search of the escapees. The ghetto authorities prevented the entrance of the Rzesza Jews. They had received promises from the Gestapo that the Rzesza camp was very vital to the war effort and that the Jews could return there and continue their work. If they did not do so, the leaders would not be responsible for their lives. The Jewish police received an order to be especially vigilant lest Josef return to the ghetto. Naturally, no one returned to Rzesza. One by one the escapees infiltrated the ghetto. They mingled among the brigade Jews returning from work. Josef also returned. A group of fighters left the ghetto to bring him back secretly. The gate guards received a sharp reprimand, though they swore on all that was dear to them that Josef would not cross the gate.

During the two weeks Josef stayed in Rzesza, he became friendly with a young poet, Hirsch Glick. They would talk for hours about armed resistance and revenge against the enemy. When Josef returned to his friends in the ghetto, he took out of his pocket a gray and crumpled piece of paper and said: "This is a gift I received from Hirsch Glick." On the paper was written: "Poem of Resistance. Dedicated to my friend Josef Glazman, who opened my eyes to the truth and taught me the right way." The Headquarters decided that this poem would be the Organization's anthem. Several days later the melody of "Do Not Say That This Is The End of the Road" echoed throughout the ghetto. Hundreds and thousands of Jews found expression for their innermost feelings in this song.

*Itzik Wittenberg, commander
of the F.P.O.*

A Burnt Offering

July 15, 1943. For several days the ghetto was in a state of great tension.
Everyone believed that a new disaster was on its way. The fighters were also
uneasy. The Organization's commander, Itzik Wittenberg, had been in hiding for
several days. Word had it that two Gentile Communist leaders in Vilna had been
arrested and one of them had revealed to the Gestapo their ties with Wittenberg and
the existence of an underground organization in the ghetto.

Kittel came to the ghetto and demanded that the leaders hand Wittenberg over
to him. They were willing to comply, but the plot was revealed in time and the
police, despite its great efforts, was unable to find the commander.

Gens invited all of the Organization leaders in for a talk. He wanted, as it
were, to tell them important news about the situation. That very evening the Betar
members were holding a small party for Josef, in celebration of his return to the
ghetto. The party took place in the workshops on 3 Oszmianska Street.

Josef did not want to take part in the meeting with Gens. He preferred to spend the evening with his friends. As always, he was quiet, serious, and gifted with a brilliant analytical sense. "The days of the ghetto are numbered," he said, "and every day and every hour we must be ready for unpleasant surprises. But the masses still delude themselves and put their trust in the leadership. They must be made to see the bitter reality so that when the time comes they will help us in the desperate battle against the enemy. The battle will be hard, with almost no chance of success, but it would be a holy war for our people and for the coming generations."

From the day he was attacked by the police, Josef did not part from his weapon; he carried his gun on the evening of the party as well. Close to midnight, Rashka burst into the room, white as a sheet. With great emotion, she whispered something in Josef's ear. He got up and his words sounded like thunder in the silence: "There has been treachery. The leaders have handed over the commander to the Gestapo." Everyone grabbed what he could and ran outside after Josef. Arriving at Rudnicka Street, near the courtyard of the Judenrat, we saw several figures in the dark. Suddenly we recognized the commander among them. His hands were manacled behind his back and he was being led away by Gestapo men. Seeing us, he lunged in our direction, shouting: "Treachery . . . they have deceived us!" A struggle broke out between us and the Gestapo men. The battle lasted several minutes. Several shots split the silence. The commander was already in the workshops, in the room where we had held our party. Hearing shots, people ran out of their homes, and panic quickly spread throughout the ghetto. People descended into their bunkers. They were sure that an action had begun.

Risking their lives, our members fought to prevent the Jewish police from entering the room that housed the commander. The police had to retreat. Pleased that we had succeeded in saving the commander, we returned to the room where the party had been held. But it was clear that the police would return soon with reinforcements. The commander was somewhat pale, but in a calm and clear voice he ordered that all the Organization's people be mobilized, that the weapons be taken out, and that the fighters take up positions. He told us how he was arrested. While they were all seated with Gens, Dessler suddenly left the meeting room and returned some time later with several Gestapo men. He pointed out Wittenberg and said: "This is the underground commander. Arrest him."

When the Headquarters people protested to Gens over this treachery, he said that the Gestapo had demanded that he turn over Wittenberg and that he, Gens, was unwilling to risk the lives of all the Jews to save one man. The Headquarters decided to hide the commander and to give him armed protection if needed. The liaisons called all the fighters to take up positions.

At 3 A.M. Gens called a meeting of brigadiers, policemen, and thugs in the courtyard of the Judenrat building on Rudnicka Street. He railed against the Fighting Organization. There was peace in the ghetto, he said, and the Germans promised that they would not harm us. "We are trying as hard as we can to help you get through this difficult period. But there is a group of stupid and crazy people among you who do not want to observe established order. Through their irresponsible acts, these people can bring disaster upon the whole ghetto. Their existence endangers the lives of all the Jews. We set up workshops for you, and jobs which are important to the Germans," boasted Gens. "We gave you the possibility of working and living in peace, because work is the only guarantee for our existence. And they, the members of this gang, not only do they want no part of this, but they are also trying to disturb us in our work. They have placed themselves outside the community and their conduct threatens to bring annihilation upon us. We must tear this evil out by the roots. Let us have no pity on them, just as they are unconcerned about us, our children, and babies. Help us, cooperate with us in our efforts to destroy them, because your lives depend on this. The Gestapo is demanding the life of only one man. We shall turn him over to them and there will be peace again in the ghetto. but if we don't do as they wish, we shall suffer for it. Draw your own conclusions."

Gens's words had their effect. The masses stormed our positions angrily. Propagandists and agents circulated among the masses, inciting them against the Organization. A terrible fraternal war was about to break out, to the joy of our oppressors who could see their own work being carried out by the Jews themselves.

In the morning hours our battalion received an order to change its positions. We walked through the streets and stones rained down upon our heads. From both sides of the street, we were attacked with clubs. Jews, whose fates were already sealed, fell upon their brethren like beasts of prey.

We had received an order not to use weapons, whatever happened. They were not to be used against our Jewish brothers. We took up new positions on Shawelska Street. The masses, headed by the police and the underworld, attacked us and were about to break through the barrier. With heavy hearts but with strong resolve, we beat off their attack.

Dessler announced from the Gestapo office: "If within several hours Wittenberg is not turned over, German tanks will enter the ghetto, planes will bomb it, and it will be utterly destroyed."

Tension was mounting; our guns were cocked. We knew that Wittenberg's arrest was just a pretext on the part of the Gestapo. They wanted to begin destroying the armed force of the ghetto to make it easier to carry out the general destruction without fear of resistance. But how could we explain the bitter truth to the masses? How could we tell this to all the Jews, incited by the leaders who preached fraternal war on the very brink of destruction instead of calling the ghetto to fight together against the common enemy?

We made desperate efforts to pacify the crowd. Some of our fighters mingled with the crowd and began explaining our position. The crowd began to listen. Perhaps they were right—these young people, ready to die fighting the enemy, thought the simple Jew. The people began to debate the matter. The inciters retreated. The murderous faces disappeared. Worry marked the faces of the Jews in front of us.

Delegations of activists, the Judenrat leaders, and other Jews began to reach our Headquarters. They wanted to be angels of peace, to mediate between the police and the fighters. The Headquarters was in constant consultation. We knew that the street was against us. The Jewish masses would accuse us of being responsible for the destruction of the ghetto. Was there no way out?

The Communist leaders and the Headquarters people decided that Wittenberg had to turn himself over to the Gestapo and thereby save the ghetto. But meanwhile contact had been lost with the commander. No one knew where he was. How could he be told about this decision?

Dessler called from the Gestapo office again. The last chance for turning over Wittenberg was 6:00 P.M. If he would not be surrendered by then, the Germans would begin to destroy the ghetto. Meanwhile several hours had passed and the tension was coming to a climax. The streets buzzed with people who believed they were about to be destroyed. The workers did not go to work.

The police conducted searches to find the commander. Leading the search was Avraham Krizovski, one of the Communist leaders and a friend of Wittenberg. His diligence amazed the fighters.

We heard that Wittenberg had succeeded in getting away from the police and reaching the Headquarters. The Communists informed him of their decision but he was unwilling to accept it. He claimed that the ghetto would be destroyed in any case, and it was best to begin the revolt immediately against the Germans. When his comrades begged him, he demanded a decision by the Communist District Center. About an hour later, one of the Communists came back with the decision: surrender. The Organization's Headquarters supported it. So Wittenberg said: "if that is what all of you want, I am willing to sacrifice myself for the ghetto."

The news spread with lightning speed throughout the ghetto. The Jews congregated in the streets to see the man who was offering himself as a sacrifice for their sake. With a calm gait and peaceful mien, Wittenberg walked through the narrow streets, accompanied by armed policemen. The fighters paid him honor for the last time. There was pain and anger in their eyes.

But the ghetto Jews breathed a sigh of relief.

In the death cars, on the journey from which none returned, they would later recall how they attacked us. They would remember the stones they threw at us and the clubs they hit us with. They would recall the human sacrifice who offered himself in vain, and the blind stupidity of the fraternal war in the presence of the common enemy, and perhaps they would find atonement for their sins.

The First Move to the Forest

Having turned the F.P.O. commander over to the Gestapo, the Judenrat leaders were now full of self-confidence. There would no longer be any contenders to their leadership. It seemed that a new period was about to begin, one of peace and quiet, which would continue undisturbed until the Liberation. The news from the fronts was very encouraging, while the daring of the partisans increased by the day. It was clear that the collapse of the Wehrmacht was not far off. Not long ago, Russian planes had bombed Vilna. Some Lithuanian policemen and German soldiers were killed, and even the ghetto received a few pieces of shrapnel from "our" bombings.

The Jews concluded that the Russians knew the precise location of the ghetto, and to infuriate the Germans, were purposely bombing all sectors of the city, except the area where the Jews lived.

The leaders decided that this was an opportune time to destroy the Organization completely. Because of the Wittenberg affair, they had succeeded in gaining the sympathy of the masses and convinced them that the Organization endangered the entire ghetto. Now they could safely expect the ghetto Jews to assist them in bleeding out the members of the Organization.

Perhaps the leaders were right. Perhaps the masses might have been willing to help destroy the Organization. Yet, in their hearts they still had the feeling that they would be deceiving themselves if they believed that the worst was already behind and that from now on the Germans would let them live to the end of the war. Something told them that the recent, tumultuous events were just the beginning of the end, and that the young people preparing for the final battle were right.

At the portentous staff meeting of July 16, in which Wittenberg decided to turn himself over to the Gestapo, the command of the Organizaton passed to Abba Kovner. The fighters were surprised at first by this appointment, for they were sure that Wittenberg would choose Josef Glazman. But after a few days, they understood. Josef was in the ghetto illegally, to the great irritation of the Judenrat leaders, and he was also the man who had convinced the Jews of Rzesza to escape.

The police were looking for him. He could not hide out for an extended period of time. If he were caught, the leaders would almost certainly surrender him to the Gestapo.

The fighters heard that messengers of the partisan commander Markov from Narocz Forest were visiting the ghetto. For quite a long time, the fighters had been debating the matter of joining the partisans, and everyone now realized that as the Organization had effectively emerged from the underground, the move of the forest must begin.

It was obvious that Josef would be among the first to leave, both for reasons of personal safety and because he was the one best equipped to establish contact with Markov and prepare the ground for the fighters who would follow. In the wake of the new situation that was created after July 16, the staff decided to start sending out groups immediately. The best and bravest fighters were chosen for the departing company named "Leon" (Wittenberg's nickname in the Organization). Included in the group were also those who would have been in danger of arrest if they remained in the ghetto.

The evening of July 24. In the prevailing atmosphere of the last few days among the Jews of the ghetto, it was not easy to slip out. One had to be very careful so as not to arouse any suspicions. Any hasty action could lead to failure.

The plan was worked out to the finest detail. Arms and ammunition were distributed. Female medics were appointed to provide first-aid. Final instructions were given. The group waited for daybreak, when the Jews of the ghetto would leave for work.

Many of the fighters envied us. Soon, we would be free men, free of all the suffering and shame, while they remained behind the ghetto walls. Miriam Bernstein desperately tried to join the group. But the number of girls was limited: no more than three were allowed to leave.

Miriam parted from me with a heavy heart. She cried and said: "I feel that we will never see each other again." This bleak prophecy turned out to be true.

The night was quiet. The ghetto was deep in sleep after a day of hard labor. For us, it was a night of vigil. At dawn, we stole out one by one through a side gate from the courtyard of 6 Rudnicka Street, the site of the Judenrat and the police. We were twenty-one men and women: the Gordon brothers, Hirsh and Leib, Berl Druzgenik, Gerson Gittelson, Tevka Halperin, David Widutski, Israelik Dubchanski, Berl and Rosa Sherezhnevski, Rachel Borakiski, Chaya Tykochinski, Chaim Spokojny, Iska Mackiewicz, Zundel Leizerson, Molka Hazan, David (Kuska) Augenfeld, Shlomo Kantrovich, Shika and Chaya Gertner, Josef Glazman, and myself.

In the street we posed as a work detail carrying axes and saws: a lumberjack force. Zundel Leizerson, dressed in a policeman's uniform, led the way. We mixed with the other brigades leaving for work and walking in the direction of Novy Vileyka.

Once out of the city, we breathed sighs of relief. Even though the situation was still perilous, at least the danger of Jews recognizing us had passed.

In Novy Vileyka, 15 kilometers from Vilna, many Jews were working. We could not avoid their seeing us there and guessing our destination. For some time, rumors had been circulating about partisans in Narocz Forest, 200 kilometers from Vilna. Fourteen young men and women working in Novy Vileyka took advantage of the afternoon break to slip out from under the eyes of the guard and join us.

To be honest, we did not receive them with a great deal of enthusiasm. Shika Gertner and his wife, who came from Narocz Forest as Markov's messengers, and who served as our guides, warned us while we were still in the ghetto not to move in large groups. They agreed to accept no more than nineteen people. Now we were thirty-five, and the new arrivals had no weapons. We had no choice but to accept the "reinforcements," and after a while the two groups merged completely with no trace of previous differences.

Toward evening we rested in a thicket of trees. Shika explained to us that the most dangerous part of the journey was already behind us. From now on, we would no longer have to pose as workers. We were partisans. During the night we would walk a distance of many kilometers and would spend the following day in the silo of one of Shika's many peasant acquaintances. The second night we would reach the area held by the partisans, and from then on we would be able to continue on our way in full daylight.

The morale of the fighters was high. Our dreams of the last few months were finally starting to materialize. We sat down to eat and prepare for the remainder of our journey.

Josef divided the group in two. The commander of one half was Iska Mackiewicz. I was given command of the other. The weapons were divided among the people, and we started off. The night was dark and suffocating. We carefully approached the village of Laboriszki, 25 kilometers from Vilna. We had to cross the Vilenka River, but it was dangerous to use the bridge because it passed through the center of the village. We threw our fortunes upon the darkness of the night and hoped we would cross without incident.

Josef sent five scouts out in front of the company: Molka Hazan, Zundel Leizerson, the Gordon brothers, and Iska Mackiewicz. The rest of the group held its breath until the command to advance was given.

Suddenly, the silence was shattered by a burst of gunfire, and murderous crossfire was showered upon us from three directions. We were only 50 meters from the bridge. Caught by surprise, the group became greatly distraught. Among us were people whose military experience consisted of a few shots fired from a pistol in the training basement in the ghetto. Even those who had had military experience lost their heads.

Our scouts fought the enemy with utmost valor. We could see the blasts of their guns and tried to give them support fire. After what seemed like a long time, when the firing had stopped, we received the order to retreat.

During the retreat into the forest, we lost contact with some of our men. Reaching a swampy area, we held a head count and found that only 13 out of the original 35 remained. Shika began to spread fear: from the direction of the bullets he concluded that the enemy was gradually encircling us and would soon start to attack us with grenades. It was imperative to keep moving.

But our minds were set. Whatever happened, we would not abandon our friends. We would not leave until we knew what had happened to them. Josef sent some people to the edge of the forest to meet those of our friends who would show up.

The shooting was getting closer. It could be heard on all sides. It seemed as if the enemy was, indeed, surrounding us. And there was no trace of our missing comrades.

Suddenly we heard a call that shocked us all: Where is Shika?

We started looking for him, calling his name, flicking flashlights—but Shika was nowhere to be found. We now realized that our situation was critical. None of us was familiar with the surroundings. No one knew in which direction to go. Shika had betrayed us. He knew that without him we were lost, yet he didn't hesitate to save himself and his wife.

Desperate and depressed, we sat down to discuss what to do. A few suggested that we return immediately to the ghetto. But the majority rejected the proposal. There was no way back for us. It would be better for us to die in the forest than to fall into the hands of the Gestapo. We must wait until dawn. Then, maybe we might find some of our friends.

The night of terror seemed endless. The hands of the watch moved at an agonizingly slow pace, as if to mock us. Echoes of nearby gunshots continued to reach us. We moved deeper into the swampy area, with our hearts heavy over the loss of our friends.

Unbridled Incitement

Gestapo collaborator Dessler, commander of the Jewish Police Force in the ghetto, lost no time, once he learned about our move to the forest, to inform the

Germans and give them time to set up an ambush. On the following day, the Gestapo demanded that the relatives of the men be turned over to them. Thirty-five kinfolk were arrested by the Judenrat and turned over to the Gestapo. (Among them were fictitious relatives who were betrayed by those who thereby hoped to get a *Schein*.) They also handed over to the Nazis the supervisors of the work brigades, from which the fighters had fled. All were taken to Ponar and executed.

The Judenrat leaders exploited the episode for broad incitement against the Organization. They did not accuse the Germans of murder, nor did they show the slightest remorse for having doomed the relatives to certain death. They blamed the heads of the Organization; were it not for them, peace would reign in the ghetto. "As it is, we are at Zero Hour. If you want to stay alive, help us eradicate this evil."

The Nazi flunkeys increased the regime of terror and oppression in the ghetto, extending the network of spies and informers. The ghetto was divided into four police districts, each subdivided into blocks, and each block into houses. These, too, were divided into dwellings and rooms. One inmate was made personally responsible for the behavior of the occupants in each of the rooms. If someone arrived late or stopped living there, he was to be reported immediately to the police.

Several days after the murder of the 35 hostages, the following item appeared in the Judenrat bulletin:

Myriads of flourishing lives have been plucked from our midst. We have shed many tears on the innocent victims of the bloody days. We clenched our fists at our cruel fate, and at times, we even berated the Almighty, as did Rabbi Levi Yitzhak of Berdichev: "Wherefore hast Thou beset Thy people Israel?"

In all of these instances, we have been confronted by external forces over which we had no control. We have been helpless against this power. Despite the tragedy of these events, their very inevitability, somehow, made it easier for us to bear our suffering. But this is not true of the 35 souls torn from our midst, so unexpectedly, last Monday. Here, we cannot take comfort in the fact that this was inexorable fate. Here it was clear that the victims were needless; their death is to be attributed to those whose irresponsible conduct led to the bloodshed of innocents. Along with our deep sorrow over the extermination of blameless men, women, and children, our hearts are filled with wrath toward those who turned their backs on the welfare of the ghetto and its important duties, though they knew they were endangering the entire ghetto, primarily their own relatives. They are the ones responsible for the spilt blood and for all the hardships we are now experiencing because of their behavior.

Let the spilt blood be a warning to all of us. Let us remember that only one course lies open to us: work output. And in this, we must go hand in hand. Let this be a warning to all the brigadiers, the group foremen, and the individual Jews, that they must report the absence of people from their units, their homes, or rooms. There is no room here for family loyalties and sentiments. This is the duty of every man assigned to the important task. He must immediately report every incident likely to do us damage. Such a report is not an informer's word, as many who are still steeped in outdated concepts seem to think. Turning in any such information is the duty of every resident in the ghetto.

The seed fell on fertile soil. The ghetto occupants began doing whatever they could to "eradicate the gang which was bringing disaster on the others." The ghetto was rife with brotherly hatred. Arrests and arms searches became a daily occurence.

After Wittenberg's death and Glazman's departure, the ranks of the Organization were thrown into dejection. There were no replacements for these stalwarts, and the new Commander did not inspire confidence. There was some doubt about his readiness and ability to lead the Organization into battle.

Two new people were added to the Organization's staff: Communist Yaakov Kaplan, replacing Wittenberg, and Betarist Lyova Ziskovich, in Josef's place. The Organization was under unremitting tension. It was not easy to forget the events of July 16, when all stood ready to battle the Germans, and fellow-Jews stormed the positions of the Jewish fighters and almost forced them to turn their guns on their Jewish brothers. Many were still bothered by the thought: was it worth sacrificing the much-loved Commander in order to have the Judenrat and the incited masses enjoy one more hour of tranquility? Would the hour of annihilation be postponed? Was it not clear that the Angel of Death was about to strike the blow?

Already, remorse was gnawing at the entrails. As atonement for the sin of handing over their Commander, the fighters swore to avenge the spilt blood of their brothers and thus commemorate their martyred leader.

The heightened terrorism made the work of the Underground very difficult. Even as the fighters gathered to train, they asked themselves: what was the use of it all, when the Organization had no definite course and its aims were obscure?

The ghetto authorities summoned the staff to inform them that the Gestapo was already aware of an armed organization in the ghetto and was demanding that its members be delivered into its hands. If the demand were not met, the Gestapo would immediately set about liquidating the ghetto. There was only one way to avert the decree: if the Organization would turn over its weapons to the authorities for safekeeping, an arrangement with the Gestapo might be achieved.

Without Wittenberg and Glazman, the staff could not give an unequivocal response to this humiliating demand. It began negotiations so as to gain time.

A Jewish girl from Kovno, a Moscow parachutist by the name of Glazer, arrived in Vilna. A longtime member of the Communist Party, with a prison record, she was known as "Albina." She was in the ghetto several days to negotiate with the Organization and to pass on instructions from the Communist Executive. She transmitted orders not to leave the ghetto or move to the forest for the time being, but to rebel within the ghetto, at the prescribed time. She promised that the Communists in the city would help supply arms, perhaps even fighting men. The main feature was that, simultaneously with the revolt in the ghetto, large-scale acts of resistance and sabotage would break out over the city, thereby considerably improving the chances of success by deflecting attention from the ghetto.

Obviously, all these instructions and promises greatly encouraged the fighters. There was joy in every heart: they would not be alone in the fighting. With the rejoicing also came impatience for the Great Day to come. The staff gave Albina tidy sums of money to buy weapons and to finance the uprising in the city.

Eventually, this dream was to go the way of the others. Reality was to prove that no trust could be places in promises of this kind, even if they came from the East, whose skies were to glow with the sun of Redemption.

Resistance in Porubanek

Vilna's Jews were quite satisfied with the benefits accrued by working for the Germans, their subjugators. Most of the Jews were working in town, in German work units. Some work centers were really vital for the German war effort, such as the Bobriszki Arsenals, the giant machine repair shop H.K.P., and the Keilis, where uniforms were produced for the Wehrmacht. But some units employed Jews whose jobs had nothing to do with the German war effort.

The Jews were virtually slaves, privately owned by the German occupation regime. Their lot was worse than that of beasts of burden, who at least were tended and fed. Jews could be enslaved without regard for their welfare.

Many Jews were employed inside the ghetto itself, in the Judenrat agencies, police, and workshops. The workers in the city itself were far better off than their brethren in the ghetto. There was always the chance of buying food and other items from the peasants or from the Germans. From time to time, they would even get gifts. Also, prices outside the ghetto walls were much lower, and many Jews lived on the difference.

The laborers inside the ghetto envied those who could afford a bit of comparative luxury. But they enjoyed one advantage: they did not have to suffer the beatings and indignities inflicted upon the "unit" laborers. Still, the ghetto Jews strove to work outside the ghetto in order to stave off starvation. Marching to work also gave them a taste of freedom, a few hours of fresh air, although the sight of herd after herd of Jews, shuffling along the middle of the street, was like a procession of cows.

All in all, there were 72 such units. In August 1943, the Germans ordered the liquidation of 54 units. Thousands of Jewish laborers were left without work. The ghetto was stupefied. Everyone realized that the move heralded final liquidation. The inmates moved about in the streets, faces furrowed with worry. Thousands gathered in the courtyard of the Judenrat and demanded an explanation. Gens and Dessler went out onto the balcony and addressed the throng: "To date, thousands of Jews have been employed in labor of minimal significance, which has contributed little to the German war effort. They worked cleaning tile floors, polishing shoes, barbering, and the like, for one German or another. As long as we could keep the Germans fooled by doing this work, we did so readily. Now the Germans are demanding that the work have a direct connection with the war effort and the needs of the military. Hence, we shall work for the Wehrmacht. Therefore, there is no cause for panic. No evil will overtake us. Let everyone go back home and continue working in the Porubanek airfields and the railway station, as well as laying new rails. There will be enough work for all the people in the ghetto; as long as there is work, we need not fear for our lives."

The name Porubanek cast fear over everyone. It was supervised by a young German named Degner, notorious for his sadism. Beatings and degradation were the daily fare of the Jewish workers. They left work two hours earlier than the others, since the ghetto was seven miles away from their jobs. By the time they came back, it was already close to midnight.

Working conditions were no better at the railway station. The work was especially heavy, and it was impossible to find enough hands for it.

To fill the quota, the Judenrat instituted compulsory service and everyone had to work at the railway station on a rotating basis, one or two days a week. The workers would return empty-handed, as there was no possibility of buying anything from the peasants.

Naturally, most Jews did not go willingly to these two places. Whoever could, tried to be sent to better jobs either by using his connections or by bribing the police. Many began to hide from the *Arbeitsamt* Police, whose duty it was to recruit the required number of workers. The ghetto leaders had to adopt various measures to force thousands of Jews to go to this undesirable work. Every morning thousands left for Porubanek and for the railway station and envied those who succeeded in finding better jobs.

It is surprising that in these two places the Jews were assigned work that certainly could not have been important for the war effort. This suspicion increased when they learned that the Germans hardly bothered to guard the Jews on the job and did not even spur them on.

The work itself was pointless: transferring rocks from one place to another, moving piles of dirt and sand, or digging up the ground for no apparent purpose.

This sense of futility bothered the Jews. However, they began to console themselves and came to the conclusion that they were deceiving the stupid Germans. . . . Meanwhile, the Gestapo, with Dessler's collaboration, was planning a new "action," the aim of which was to send the Jews from Vilna to the labor camps in Estonia. According to the plan, 2,400 people were to leave on the first transport.

On August 5, the ghetto residents went to bed, unaware that something terrible was about to happen in the next few hours. At 11:30 P.M. all the members of the police were called up and put on the alert. The *Arbeitsamt* Police had forwarded lists of people who had been absent from work during the last days, as well as a list of people with criminal records from before the war and during the ghetto period. The police divided up into groups according to areas and set out to find the people on the lists, arrest them, and imprison them in Lidski. Within two hours the police fulfilled their duty. About 450 people were imprisoned in Lidski.

At midnight a rumor circulated throughout the ghetto that a new "action" was starting. The people woke up from their sleep in terror. Those who had prepared hiding places grabbed some possessions and ran off to hide. Those who had no hiding places went out into the street to see what was happening. The panic and commotion increased by the minute. Overcome with fear, the people waited for the Germans to come.

The prisoners in Lidski announced that if the Germans came to get them, they would resist with force, and the first object of their anger would be the ghetto leaders and the police. Thousands of people crowded in the narrow streets and around the jail, threatening that they would not let the prisoners be taken. The situation was explosive. It seemed that the crowds would soon attack the police, lynch them, and free the prisoners by force.

The leaders were not ready to take risks. At 4:30 A.M. they gave the order to free the prisoners. At the same time they warned all the people that if they stayed away from work, they would be punished, even turned over to the Gestapo.

The Jews naïvely thought that the incident was over. They were proud of their victory over the leaders and the police. Everyone went to work, even those who up to now had not been meticulous in following the orders of the leaders.

When the groups of workers were already in the city streets outside the entrance to the ghetto, they were suddenly surrounded by large forces of Germans, Estonians, and Lithuanians, armed with automatic weapons. There was no point in resistance now. They were led to the railway station, where the train cars stood ready to take them away.

Thousands of workers in Porubanek were also surrounded by army forces after they arrived at the airport. In the beginning, they were confused by the sudden appearance of the soldiers, just as they were ready to leave. Then suddenly they heard shouts: "Jews, they are taking us to Ponar to slaughter us like sheep! Let us resist the murderers! There is nothing to lose! Let us scatter and escape!"

Like madmen, the Jews attacked the army cordons. They struck blows left and right and broke their way through. The Germans were surprised at first. They were not used to such behavior on the part of Jews. But they soon came to their senses and opened fire on the escapees. Dozens of shattered corpses lay in the roads.

A thousand escapees scattered throughout the city looking for hiding places. Hundreds streamed towards the ghetto. Only a minority was caught by the Germans and taken to the railway cars. Those who had succeeded in reaching the ghetto were arrested by the Jewish Police near the entrance. When their numbers reached several hundreds, notice was sent to the Gestapo, which immediately sent vehicles to collect them. But the prisoners and their relatives in the ghetto fought like wild animals to get out and most of them succeeded in escaping. In the end, about 200 people were left, and these were turned over to the Germans. But the Jews continued to resist. One Jew, named Berka Kasoi, injured two Estonian soldiers with a bottle and, in the ensuing uproar, escaped with dozens of other Jews.

Every ghetto Jew experienced the sweet taste of "victory" over the Germans that day. It was the first time in the history of the actions that Jews had resisted en masse. And instead of 2,400 people, only about 800 people fell into the hands of the Germans.

Yet, together with the sense of pride came a feeling of depression. It was clear now that there was no hope for a better tomorrow. The Germans were resuming the slaughter and this time they probably would not cease until no one remained.

The Jews debated on how to escape the trap. Those who had no bunkers had no alternative but to come to terms with their bitter fate. After all, were they any better than the tens of thousands of their brethren who had been killed in Ponar? And perhaps, said the Jews, the murdered ones were better off, for they were free from fear and torture.

Shlomo Brand, a leader of the Second Organization and member of Betar.

Borka (Dov) Friedman, an organizer of the Second Organization and leader of Betar.

The Second Organization

In the beginning of 1943 a second Fighting Organization was set up. Its founders wanted to organize and arm the youth to prepare them for their departure to the forests.

If the F.P.O. was selective and checked everyone thoroughly before accept-

Shmuel Levin.   *Leon Bernstein*

ing him into its ranks, the Second Organization strove to be a mass movement. The F.P.O.'s ideology was based on preserving Jewish dignity and retaliating against the enemy within the ghetto for the spilt blood and the sullied honor of the people. The F.P.O. believed that when the day came, the masses would follow it into battle. In contrast, the Second Organization did not believe in the possibility of resistance within the ghetto. It believed that everything possible should be saved and that any able-bodied Jew who had stopped believing the promises of the Germans must save his life by going to the forests. Naturally, a great amount of courage was needed to leave the ghetto for the unknown. The Second Organization believed that the Jews would go because they had nothing to lose.

There were hundreds of young people in the ghetto who, before the war, had belonged to youth parties and organizations that were unaffiliated with the F.P.O. Among them were people unfit for work in the Underground, and those who could not bring themselves to join the F.P.O. or remained outside for personal reasons. Dozens of such youths, who were well aware of what was going to happen, could not sit idly by. Thus, the Second Fighting Organization was set up in the Vilna Ghetto. Its main organizers were Shlomo Brand, a veteran Betarist and a leader of the Workers Brigade working in the Gestapo warehouses; Leon Bernstein, a public activist and director of the Judenrat cultural department; Natan Ring, chief of Police Station No. 1 in the ghetto; and Borka (Dov) Friedman, one of the leaders in the former Vilna Betar branch. They were later joined by Ilya Scheinbaum, representing the "Dror" labor party of the Zionist Socialist (Z.S.) Federation.

In the ghetto were several Betarists who opposed joining the F.P.O. because they did not trust its new commander. They felt that he would exploit both his position and the sincerity of the members of other parties to further his own movement, Hashomer Hatsair. They furthermore claimed that he was not a military man and that there was no point in joining an organization headed by a man with dubious military skills.

On the eve of the establishment of the F.P.O., when negotiations were still underway with representatives of the various organizations, the Hechalutz representative, Mordechai Tenenbaum, announced his refusal to join the organization. His position was that Jews were living in peace and quiet in the Polish ghettos; therefore, it was best to organize an evacuation of all the youth from the Vilna Ghetto to the Polish ghettos. Tenenbaum did as he preached and went to Warsaw. Thus, the Hechalutz people and the Zionist Socialist Federation remained outside the F.P.O. Some time later they asked to join the organization, on the condition that they be accepted not as individuals but as organized bodies whose representatives would be included in the leadership. This condition was rejected. The Second Organization, therefore, had a reserve of hundreds of organized Jewish youths and hundreds of unaffiliated ones, who did not join the F.P.O. Like the F.P.O., it, too, had great difficulty obtaining arms. Lacking financial resources, it decided to turn to Gens and ask for his help. Brand, Bernstein, and Ring approached him and, surprisingly, he agreed and gave them half a million rubles.

With this money the first guns were purchased. Gens asked that a good gun be bought for him as well. For a long time Gens's gun lay in the general warehouse of the Second Organization. Eventually, when the ghetto police began arms searches, it did not overlook the Second Organization. Generally, however, the Organization had good relations with the police and in most cases received prior information on what was going to happen.

When Gens asked the Second Organization's leaders to give him all its arms and place their warehouse under his supervision, they vehemently refused. They gave him his gun and stood their ground, despite his threats. When Josef Glazman was sent to the work camp in Rzesza, Janek Faust of the Second Organization, who was a police officer, was also sent there. But several days later he returned to the ghetto, thanks to the intervention of the leaders of his organization.

The main source for acquiring arms was the Gestapo warehouses, where several members of the Second Organization worked. Those working for the Gestapo had certain privileges. Every so often they received permission to bring to the ghetto several wagonloads of items for their families. The gate guard did not check these wagons and the Organization's members took advantage of this to hide in them the weapons they stole from the Gestapo warehouses. One day they even succeeded in stealing a gun belonging to Martin Weiss, the man chiefly responsible for the massacre of the Jews.

After the Kovno action, the Second Organization's Headquarters decided to send a unit of fighters into the Rudnik (Rudnicki) Forest near Vilna. This unit had to scout the area and prepare bases for the fighters who would follow. Eight people set out, headed by the Betarist Borka Friedman. This exit caused a minor sensation in the ghetto and angered the leaders, particularly since the departees included a police officer from the gate guard named Frida, who took his wife with him. This meant that the loyalty of the police could no longer be trusted. From now on every policeman and officer was suspect, lest he form an alliance with the Underground and weaken the authority of the ghetto leaders. The average Jew reached a similar conclusion; if police officers stopped believing in the leaders, why should he believe in them? After all, police officers know better, as they were closer to the leaders. . . .

I learned about the fate of four members of the group only much later, when I arrived with members of the first company from the Narocz Forest to Rudnik Forest. ''Batya'' told me that several days previously, the fighters met up with a strong guard of the German Army, and in a short but fierce battle, four of them fell: Borka Friedman, Shmuel Levin, and Frida and his wife.

In the summer, negotiations began between the F.P.O. Headquarters and the Second Organization's Headquarters regarding a merger. Representatives of the Second Organization were somewhat wary, for they were firmly resolved to begin

Ilya Scheinbaum, one of the leaders of the Second Organization, representing the Zionist-Socialist Federation.

the immediate evacuation to the forest, but if the revolt broke out before they could leave, they would naturally take part in it alongside the F.P.O. Meanwhile, strong ties had developed between the two organizations. Shlomo Brand joined the F.P.O. Headquarters as liaison. Relations grew warmer, and when the Gestapo demanded the surrender of Commander Wittenberg, Natan Ring was the one who brought the first information about this, thus enabling Wittenberg to go into hiding.

In the final period of the ghetto's existence, there was full cooperation between the two organizations, and a virtual merging of the two commands that blurred the borders dividing the fighting companies of the two organizations. But the members of the Second Organization were quickly disillusioned by the new commander's behavior and began to operate separately again. They sent companies into the forest and succeeded in saving most of the members of their organization.

The Estonia "Action"

The Gestapo's decision to carry out the action in Porubanek outside the ghetto walls was a direct indication that they knew about the existence of an armed organization. Some said it was Dessler who gave the advice to carry out the "action" outside the ghetto to prevent armed resistance. But as the attempt to kidnap Jews in the streets and in their places of work did not succeed, the Gestapo now decided to adopt a new tactic.

On August 7, one day after the action in Porubanek, Gestapo Chief Neugebauer appeared in the ghetto with his entourage. He ordered that the brigade workers be assembled in the theater hall and gave a speech. The people who were kidnapped the day before, he said, were sent to Estonia to do very important work for the Wehrmacht. They would live and work there under good conditions and there were no grounds for fears. In the future, he promised, there would be no more kidnapping. If a new shipment of workers was requested, the Jews would receive written invitations in their homes. He hoped that the Jews would be clever enough to report by themselves. There would be no more "actions" ending in massacre, he promised. Germany needed many work forces to overcome her enemies and win the war.

When Neugebauer and his entourage came to the ghetto, Lyova Ziskovich proposed killing them. Ziskovich told the commander that according to the bylaws, the Organization should begin the revolt when it was clear that the final liquidation had begun. He said that an opportunity like this would not come again and there were good chances of success. The Gestapo people would be caught unawares and the Organization would have the upper hand. After the "action" of the previous day, the Jews could no longer believe in the promises of the Germans and, thus, one could expect the sympathy of the masses and their participation in the revolt. But the commander preferred to wait. In his opinion, the time was not yet ripe. The near future would prove that the time would never be ripe enough for him. . . .

Several days later, Brigadier Hyman, head of the work brigades in Porubanek and the train station, returned after accompanying the first transport to Estonia. He said that the Jews were living in good conditions. He brought with him many letters from the transport people to their relatives in the ghetto. The letters confirmed what he said, and the mood in the ghetto improved. The last kidnapped people were not taken to Ponar, after all. If so, the situation was not so bad. . . .

Meanwhile, the Judenrat registration office was busy preparing lists of the relatives of the people already in Estonia. It also prepared lists of Jews from the surrounding towns now living in the ghetto. Over the next few days, close to 3,000 invitations were sent to Jews to report to the assembly-points designated by the Judenrat to go to Estonia. Relatives were happy to receive the summons, since they wanted to join their children and spouses. But the town Jews tried to avoid the transport and the police began looking for them in the houses. The ghetto inmates were held collectively responsible. They had to find the wanted people. If someone was hiding in a bunker, someone else would be arrested in his place. This system led to a new bout of internal terror. Everyone was afraid of his neighbor and everyone was ready to inform on those in hiding.

The leaders appointed a complaints committee, to which anyone who received an invitation to leave could turn, despite the fact that he had no relatives in Estonia and did not come from the towns. Bargaining over human lives began anew. People paid huge sums to save themselves from deportation.

The Organization's Headquarters issued an announcement addressed to the fighters, but directed, in fact, to all ghetto Jews. The announcement said:

Vilna Jews,

The hour of the final liquidation has come. The German and Lithuanian murderers will soon break into the ghetto to kill us. We shall soon be led through the gates, group after group.

So were hundreds of Jews taken away on Yom Kippur. So were they taken away on the nights of the white, yellow, and pink *Schein*s.

So were our brothers, sisters, mothers, fathers, and children led away.

Let us not stretch out our necks like sheep about to be slaughtered.

Jews, defend yourselves with weapons!

Do not believe in the deceptive promises of the murderers; do not believe the words of the traitors.

Whoever passes through the ghetto gate goes only one way: to Ponar.

And Ponar is Death.

Jews, we have nothing to lose. Death will reach us in any case. Does anyone still believe that he will remain alive while the murderer is systematically destroying us? The hangman will get every man and every woman. Flight and fear won't save your lives. Only armed resistance can save our lives and our honor.

Brethren,

It is better to fall in battle in the ghetto than to be led like sheep to Ponar. Know that there is an armed and organized force in the ghetto which will revolt.

Help the revolt!

Do not cower in the hiding-places and bunkers. In the end you will fall like rats into the hands of the murderers.

Jewish masses: Go out into the street! Those who have no arms can wield an axe and those who have no axe can grab a pipe, a rod, or a stick.

Vengeance for our parents!

Vengeance for our murdered children!

Vengeance for Ponar!

Strike down the enemy!

In every street, in every yard, in every room, in and outside the ghetto. Beat the dogs!

Jews, we have nothing to lose. We won't save our lives if we don't destroy the murderers!

Long live freedom!

Long live armed resistance!

Death to the murderers!

The effect of the manifesto was tremendous. The fighters were tensed for battle and waiting for the arrival of the enemy and the order of the commander. But the F.P.O. commander appointed Abrasha Krizovski, one of the Communist leaders, to negotiate with Police Commander Dessler. If Dessler promised that none of the Organization's members would be removed from the ghetto, the F.P.O. would agree not to disturb the police in carrying out the "action." They came to an agreement. Hienna Borowska was sent to the assembly point on 1 Shawelska Street as the F.P.O. representative to see that the agreement was kept. If she saw one of the Organization's members being taken away, she would order his release.

The rank-and-file fighters did not know about the agreement. They wondered why they did not receive an order to prevent the mass deportation. But they trusted the commander.

On August 22 the "action" was completed. A total of 1,400 people were sent to Estonia, instead of the 3,000 demanded by the Germans. Letters arrived within a few days from the people of this transport as well. They affirmed that they had arrived safely and had rejoined their families in the work camps. But the Gestapo was dissatisfied with the slow progress of the "action" and its meagre results.

During the very days of this "action", Gens gave a speech before the ghetto Jews in which he said: "I am very well aware that the Gestapo is not satisfied with our work but I am not worried about this. I am deliberately trying to postpone the action so as to gain time, which is so precious to us. Time is working in our favor. I am convinced that the Red Army will reach Vilna by December of this year. And if the ghetto still exists by then, even if only a few are left, then I will know that I have done my duty. With a calm heart and a clear conscience I can announce that I did my duty towards my people and towards the future. Jews, try to hold out until the end and believe that we shall see better days."

One day after the completion of the "action," Gestapo officer Kittel visited the ghetto, accompanied by several of his men. All of them were armed. He ordered the closing of all the entrances and breaches through which the Jews brought food into the ghetto and maintained contact with the city. He went from yard to yard, and under his supervision, people sealed the entrances with stones and barbed wire. Outside, in front of these places stood plainclothes Lithuanian detectives whose duty it was to make sure that there was no contact between the ghetto and the city. This caused great anxiety among the Jews. Everyone understood that something terrible was going to happen, and that when it did they would be unable to escape.

In this tense situation Dessler summoned the police and spoke to them about their duties. He explained that the surveillance outside the ghetto was not directed against the Jews but rather against the Poles. The Germans were about to embark on a big manhunt for Poles to send them to work in Germany. It was feared that some Poles would want to infiltrate the ghetto to hide there. The ghetto entrances were sealed off to prevent provocation by the Poles, which could end in disaster for the Jews. He added that many Latvian and Estonian soldiers were coming to Vilna to take part in the action against the Poles, and perhaps to move against the partisans. He asked his police to calm the Jews down and guard against penetration by Poles. He ordered an increase of the guard, especially at night. Those responsible for the yards were ordered to hold a roll call of the tenants every night.

Rumors reached the ghetto about the kidnapping and arrest of Poles. People relaxed somewhat and started to believe Dessler. They were amused by the thought that things had reached such a state that Poles would seek safety among Jews. One day the police arrested two old Polish women wearing yellow patches, who entered the ghetto to bring food to Jewish friends. This was seen as further proof that Dessler was right and that there was, indeed, danger of penetration by Poles into the ghetto.

In the early morning of September 1, the Jews woke up, little imagining that the day would raise the curtain on the final disaster.

Last Chance for Revolt

At 5:00 A.M. the ghetto was surrounded by troops. The gate was closed and no one was allowed to enter or exit. When the Jews got up to go to work, they were shocked to see many Estonian soldiers inside the ghetto. The soldiers immediately went into action. They kidnapped men and brought them to the gate. Everyone realized that the end had come.

Within minutes the narrow streets were empty, as if the ground had opened up and swallowed everyone. The Jews hid in bunkers, attics, chimneys, and cellars. Aside from the Estonians and the Jewish police, no living being was to be seen. And since the Estonians kidnapped only in the streets, they did not find many victims. In several hours they rounded up only 300 people. Considering that the Gestapo wanted to collect 5,000 people this time, these results were minimal.

At 11:00 A.M. Paulhaber, a high-ranking Gestapo officer and chief of the Main Headquarters of Lithuania, entered the ghetto. He told Gens that if 2,000 were not rounded up that day, he would order the ghetto to be blown up. Gens promised that he would do his best, providing the army would leave the ghetto and the Jewish police would carry out the "action" alone. Paulhaber began to rant and rave and to scream that he did not understand the disappearance of tens of thousands of Jews who, to the best of his knowledge, had to be in the ghetto. He screamed: "I am sick of all the tricks of the damned Jews! I will carry out the action myself." He ordered the Jewish police and the army to begin house-to-house searches. Six hundred to 700 soldiers and police took part in the searches but came up with nothing. When Paulhaber realized that he had failed, he ordered the army out of the ghetto, leaving 25 Gestapo men, who concentrated near the gate. Afterwards he, too, left the ghetto.

At 5:00 A.M. when the Organization Headquarters learned that the ghetto was surrounded, it issued a mobilization order. The fighters took up their positions on 6–7 Straszun, 8 Oszmianska and 4 Szpitalna Streets. The Headquarters discussed how to get arms from the warehouses and divide them among the fighters. The operation entailed tremendous difficulties, for there was no one on the streets except the Estonian soldiers. However, since the Jewish police were allowed to walk in the streets, seven policemen who were members of the Organization were mobilized for this purpose. Several other fighters put on police uniforms and went out to distribute the arms.

The second battalion of the Organization, numbering about a hundred people, was concentrated in the yard of 4 Szpitalna Street, and even before they could be given arms, the army surrounded them on all sides and began to take them to the gate. The fighters resisted for several minutes, but naturally they could not stand up empty-handed against soldiers armed with automatic weapons. Only a few fighters succeeded in getting away. This was a heavy blow for the Organization. In one stroke a considerable number of fighters had been lost without battle. Nevertheless, preparations began for the confrontation. The arms were distributed, the submachine guns set up, and clubs and iron rods were given to comrades who had no firearms.

The main force was concentrated on 6 Straszun Street, the site of the Headquarters, at the edge of the ghetto. The front position was in the school auditorium on 12 Straszun Street. A company of fighters was sent there, made up mainly of members of the Second Organization. (That same day the two organizations merged completely.) Ilya Scheinbaum, a leader of the Second Organization and a former officer in the Polish Army, was chosen as commander of the position. The choice was a good one. A professional stood at the place which would be the first to encounter enemy forces.

The F.P.O. commander was upset by the appointment. He wanted members of his own movement in command. At the last minute, he appointed as commander of the position Rozka Korczak, despite her lack of military knowledge, and made Scheinbaum her second-in-command.

By order of the Headquarters, the fighters passed the buildings and yards and called upon the Jews to be ready to resist. The ghetto women answered the call. They began to boil water and prepare various objects to throw at the Nazi enemy. The ghetto masses knew that this was the beginning of the end, and they were resolved not to surrender willingly to their oppressors. Though some of them hid in bunkers, most of them knew that the bunkers would not save them, and they decided to resist. Had the signal been given and the Organization gone into action, a large-scale revolt would have erupted. But the signal was not given. Both the fighters and the masses were amazed when an hour later, the calls for mass resistance stopped.

No one knew that an agreement was renewed between the Organization commander and the police chief, Dessler. The Organization commander promised not to begin resistance operations if the Germans did not reach the fighters' positions, and Gens and Dessler did their best to ensure that the Germans did not enter Straszun Street. Throughout the day, the women fighters walked along the streets, from time to time relaying information about the situation. The policemen who were Organization members would also appear occasionally and report the steps about to be taken by the ghetto authorities. The policemen said that they could kill many of the enemy, without it becoming known, for they accompanied small groups of Nazis into attics and other isolated places. But the Organization commander forbade them to carry out separate actions, as it could interfere with the Headquarters' plans. The fighters in the positions also received instructions not to go into action unless the Germans approached their positions.

When Paulhaber left the ghetto and took the army with him, Gens understood this to mean that the Nazis accepted his proposal. He gathered together the Jewish policemen and told them: "The Gestapo has demanded that I turn over 5,000 people. I agreed to give them 1,000 people on the first day of the "action" and a thousand on each of the next three days. They promised me that after the four-day "action" there would be peace in the ghetto for seven months, and meanwhile the Redemption might come. But now we have no alternative but to remove the Jews from the bunkers and deliver the demanded amount. If my order is not carried out, I will have no recourse but to leave the ghetto, and tomorrow the Germans will come in and begin the final liquidation."

Gens's words did not convince the policemen. Nevertheless, they dispersed among the narrow streets and got down to work. Gens and Dessler directed the "action." But they were not successful. By 4:00 P.M. five people had been caught.

Around 4:00 P.M. Dessler came to the corner of Shawelska and Straszun Streets, where 50 to 60 policemen were standing. They surrounded him to hear what he had to say. He appeared very depressed and said: "We have about two more hours. If during that time we don't come up with the required number, Gens and I will leave the ghetto, and then the Germans will come and begin the liquidation. Therefore, I am asking you as a friend: Do any of you have a practical suggestion how to get out of this mess?" No one answered.

Meanwhile, Krizovski, the liaison between the F.P.O. and the police, appeared and was asked the same question. Krizovski replied: "You should know better than I. You are the police chief." Dessler said that, in his opinion, there was no alternative but to make another effort to round up the required number. Only in this way was it possible to save the ghetto. And he ordered the policemen to continue their work. He warned them that their lives, too, depended on their success. This time the policemen went to work with vigor. Within a half hour they caught 250 people.

Gens, walking along Straszun Street, came across two fighters in police uniform carrying packages containing arms. Familiar with his men, he saw at once that these were not policemen. He went up to them and wanted to take away the packages and arrest them. The two fighters took out guns and ordered him to go away. Gens retreated and the fighters ran to the position on 12 Straszun Street. Many policemen witnessed the scene but did not intervene. Gens was furious. He summoned the police on Rudnicka Street, near the gate, pulled 12 policemen from the ranks, and turned them over to the Gestapo. The rest returned to work, but he warned them that if they did not take their duties seriously, he would turn them over to the Gestapo as well.

At dusk several Gestapo men and Estonian soldiers came to the ghetto, and together with Gens and a number of Jewish policemen, approached the house on 12 Straszun Street to conduct a search, having heard that a lot of Jews were hiding in the yard.

Ilya Scheinbaum stood at the window and saw the Germans approaching the building. According to plan, he fired shots and threw a grenade. But the grenade did not explode. The Germans retreated momentarily but then opened heavy fire on the position. A bullet struck Scheinbaum, killing him. Rozka, the commander of the position, gave no order to the fighters. She ran to the Headquarters and said that everything was in order at the position and did not relate what had happened.

The fighters at the position were confused. They waited for instructions which did not come. Though they saw that the building was about to be blown up, they did not leave it. Chaim Napoleon was killed in the explosion and several other fighters were seriously wounded. The fighter Feigelson jumped out the window at the last minute and was mortally wounded. Dozens of Jewish tenants were buried under the rubble.

The Germans blew up other buildings: 15 Straszun, 8 Oszmianska and 4 Szpitalna. The Organization commander still gave no order to begin fighting, though even according to the agreement with the police, he was entitled to begin resistance if the Germans attacked the fighters' positions. The people in the positions were ready for action. They awaited an order, but to their great dismay none came.

There was great panic in the ghetto. Dozens of Jews were killed and wounded in the explosion of the buildings. Only when the "action" was over, late that night, was it possible to dig the bodies out of the debris and give the survivors the required aid.

Gens and Dessler recruited several hundred people as auxiliary police and called upon members of the underworld to help carry out the action. By evening the operations were completed. Nine hundred sixty people were turned over to the Gestapo. The Jews stopped resisting. Disappointed with the lack of organized action, they gradually accepted the situation. There was only one case of resistance: on 6 Shawelska Street lived a hunchbacked Jew, and when the police came to take him, he resisted with the little strength he had. Naturally, his resistance did not last long.

When the fighters learned that Rozka had left the position on 12 Straszun Street, they were very angry. Several members of the Headquarters wanted to try her, but the commander would not agree to a trial. After the action, a meeting of the fighters was called and he announced that as punishment for Rozka's unfitting behavior, her gun would be taken away until further notice. The commander of the cell, Grisha Jaszunski (one of the leaders of the Bund in Poland), was likewise punished. He was demoted to the rank of private.

Kovner, the commander, analyzed the situation in a speech he gave before the fighters and he said: "In my opinion, the actions of the final liquidation have already begun. This night all the fighters must prepare candles and bottles of water, for the Germans might stop the supply of water and electricity to the ghetto. The Organization could not begin the revolt today, because the masses were against us and against any action on our part. It seems there will be considerable pauses between one action and another, so we can still operate. We have two alternatives before us. One is to blow up the gate on Lidski Street and break our way through the enemy cordon surrounding the ghetto, cross the city, and go into the forests. But from the military viewpoint, we should not do this, as we lack arms and military training. Moreover, we will be forced to make our way on foot, while the enemy has many vehicles. We might all fall in battle before we are able to kill even one of them. Therefore, we should hold out until the end of the actions and leave the ghetto in an organized manner and surprise the enemy with our shooting, and then we shall have chances of success."

The fighters heard Kovner's words with great disappointment. Everyone realized that the last opportunity had been wasted. In vain they had prepared long months for the beginning of the revolt.

The Treachery of the Headquarters

The next day, on September 2, the Jewish police continued to carry out the actions. Germans and Estonians did not appear in the ghetto that day, but ten

Lithuanian policemen and four demolition experts equipped with large quantities of explosives concentrated near the gate under the command of a German Gestapo officer. The police looked for the bunkers, and when they succeeded in discovering one of them, they removed the Jews hiding there and sent them to the gate where they were turned over to the Lithuanians. The police asked the ghetto people to help uncover the bunkers, and all those who accepted this invitation would wear a special band on their arms and work with the police. During the day an "auxiliary police" formed, numbering several hundred people, and they carried out their work with devotion and enthusiasm, in the belief that in so doing they were saving their own lives.

The Jews were led to the gate with no baggage or possessions. The Lithuanians searched them and took away their money, watches, and other valuables. By car or by foot they were taken to the train station and from there sent to Estonia. All the way they were beaten mercilessly by the Lithuanians.

German sappers went from house to house together with Gens and several policemen. They shouted warnings to the Jews to come out of hiding, for the building was going to be blown up. The Jews, experienced from the day before, knew that this was no idle threat. They ran out of their hiding places and surrendered. There was no resistance, for they knew that they were going to Estonia.

After they left the houses, the sappers laid explosives to frighten those hiding in other places. But the houses were not harmed or hardly so; most of the time the charge was enough only to blow up the windows.

Gens asked the Gestapo officer to stop the explosions because it would be difficult to live in houses without windows in the winter. He did not imagine that by winter the Vilna Ghetto would no longer exist. The Gestapo officer granted Gens's request, and some time later the sappers were equipped with explosives powerful enough to scare the people rather than cause damage.

The action was carried out in the same way the next two days, and each day the Germans received their promised quota.

On September 4, in the afternoon, the policemen saw that the results of their searches were meagre and they would not be able to supply the necessary number of people. Gens ordered the police to gather in the courtyard of the Judenrat. He placed the regular police on one side and the auxiliary police on the other. The entrances to the yard were guarded by the *shtarke* (strongmen), members of the underworld who had also been recruited for this dirty work. Some time later the regular police and 50 members of the auxiliary police were given pink slips and told to leave the yard and gather in Rudnicka Street. The rest of the auxiliary police, about 400 people, suddenly found themselves surrounded by the "strongmen'' who took them out of the yard. When the unfortunates reached Rudnicka Street, the regular police also joined in the treacherous action against them. They were taken to the gate and turned over to the Lithuanians. One of them tried to escape and a Jewish police officer, Taubin, shot and killed him.

At that same time, 50 members of the auxiliary police, who led a group of kidnapped people to the police station, returned to the ghetto. They, too, were turned over to the Lithuanians. Thus, they fulfilled the proverb: ''Because thou drownedst others, they have drowned thee,'' just as the regular police would fulfill the second part of the saying: ''and at the last they that drowned thee shall themselves be drowned.''

A war of nerves raged among the ghetto Jews. The police spread rumors that anyone who continued to hide would be shot. They said that those who went to Estonia were better off than those remaining. Because there were mainly women left in the ghetto, the ghetto would be unproductive and would not last long, whereas a long life was assured for all the Jews taking part in the productive work in Estonia.

The Jews were tired of sitting in the bunkers. They could no longer stand the constant tension. They began to leave and surrender of their own free will.

By 5:00 P.M. the ''action'' was over. Gens published two announcements to the ghetto inhabitants. The first, that after many efforts the leaders were able to get the Gestapo to agree to a shipment of 1,000 women to Estonia, where they could join their husbands. Any woman interested in going had to appear the next morning in the Judenrat yard with her baggage. Priority would be given to those women whose husbands were seized in the actions of the four previous days. Gens promised that no woman who had the right to travel would be denied it. He, himself, would oversee the organization of the transport. The second announcement stated that anyone wishing to send food and clothing packages to their relatives who were abducted the four previous days must prepare the packages so that the Gestapo could bring them to their destination.

On September 5, in the morning, a large crowd gathered in the Judenrat yard. Hundreds of women came to ensure their right to leave. They crowded and pushed so as not to miss the opportunity, Heaven forbid. Several women bribed the police and *Arbeitsamt* officials to put them on the list of passengers. Groups of several hundreds each left, one after another, through the ghetto gate and from there to the train station. The women took only small bundles with them. The heavy baggage was to be transported in cars supplied by the Gestapo.

Several hours after the registration began, women discovered that it was not hard at all to be accepted for the transport. On the contrary, the police were walking around the ghetto urging women to go to the *Arbeitsamt*. Rumors spread that the women were not taken to Estonia, but to Riga instead. The proof was the fact that Estonian soldiers were no longer seen near the gate, only Latvians. The women, including those who were already registered for the trip, began to slip away and hide. The police embarked on a woman-hunt and only in the evening succeeded in fulfilling its quota. This was the end of the "action." All in all, over five days, more than 7,000 men and women had been rounded up.

From the second day of the "action," everyone knew that the house on 6 Straszun Street, the Headquarters of the Fighting Organization, was a safe place. People heard that there was an agreement between the Organization and the police chief. It was an open secret among the fighters as well, who were upset that the Command had betrayed the idea which they had nurtured for long months. Once they realized they could no longer expect a revolt or resistance, they hurried to bring their parents and other relatives to 6 Straszun Street. They wanted to save, at least, their families.

When Gens learned that hundreds of Jews were hiding in the Headquarters, he contacted Krizovski, the liaison between the Organization and the police, and told him that the agreement applied only to the fighters and in no way would other Jews be allowed to hide there, for this would lead to demoralization within the ghetto and disturb the course of the "action." Gens wanted to go and see for himself if it were true that the Organization was giving shelter to Jewish non-fighters. Krizovski announced that he would have to ask Headquarters about this. After a long discussion, the Headquarters agreed to a visit to the main position by a police committee. Following this decision, the commander wanted to remove the Jews who were in the house, but did not want to anger the fighters. He ordered all the armed fighters to gather in the library of the building, while those without arms, as well as the relatives, would gather in the bathhouse in the same building and enter the bunker there, which could accommodate 200 people. He also warned the fighters against any separate action that might cause an exchange of fire. He told them that when they would see Germans and Lithuanians approaching, they should leave that position and gather inside the house. Indeed, several times Germans walked around the area and the fighters received an order to lie down on the floor.

The next day the position was visited by a committee of police officers, headed by Nussbaum, the chief prosecutor of the police and one of Dessler's admirers. They had come to check whether the fighters were keeping their part of the agreement. Nussbaum went around all the rooms, surveyed the armed fighters, and with characteristic cynicism remarked: "It makes one proud to see Jewish boys who know how to handle arms." The commander gave Nussbaum permission to enter the position any time he pleased.

Two hours after this inspection, Nussbaum showed up again and found several hundred unarmed Jews and several dozen fourteen- and fifteen-year old Komsomol members. He said that he thought that the Organization's Headquarters would be gentlemanly enough to keep its side of the agreement faithfully, and left the building in a huff. Some time later Krizovski announced that Dessler was demanding the removal of the children and the other Jews hiding in the building. The Headquarters met to discuss this but reached no decision. So Hienna Borowska, one of the Communist leaders, ordered that the children be taken to the yard of 13 Lidski Street. The children innocently believed that they were being transferred to a new position, and when they passed Borowska, they saluted in her honor. One fighter accompanied the children to Lidski, and after arriving there, left hastily.

Evacuation

Anger spread among the fighting ranks over the command's treachery. Many gave loud expression to their bitterness. One evening the commander ordered the fighters to hand over their arms for inspection. Most of them received their arms back but some weapons remained in storage. The commander said that these weapons were to be used for special assignments. But, "by coincidence," these belonged to the fighters who complained against the Headquarters.

The Headquarters was planning an exit from the ghetto. The idea was to hire cars to take the fighters to the forests, or if this did not succeed, to break into the German camps and seize the cars by force.

For the last two nights the guard around the ghetto had been less vigilant. Advantage was taken of this to strengthen ties with the city and to purchase additional arms. The new weapons would not be brought into the ghetto; they would remain in the city. Ways were also sought to remove part of the Organization's arms from the ghetto.

On the evening of September 5, after the "action" was over, a call-up was held of all the members of the Organization, and Kovner gave a speech, in which he said: "The 'action' has been completed and it seems we shall now have a long period of peace in the ghetto." He spoke at length about the Organization which should have revolted but was unable to because of the strong opposition of the Jewish masses. And from now on, he said, even the approval of the Jews would not help any more because there were no longer enough men in the ghetto to organize a successful revolt. He believed that the only way was the evacuation of the whole Organization to the forests to continue the war there.

The ghetto remained closed after the "action." Entrance and exit was barred. The Jews no longer went to work in the city. Gens announced that from now on all the Jews would work within the ghetto. He was still convinced that the ghetto existed thanks to the benefit it brought the Germans through its labor. Therefore, he made great efforts to find jobs. After much persuasion, he got the approval of the Germans to open new workshops in the ghetto. Suitable places were prepared so that hundreds of Jews could find work. Even the big sewing factory in the city, which employed hundreds of Jews, was to be moved into the ghetto. Large orders were received from the Wehrmacht, work for many months. There was also great improvement as far as housing and food were concerned. The Germans were wont, after each "action," to increase the food rations of those who remained. The Jews once again began to build secret passages enabling them to bring in various food items, despite the police and army guards.

Encouraging news reached the ghetto regarding the successes of the Russians on the fronts. All of this cheered the Jews and awakened new hopes in the future.

The F.P.O. commander held a referendum among the fighters: to remain in the ghetto or to begin leaving for the forests. As no one believed any longer in revolt within the ghetto, the majority voted for evacuation. Yet, exit from the ghetto was not such a simple matter. First of all, Aryan papers had to be prepared for some of the fighters so that they could go to the city to search for safe exit channels. The matter of removing the arms also had to be dealt with. The only people who could leave the ghetto now were the dead. Yehuda Kushinski went out every day with the funeral wagon, as a helper to the gravedigger, and brought out quantities of arms and ammunition with him, which he hid in the cemetery. The departing companies of fighters would first go to the cemetery, arm themselves, and from there continue on their dangerous way.

At the same time, several Jewish boys, almost all of them from Swiecany, came to the ghetto by order of Markov, the partisan leader in Narocz Forest. Their task was to take Jews out of the ghetto and bring them to the forests. They spoke highly of life in the forest, of the partisans, their weapons, and the operations against the Germans. They also said that the partisans believed that redemption was near and that the Russian Army was making rapid advances all along the front. Their words excited the fighters. All of them imagined themselves as heroes in the forest.

By order of the commander, the emissaries were kept on 6 Straszun Street so they would not come into contact with the masses in the ghetto and organize groups of nonfighters to leave for the forests. The emissaries were told that for their own safety they must not be seen in the ghetto.

The fighters began to organize companies to leave. According to the original plan, a member of the Headquarters had to accompany each group. But the command, believing that the ghetto would last many more months, decided to remain, together with several dozen fighters who chose not to leave, whether for ideological or health reasons or because they were not ready to part with their loved ones.

Once again an agreement was made with Gens. The latter promised that he would not hinder the exit of the fighters, providing the Organization did not allow the exit of nonfighters. Gens claimed that if a mass exodus began from the ghetto, the Germans would begin the final liquidation. Following the agreement, he gave the Headquarters the key to the gate on Yatkever Street.

The exodus to the forest did not remain a secret for long. Every time a group left, the masses ran after it and wanted to join it. But according to Kovner's orders, a thorough search was conducted at the exit. The Jews were driven from the gate and only rarely did one of them succeed in mingling with the fighters and leaving with them. It is interesting that among those ''illegals'' were later to be found some of the best fighters in the forest.

The Jews began to complain about the F.P.O. commander. How was he any better than the police chief? One chose who would die and the other chose who would live. . . . Hundreds of Jewish youths were to be killed who might have made important contributions in the war against the enemy. And the Jews were the ones who shut the doors to rescue in their faces.

During the second week of September, three companies left, accompanied by two members of the Headquarters: Lyova Ziskovich of Betar and Nissan Reznik of Hanoar Hatsioni.

One day a letter arrived from Josef in the Narocz Forest. He wrote that there in the forest, among the non-Jewish partisans, he once again learned how correct was the F.P.O. premise that the revolt had to be made within the walls of the ghetto. The war in the forest, he wrote, is not our national war. Anti-Semitism is rampant even among the partisans. He also wrote about the scant arms and equipment of the partisans and ended his letter with the following words: ''If the whole Organization came with its arms to the forest, we would be a military force of the first order. We would assume an important position and would do great things.'' The letter was not publicized among the fighters. Nonetheless, groups of fighters were no longer sent to Narocz Forest, since in the interim information had arrived about partisan bases in Rudnik Forest near Vilna, which was much more accessible.

To form ties with the partisans around Vilna and to check the access routes to them, the Headquarters sent out two women fighters, Niussa Lubotski and Tamar Reshal. Meanwhile, two companies from the Second Organization left for Rudnik Forest.

On September 14 Gens and Dessler were called to report to the Gestapo. Dessler returned alone in the afternoon. When asked where Gens was, he replied: "Gens was arrested."

Late that night, Kemermacher, a member of the Jewish labor brigade who worked at the Gestapo offices, arrived in the ghetto and reported that Gens had been shot by the Germans. He said that Neugebauer and Paulhaber, two Gestapo leaders, went with Gens to Rossa, the site of several important Gestapo departments. Gestapo leader Neugebauer told Gens that the ghetto was about to be liquidated and, therefore, he was no longer needed. But he added that since Gens had fulfilled his role faithfully, he would have the honor of being shot by the Gestapo leader himself. And with these words, he shot him.

In the ghetto the story was that several high officers in the Gestapo, including the famous hangman, Weiss, had warned Gens in advance and advised him to escape. They had even offered him help. But Gens did not want to leave the ghetto until the last minute and remained firm in his decision, despite all attempts to persuade him otherwise. It was also said in the ghetto that Dessler informed on Gens, saying that he had helped the Underground. In any case, Dessler knew in advance what was going to happen but he did not tell Gens.

The news raised panic in the ghetto. Everyone saw this as a sign that the remaining Jews were about to be exterminated. They had heard about other places where the Germans first killed the ghetto leader and then the rest. The Jews grieved over the tragedy of Gens. One could say that he was wrong, but everyone knew that he was not a traitor. Whatever he did as head of the ghetto, he did for his people. His methods were wrong and one cannot find any justification for turning Jews over to the Gestapo under any conditions. But he did not sell himself to the Germans. He truly and naïvely believed that he could deceive them, and that through a policy of concession and postponement he could keep at least a small number of Jews alive.

Everyone knew that Gens had had many possibilities to save himself. He was once captain in the Lithuanian Army and he had many Lithuanian friends who would gladly have helped him. His Lithuanian wife could have also saved him. But he gave up his personal security to devote his life to the ghetto. He believed in his ability and was convinced to the last moment that he would be able to save the remnant. People still remembered his proud attitude before the Germans. Several times they threatened to kill him, but he remained calm and smiling in the face of all their threats until the murderers withdrew. Everyone believed that if Gens had been convinced that the end had really come for the ghetto, he himself would have organized an exodus to the forests and would have placed himself at the head of the fighters. They remembered that several days before his death, he left the ghetto on a bicycle and scouted the boundaries of the city to inform the Organization Headquarters whether it was possible to go out that day and along which route. Everyone was convinced that Gens had died deeply regretting his mistaken course of action, with no consolation save the fact that he sacrificed his life for the Jews in the ghetto.

The next day, Gestapo officer Kittel came, summoned the police, and made a speech before them. Kittel was the only one among all the Gestapo people who behaved towards the Jewish police like a military leader, demanding that they submit reports and that they salute him.

He announced that Dessler had been appointed ghetto leader, as Gens had been shot the night before. But this had no connection whatsoever with the fate of the ghetto. Gens's death was a result of a personal quarrel between him and Neugebauer, which had been going on for some time. Gens was a captain, while Neugebauer was only a lieutenant. And when Gens would address him as "Lieutenant," this would anger Neugebauer. He waited for an opportunity to pay him back and the time came the day before, when several Jews were caught escaping to the forest, who under interrogation confessed that Gens had helped them. (It was true that several Jews who tried to leave in an unorganized way had been caught.)

Kittel asked them to tell the Jews in the ghetto that the actions were over and no one would be sent away, not even to Estonia. The Jews would work in the ghetto and if they did well, a cinema would be opened in the ghetto at the end of the war. . . .

Most of the policemen believed Kittel and were consoled. And the ghetto Jews were also ready to believe him. They forgot the latest events and even the death of Gens. It seemed to them that a ray of light was shining through the dark clouds.

The Day of the Attempted Liquidation

On Saturday, September 18, the Jews saw that the ghetto was surrounded on all sides by a Latvian military force. In front of the ghetto gate stood several hundred Latvian soldiers, armed to the teeth. Everyone was seized with fear. Whoever had prepared a bunker ran to hide in it. But the large majority of ghetto inhabitants were helpless. Once again they discovered that the German promises were lies. The police, too, were in great confusion. Their confidence was shaken and doubt began to gnaw at their hearts. Could it be that they would not be spared after all?

Dessler gathered the police in the Judenrat courtyard, and everyone expected to hear an explanation for the army forces around the ghetto. But Dessler said nothing. For about an hour he walked back and forth and finally he spoke. He told the police to walk through the ghetto two-by-two and inform the people that all artisans must register in the Judenrat offices and report near the gate, for they were going to be taken to special blocks outside the ghetto.

Later Weiss came and talked with Dessler for over an hour. The police were still walking from yard to yard, urging the Jews to report, when suddenly they heard a rumor that Dessler, together with his parents and friends, including Nussbaum, had escaped from the ghetto. This was a hard blow, though they knew that Dessler was a submissive servant of the Gestapo and would do anything to save his life. They knew that he had never thought about the good of the community. He was always hardhearted towards the Jews and treated them cruelly. He wanted to find favor in the eyes of the Germans to save his own skin. Naturally, the workers did not report. In wild fear, each sought a hiding-place. The policemen, too, scattered after hearing about Dessler's escape. They looked for ways to save themselves from both the wrath of the masses and the threat of extermination.

At 3:00 P.M. the first units of the Latvian Army entered the ghetto and took positions at the street corners. Kittel tried to reorganize the Jewish police. After repeatedly promising that nothing would happen to them, he was able to round up several dozens of policemen, and under his command they began to grab Jews and load them onto vehicles. The police did their work without any enthusiasm. An hour later they had only 30 people.

When the Latvian soldiers entered the ghetto, the remaining fighters were mobilized. About fifty of them appeared at the call-up which took place on 6 Straszun Street. The Organization's commander, Abba Kovner, announced: "The time that we feared has come. This is the day of the final liquidation." He stressed that most of the fighters and the arms were no longer in the ghetto. Part of them had already reached the forests and part of them were still on their way. "We, the remaining ones, have been fated to keep our vow of resistance." Despite the scarcity of arms and men, they would begin the revolt.

He selected 20 people for the grenadier company and sent them to Rudnicka Street to take up positions on the top floors of the buildings, near the gate. If strong army forces entered the ghetto, the grenadiers would go into action. A small 5–6-member unit would take advantage of the confusion to start throwing grenades and to open fire on the enemy. With the help of the ghetto people, it would try to push the army outside the ghetto. The rest of the fighters would try to persuade the people to set fire to their homes in order to increase the confusion, which was the only chance for success.

The fighters received instructions to fight to the end, but when the resistance would break, they were to force their way out and make their way to Rudnik Forest. The fighters were given exact details on the routes they would have to take to get from the ghetto to the forest. Everything seemed in order, but several days later, the fighters learned that there was an exit from the ghetto through the sewer system which could be used on the day of the final liquidation. But why did the Organization's commander conceal this fact from them? Why did he not tell them that an exit existed which could save the lives of those who survived the armed revolt?

The fighters took up positions. But suddenly came unexpected salvation. The enemy was leaving the ghetto, freeing even the Jews who were already in the cars and removing the guards around the ghetto.

An hour later it was learned that Italy had surrendered to the English and the Americans. What joy! At first, it was believed there was a connection between this event and the sudden interruption of the action against the ghetto. However, the next day it was learned that the Gestapo and the army had received orders from Riga to stop the operation in the ghetto immediately and to hunt for partisans in the Narocz Forest. The liquidation was postponed until after the hunt. The Vilna Jews called this day "the attempted liquidation."

The next day large quantities of food were brought to the ghetto. The Jews made calculations and found that the food was sufficient for a considerable period and, therefore, drew the conclusion that the ghetto would remain for a long time. The police officers held a meeting and decided to appoint as ghetto leader Borya Binikonski, a Kovno Jew and one of the directors of the workshops in the ghetto. Binikonski announced that he was willing to assume the responsible position. He promised that as long as he headed the ghetto, the police would not carry out actions and would not even help the Germans remove Jews from the ghetto. At that same meeting, Gens's brother, Solomon, made a speech in which he accused Dessler of the death of his brother and said that Dessler had told the Germans the true views of the ghetto leader, and on the basis of this they executed him. Solomon Gens, who was one of the police officers, called upon his fellow policemen to find the hiding-place of Dessler, bring him back to the ghetto, and hang him for all the Jews to see. The police received his words enthusiastically and expressed their condemnation of Dessler.

The next day, three hundred new sewing machines were brought to the ghetto to enlarge the sewing factory. The Germans also brought trucks loaded with cloth.

The work would suffice for many months and the Jews hoped that this meant a long period of peace. But doubt still gnawed at them. Something told them that the ghetto's days were numbered. It was as if they could see the wings of the Angel of Death gradually eclipsing the sun, as if they could feel his sickle against their necks.

During the time the transfer was completed of the Jews working in the Keilis, the Gestapo, the Spanish Army Hospital, and the H.K.P. to special blocks in the city. Jews paid enormous sums to be among those transferred and to get a postponement of their death. The week before, the last group of the F.P.O. made several attempts to leave the ghetto. But the Lithuanian and Ukrainian police and Gestapo men guarded all the exits. In the evening of September 22, the people tried to leave the ghetto through the sewer system but decided against it at the last minute, after hearing news about the serious danger along the escape routes.

We were to hear about Dessler several weeks later, when we were in the forest. The Gestapo discovered the bunker in which he and his relatives were hiding in the city. What surprised us more was that Abrasha Krizovski was also in the bunker. But Krizovski succeeded in getting away from the Gestapo and reaching the Narocz Forest.

Dessler's charm for the Germans did not fail him. The Jews living in a special block in the city, even after the liquidation of the ghetto, saw him frequently with Gestapo men. It turned out that he was working for them in the city, among the Poles. Only several days before the Liberation, when the remaining Jews in the city blocks were killed, Dessler was shot by the Gestapo officers.

The Final Liquidation

We heard several details of the events of these last days only much later. After the Liberation, in the summer of 1944, the Russians captured the Gestapo officer, Franz Müller. During the interrogation he confirmed that it was because of the hunt for partisans that the liquidation of the ghetto had been postponed for several weeks.

But Kittel wanted to rise in rank by showing his diligence. He announced to the main headquarters in Riga that the Fighting Organization and the resistance movement had already been broken. He was ready to carry out the liquidation of the ghetto if he were given 150–200 Ukrainian soldiers. In his opinion, there was no reason for delay. He asked for permission to carry it out. Permission was granted. On September 23, 1943, Kittel began the final liquidation.

At midnight of September 23, the Gestapo informed the new ghetto leader,

Binikonski, that the Vilna Ghetto would be totally destroyed and all its inhabitants would be taken to work camps in Estonia. He was promised that after the action, the police and their families would be taken to the blocks of Keilis and the H.K.P. By 4:00 A.M. every ghetto Jew already knew what awaited him. The self-confidence which had sustained them all these difficult years disappeared. All the spiritual strength which had enabled the Jews to undergo hell and keep going evaporated in an instant. Their belief in the morrow was shaken to the core. They knew that this was the end. From now on nothing would help them—no tricks or tactics.

Their senses were blunted. All bedlam broke loose. People no longer knew what lay in store for them. They only knew one thing: they had to fight death off to the very end. They had to postpone the death sentence as long as possible. The Jews frantically began to grab onto anything that seemed a possible anchor of safety. The Jews hid in every place they could find shelter. Though most of the hiding-places were well known to the Jewish police, it was hoped that this time the police would not cooperate and would not reveal them to the Germans.

At 8:00 A.M. Gebitskommissar Hingst arrived in the ghetto with Gestapo officer Kittel. In the courtyard of the Judenrat, they found the police and several hundred Jews who had not found hiding-places and were already sick of sitting in the bunkers. They announced that all the Jews would be transferred to Riga, Kovno, and Siauliai (Shavli). Everyone had to be ready to go by 11:00 A.M. Each person could take only a small bundle; heavy packages had to be left near the homes and the Gestapo cars would bring them to the police station.

The Germans promised that this time families would not be parted. The transports would leave that day and the traveling conditions would be much more comfortable than on the previous transports. Anyone not reporting of his free will would be shot by the Ukrainians who came to the ghetto to oversee the execution of the order.

At the same time Gebitskommissariat clerks came to the ghetto to receive from the ghetto management the funds, workshops, and other property. The clerks carefully checked if the books were in order.

Confusion reached a climax. No one knew what to do. It was clear to all that they would not be taken to Ponar, but should they believe the Germans and go or perhaps it was better to remain in the bunkers and take their chances? They asked one another's advice. Everyone wanted to see what the other would do. Several women even went to Kittel and asked his advice.

A meeting of the police was held that day. One of the officers announced that the police should hurry up the ghetto inhabitants so as to meet the deadline. He added that the policemen's families did not have to leave the ghetto and that they would be taken with the police to blocks in the city. Naturally, this was on condition that the police carried out their duty. These words had their effect. The policemen scattered among the yards and urged on the residents.

At 10:00 A.M. the ghetto was surrounded by Ukrainians. The Jews began to prepare to leave. The majority had packed their belongings and had gathered near the gate. From there they would be sent in groups to Rossa. Before leaving they broke into the Judenrat warehouses and grabbed the food there. Everyone wanted to take full advantage of the confusion. Close to 11:00 A.M. the narrow streets began to empty of people. The police gathered their families at 11 Szpitalna Street, at the Second Police Station. At 11:00 A.M. the Ukrainians broke into the ghetto with savage cries, like starved animals who smelled their prey.

From early morning the fighters were located at 6 Straszun Street. For several hours they waited for the commander's order to begin the revolt. They believed that this time the order would be given, for there was no longer any doubt that the final liquidation had begun. But instead of issuing orders to begin the revolt, the commander and the Headquarters officers were making preparations to leave the ghetto. They had decided to go to Rudnik Forest.

At 11 A.M. all the cell commanders received instructions to tell their fighters to go to 13 Deutscheshe Street and enter one of the Judenrat workshops in the courtyard. According to the order, they had to go there quietly and inconspicuously so as not to draw the attention of the residents. The exodus had to be carried out with complete secrecy, and if someone tried to take his parents or family with him, he would be left behind in the ghetto. The fighters were told that the route must be guarded only for those who were leaving to fight and not for run-of-the-mill Jews who only wanted to save their own lives. For the same reason the fighters were not allowed to say goodbye to their loved ones.

Several fighters asked permission to take along relatives who were ready and able to fight, but the commander refused. He reminded them that when they bound their fates to that of the Fighting Organization, they promised to remove all sentiments from their hearts and to devote themselves only to the common cause. And to set an example to the others, he left behind his mother and brother, who were in the same category.

Despite all the precautionary measures, the ghetto people learned that the fighters had gathered in the workshops and were preparing to leave. Dozens of healthy and strong youths gathered in the courtyard and begged to be allowed to join those who were leaving, but in vain. The commander threatened them with his gun and chased them away. He also chased away two girls, aged 16–17, who belonged to the F.P.O. cells, despite the fact that several days before it had been agreed that they would leave the ghetto with Aryan papers. Their exit was prevented at the last moment because strong German and Ukrainian guards were stationed near the ghetto. All their pleas were for naught. They promised to go to the forest alone, so as not to be a deadweight on the fighting force. But the commander was adamant: exit was for fighters only.

At noon the final call-up took place, attended by about 50 people. The arms were checked, the last instructions were given, and immediately afterwards the fighters began to descend into the canal. Armed guards stood at the opening, lest, Heaven forbid, an "illegal" Jew infiltrated. While they entered the canal, they heard the cries and shots of the Ukrainians who had scattered throughout the ghetto to find hidden Jews. In this way the commander "fulfilled" Paragaph 22 of the Organization's constitution, which said: "We shall go to the forest only as a result of battle. After we carry out our mission, we shall take with us the largest possible number of Jews and break our way to the forest, where we shall continue our war against the murderous conqueror, as an inalienable part of the general partisan movement."

The Destruction of "Jerusalem of Lithuania"

The Ukrainians carefully checked every corner of every building. Among the policemen were several who rushed to help them, but the Ukrainians treated them with contempt, as if they did not exist. With particular cruelty they stormed the hospital, the orphanage, and the childrens' dormitory which had been abandoned during the evacuation. They beat up and reviled the patients and children and threw them into cars, which took them away from the ghetto, apparently to Ponar. Afterwards, they began to riot and pillage the homes. They broke down doors, smashed windows, broke furniture, and threw all the movable property out of the windows. The air suddenly filled with feathers from the pillows they tore to shreds in their search for hidden treasure. The streets were blanketed in white, as if snow had fallen. From time to time the air shook with the sound of dynamite. The Ukrainians set off bombs to frighten the Jews and make them leave the bunkers.

Meanwhile German cars came to the ghetto and began to take away the property in the workshops and the homes. They took the kindling wood which the Judenrat had prepared to distribute in the winter. The Jewish police tried to help them. They were confused, frightened for their own lives and the lives of their families, and ready to do anything to be of use. There were no longer any Jews in the ghetto and the guards around were growing more numerous. Every entrance known to the Germans was carefully guarded. By nighttime the last Jews who had been discovered by the Ukrainians during the day were taken out. The Ukrainians left with them.

A great darkness enveloped the sad streets. An offensive and suffocating smell of explosives filled the air. Light rain fell, as if the skies themselves were mourning the mortals who had been taken to the unknown. The wind wailed through the windows and doors which were left open in the deserted houses. The feathers scattered on the sidewalk gleamed white, like death shrouds. Electric lights shone from many windows like memorial candles to the people who had filled these narrow streets for hundreds of years and whose time had come to ascend to heaven. Here and there human shadows crept by—Jews who left their bunkers and who were looking for safety in the darkness of the night.

At 11 Szpitalna Street, the families of the policemen were gathered as well as other Jews who had left their bunkers and had made their way there. All together there were 2,000 people. They still hoped that in the morning they would be taken to the Keilis and H.K.P. blocks.

At 3:00 A.M. the Jewish police took all those remaining into the large hall of the ghetto theater and began to conduct a selection. Those closest to them they sent to a side room. They thought that they would have better chances of survival if the number of "privileged ones" would not be too great. Those remaining in the large hall saw this as a bad omen and tried with all their might to push into the side room. A fist-fight broke out between those condemned to death and those chosen to live. Everyone fought for his right to live. Many blows and insults were exchanged in this struggle between Jew and Jew, which lasted for several hours.

On Friday morning, September 24, several Germans entered the ghetto. At their order the guards were removed from the side room and all the Jews, including those in the big hall and the policemen and their families, were moved to Rudnicka Street. The Jews in the hiding-places "smelled" that the police were being taken out and rushed out of their bunkers to join the "fortunate ones."

At 7:30 A.M. the Ukrainians came, armed to the hilt. They set up machine guns everywhere and surrounded the Jews on all sides. For an hour and a half they maltreated their victims and took away their money, watches, and all other valuables they had. At 9:00 A.M. they were taken out of the ghetto and driven to Rossa, where all the Jews who had been removed from the ghetto the day before were gathered.

The wind rocked three corpses hanging from the trees. When the fighters emerged from the sewer, some of them encountered Germans. Two Headquarters officers, Abrasha Hvoinik and Yaakov Kaplan, and the fighter, Asya Bik, opened fire but were caught by the enemy. To strike fear into the hearts of the Jews, the Germans hanged the three in sight of all the Jews in Rossa.

For three days and nights about 10,000 Jews stayed in Rossa under the open sky, shivering with cold and soaked to the bone from rain, hungry and depressed. During this time, the Germans conducted a selection: children, old people, and weak people were sent to Ponar or Majdanek. The rest were sent to the labor camps in Estonia.

"Jerusalem of Lithuania," the city of scholars and writers, the city of Torah and progress, the city which for generations had been a light for Jews of the world, was no longer.

Part Two
The Forest

First Encounters

"There is no way back," said Josef.

We, 13 of the 35 who had left the ghetto to join the partisans and to strike the enemy, were in a woods, surrounded by enemies. Our situation was desperate. Shika, our guide and the only one with a map and compass, had deserted us. None of us knew the way. We were still stunned by our losses. We were unable to grasp the fact that so many of our brave comrades were no longer alive.

We were enveloped by fear and the shadow of death. The enemy's shots were heard on all sides. Any minute they could attack us with grenades and kill us off. But Josef strongly rejected any proposal to return to the ghetto. The weak of spirit could return. The rest would break a way through.

The horrible night passed. Morning broke and our situation became much worse. In daylight the Germans could enter the forest and discover our hiding-place. Several people went out to survey the area, and when they returned, we went further into the forest. We lay down to rest in a place where the trees were dense. During the retreat at night, most of the people had lost their backpacks and we were beginning to feel hungry. We set up guards all around. We were exhausted and dejected from the night's adventures. Our limbs felt like lead. With our remaining strength we fought off sleep, but it eventually overcame us and one by one we dozed off. Even the guards could not keep their eyes open. They, too, fell into a deep sleep. Suddenly, as if bitten by a snake, we jumped to our feet. The sun was high in the sky and before us stood two young men from the nearby village who were gathering mushrooms. They said that a fierce battle had taken place in the night between partisans and German soldiers, aided by Lithuanian policemen. Three policemen were killed and several were wounded. Two partisans lay dead near the bridge. Others were taken prisoner and sent to Vilna. The Germans and Lithuanians were searching the whole area now. They were waiting for reinforcements to penetrate the forest. The two young men offered to take us to a safer place.

We followed them to an area in the forest bordering corn fields. There was no village to be seen. After a discussion, one of them promised to return at noon to bring us food. He would also tell us whether he could take us out of there. In fear, we awaited his arrival. Would he return? And if so, would he bring Germans? We cocked our guns to be ready for the last battle.

He appeared at the appointed hour, carrying a basket of food. He apologized to us for the small quantity; he had brought only what was in the house and he took it without his parents' knowledge. He did not want to buy additional food from the villagers so as not to arouse suspicion. He sat with us for a long time and told us the exaggerated rumors floating around the area regarding the battle of the previous night. He promised to return by evening to take us across the river. We were relieved, despite the shots which still could be heard.

Two of the young men who joined us at Vileyka and F.P.O. member Chaim Spokojny announced their decision to return to the ghetto. We gave them the remaining food and wished them well. (Some time later we heard that the three had been captured by Germans.)

We crossed the river at dusk. Our guide brought us to a place where the water was neck-high. We held our weapons over our heads, so as not to wet them. In the distance we saw the bridge which had cost us so many casualties in our attempt to cross it. We continued on our way through the fields. The walking was very hard. Our clothes were heavy with water. Our shoes were wet and covered with mud. But we walked quickly to get as far away as possible from the dangerous area. Night fell and we breathed a sigh of relief.

Several kilometers later we reached a forest, and the young man told us that he had to return home. We gave him a reasonable sum of money and thanked him profusely as we parted. Yes, there were still some "righteous gentiles." And if this *sheigetz* was so good, then the non-Jewish partisans had to be even more so. Without a doubt, we would be accepted as brothers.

That night we crossed many kilometers. At dawn we chose a resting place for the day. We naïvely thought that our misfortunes were over and that we could now continue on our way without many mishaps. We were wrong.

There was unusual movement in the forest from time to time. We heard heavy shooting. The Germans had not stopped looking for us. For three whole days we remained in the same spot without food or water. Only on the third night did a silence fall in the area. We continued our trek, tired and exhausted. We had to wait until the next night to get a little food. We made our way as follows: in the morning two of us went out dressed as peasants to scout the area. Sometimes the scouts were able to buy a little food. At noon they would return, and at night we would advance along the same bit of route which the "peasants" had gotten to know. We did not dare go any further. Hence, it was not surprising that we took fourteen days for a journey of five days.

One day we rested in a woods between two small villages. Throughout the day the local peasants observed us, and after some time, the two village heads came to talk with us. They wanted us to decide to which of the villages the woods, in which we were hiding, belonged. Each of them was interested, naturally, that the woods belong to the other village. We calmed them down and assured them that we would leave the place that night. They were so pleased to hear this that they brought us bread, roasted meat, and confections.

The Viliya River, which crosses several dozen kilometers of the Narocz Forest, was the natural border between the partisan territory and the German-controlled area. The Germans did not dare cross the river, except with large forces. The partisans had burned all the bridges to make it difficult for the enemy to penetrate their territory. We finally reached the river and crossed it in the evening. On the other side, we met up with a Russian fellow named Misha. He told us that he was a lieutenant in the Russian Army, had escaped after being captured by the Germans, and was now living in one of the local villages. When we asked him if he, too, was going to the forest, he replied that he was a liaison for the partisans and, knowing the area well, would be very happy to help us. He said that he had a friend living in the nearby village, who was also a Russian officer, working in a similar capacity. He wanted his friend, too, to help us. The two of them would accompany us to the woods and bring us safely to the partisans.

There were those among us who were inclined to believe Misha. He was so warm and spoke such a fluent Russian. Nevertheless, we were wary, and when Misha went to call his friend, we left the place and hurried on our way. Some time later, when we were already in the forest, we heard that Misha and his friend had been captured by the partisans and executed for spying for the Gestapo.

The Jew Is Alone Even in the Forest

The partisans of Markov's brigade received us cordially. They had already heard about our clash with the Germans and about everything we had undergone. In the forest we found several dozen Jews who had escaped slaughter in nearby villages. Josef immediately began to set up a Jewish partisan unit. He met with Markov and tried to win him over to the idea. He also met with the commander of the Lithuanian partisan movement, a Jew named Ziman, from Kovno, and a well-known Communist leader, editor of the Communist paper *Tiesa* (Truth), and a regular contributor to the Yiddish paper *Folksblatt*. His name was now Yurgis. Josef and Yurgis had known each other before the war. Yurgis promised to help set up a Jewish unit. He also promised to supply arms. After long negotiations, Markov also gave his approval.

The Jewish battalion numbered 70 people. Markov appointed Butienas, a Jewish Communist from Lithuania who had arrived not long before from Moscow, as its commander. Josef was appointed chief of staff. The battalion was divided into two companies. I was in charge of one of them. This was the first fighting Jewish unit in these forests.

Several days later a swearing-in ceremony was held for the commanders of the various partisan battalions in the Narocz Forest. We vowed not to rest until we had expelled the Nazi invader from White Russia. The brigade commander, Markov, gave a stirring speech. He spoke at length of the terrible Jewish tragedy and ended by saying: "Who, more than you, must fight against the Nazi enemy and avenge the spilt blood of your brothers and sisters? Try to be good, brave, and loyal fighters. We shall help you with all the means at our disposal: guides, arms, instructions." He suggested that our battalion be called "Vengeance."

We were somewhat embarrassed that a non-Jew should tell us to avenge ourselves on the Nazis. The simple Gentile had reached logical conclusions which the thousands of Jews standing on the brink of destruction had not yet reached. But we consoled ourselves with the fact that we had, indeed, come to fight and we would not shame the name of our nation nor disappoint the hopes pinned on us.

With high spirits we returned to the camp and with renewed vigor set about arranging our new lives. We were full of hope. The reception held for us by the partisans made a great impression on us, especially since we had gotten used to being treated like dogs. We had almost lost our human image in the ghetto. And here we were equals among equals. We would soon fight shoulder-to-shoulder alongside the other partisans in the war against the common enemy.

Several days later partisan groups from all the battalions left Narocz Forest, under the direct order of Markov, to attack the town of Miadziol. We, too, were asked to take part in the attack. One of our companies, led by Josef, was very active in wiping out the German garrison in the town. Among our men was a native of the attacked town who served as a guide. He entered the town and set fire to his parents' home, which had in the meantime been converted into a German police station. After the operation we received our share of the booty taken from the Germans.

The initial romantic period did not last long. Our daily life was gray and full of hardships and disappointments. The lack of food and arms bothered us. The arms we had brought with us from the ghetto were for close range. Naturally, one could not wage war with pistols alone. Moreover, the Soviet partisans were beginning to show great interest in our guns. They had a kind of competition as to who had the nicest gun. We wanted to take advantage of the opportunity and to give them our guns in exchange for a promise that in a day or two they would bring us rifles. We were very naïve and lacked partisan experience. We thought that the elementary rules of human decency existed in the forest. But after a short time we learned that the partisans did not keep their word. They did not bring the promised rifles—and this was still during the relatively idyllic period, in comparison with what was to follow.

One after another, groups of youths arrived from Vilna. Most of them were members of the F.P.O., but there were also groups that were organized under their own initiative. The majority of their members came from the small towns around Vilna. Thus, the number of fighters in our battalion grew steadily: instead of 70 we already numbered several hundred.

Every day there were incidents of robbery in the forest. At first we did not understand what was going on. One of our boys returned to camp barefooted. He said that he had met up with Russian partisans in the woods and they ordered him to take off his boots. While one took his gun, another removed his watch. There were incidents of murder as well. Several Jews were found dead in various places in the forest. There were also more and more cases of anti-Jewish outbursts. Insult, scorn, and ridicule were the daily bread of the Jewish fighters. We complained to the High Command but nothing came of it. We grew embittered. True, we had been used to such an attitude in the ghetto. There it had been natural, almost self-evident. But in the forest it was hard to take insults from the Soviet partisans from whom we had expected so much. Still, the only hope of survival for the Jews lay in the forest.

During these days Josef sent two partisans to Vilna to report to our comrades in the ghetto on our life in the forest and to call upon the Jews to leave the ghetto en masse and join the partisans. Soon afterwards, I left Narocz Forest with a group of partisans. We had received orders from Commander Yurgis to go to the forests near Vilna and set up a partisan movement there. We were nine in all: four Lithuanian parachutists who had recently arrived from Moscow, including a man and a woman radio operator with two transmitters, and five Jews from the Jewish camp "Vengeance"; Gershon Gittelson from Vilna, Abrasha (Lyovka) Svirski from Glubokoye, Sasha and Chaim Meltzer from the Narocz environs, and myself. (Only one of the five would survive in one piece to see the liberation. One was killed, one lost an eye, one lost a leg, and one lost a hand.) We were equipped with as much modern automatic weaponry and ammunition as we could carry.

The day we set off, we were called in to see Commander Yurgis to give him biographical details and receive final instructions. The head of headquarters of the Jewish partisan camp, Josef Glazman, and the political commissar, Berl Sherezh-nevski were there as well. Yurgis asked if I belonged to any organization before the war and I answered: "I am a Zionist and belong to Betar." He was somewhat surprised by my candor, but did not seem upset by the answer.

My parting from Josef was very difficult. We had undergone many experiences and hardships together, both in the ghetto and in the forest. We had both been imprisoned and beaten. We left the ghetto together and were attacked in an ambush. We starved together, and together we built the Jewish partisan camp in the forest. These common experiences bound us closely.

Josef looked at me sadly and said: "Who knows if we shall ever see each other again. Try to keep the flame alive, come what may. No matter what the situation or what the condition, remember your nation. Draw your strength from it and hold out through difficult times." With these words we parted. I went to Rudnik Forest and he later took "the road of no return."

One day an official announcement came from Markov's headquarters that by order from Moscow all the separate national battalions must be disbanded, and first of all, the Jewish batallion. Its name was changed from "Vengeance" to "Komsomolsk" and the Jewish command was replaced by a non-Jewish one. The Jewish fighters were promised that they would be included in the general battalions and would receive their share of arms, and that there would be no discrimination between Jew and non-Jew.

One day all the Jews were lined up and led to Markov's headquarters. They were met by a strong guard. One by one the Jews were led to the Headquarters cabin. All the Headquarters officers and several of the commanders were there. Each and every one of the Jews was told that because the times were growing harder from day to day and there were not enough arms for the experienced fighters, the Jews must hand over their arms, and all their money and valuables to buy more arms. Each of them was searched. Their boots were removed, their good clothes were taken away, and their valuables were confiscated. The robbed people were let out through a second door so they could not tell their friends what had happened to them. Some hours later one could see a whole mourning procession of several hundred half-naked Jews, without arms and fearful for their future. One thought filled their minds: how were these partisans any better than the Germans? Afterwards, the Jews saw the girlfriends of the Soviet commanders and commissars sporting the clothes taken from the Jewish women partisans and wearing the watches taken from the Jews.

Commander Yurgis claimed that he could not intervene on behalf of the Jews because the Jewish camp was under Markov's authority.

Josef's Death

Frightening news came in the autumn of 1943 that the Germans were concentrating about 70,000 soldiers in the area and, with tanks and guns, they planned to rid the forest of partisans. Markov issued an order which said: "As we cannot enter battle against such enormous forces, all the partisans must leave the forest and find hiding-places until the storm is over. At the end of the German operation, all of you must come back and resume your fight against the enemy."

Thousands of partisans began to leave the forest in groups of three to five. They took their arms with them and scattered in various directions. Many of them had acquaintances and relatives among the villagers in White Russia. The over-whelming majority knew the terrain and knew where to go. But the Jews were left to their own devices. No one was interested in their fate. Those among the Jews who came from towns in the area still had a chance of finding shelter. But most of them went deep inside the swampy area, hoping that the Germans would not reach them there. Their request to receive arms or join partisans units leaving for other areas met with no response. Derisive remarks were made about the Jews and their bravery. Several Jews who tried to join the departees were shot and killed. Only a handful succeeded in being accepted by the departing units.

The forest emptied and the Germans were moving closer. Yurgis, too, gathered his people—about forty of them—and prepared to set off. Ten times a day Josef importuned him about arms, hoping to touch his Jewish heart. But Yurgis's heart was as hard as stone. As it turned out, due to the flight from the enemy, many arms had to be left in the forest. On the day of his departure, Yurgis called Joseph over and said: "I am giving you enough modern automatic weapons for ten people and I advise you to go in the direction of Kazian Forest (120 kilometers east of Narocz, deep inside White Russia. In the Kazian Forest were strong partisan bases). I, too, am going in that direction and we shall probably meet there in a few days. Unfortunately, I cannot take you with me because it is dangerous to go in large crowds." How could Josef imagine that this was a trap and that the Jew Yurgis, of all people, would deceive him?

Josef took eighteen people with him. On the way they were joined by other Jews and in the end the number reached thirty-five. They went along the route Yurgis told them to follow.

The trek was very dangerous. German planes constantly surveyed the roads. The thunder of mortar and tanks filled the area. After much tribulation, Josef and his people reached Kazan Forest. But while debating whether to enter the forest, he met Kazimir, a former minister in Soviet Lithuania who was now responsible for the partisans throughout Lithuania, as the latter was leaving the forest. Kazimir was amazed to see Josef and his people. When he heard that Yurgis had sent him and promised that he, too, would come, Kazimir said: "First of all, Yurgis won't come because he went in the direction of Rudnik Forest near Vilna. Secondly, you must turn back immediately because the Germans have begun an attack on this forest as well.'' After a hasty farewell, Kazimir and his people disappeared.

A triangular cordon of the German Army entered Narocz and Kazan Forests from two sides. There were only a few meters between each soldier and two days' walking distance between each cordon. Whoever succeeded in sneaking through the first cordon would run up against the second, and if he avoided the second, he would meet up with the third. The Germans combed the forests and wiped out all the positions and bases left by the partisans. They also set fire to dozens of villages whose inhabitants were suspected of aiding the partisans. Two army camps moved towards one another and the ring grew even tighter. Between the two jaws were Josef and his people. Their situation was desperate. There remained only one ray of hope: if they succeeded in crossing the railroad to Polotsk, halfway between the two German forces, they might get out of the straits.

On Kol Nidre night, 1943, they approached the railroad tracks. The railway was well guarded by the Germans, but the sky was clouded and the darkness gave them protection. One by one they crawled across the tracks and reached the other side safely. Now they had some chance of survival.

At dawn they reached a wood far from the tracks and hid there throughout the day, before continuing on their way the next night. The thunder of cannons and rattle of machine guns and tank wheels was already behind them. Their tension subsided, but their arms were still ready should the enemy discover their hiding place.

Suddenly German steel helmets appeared among the trees and the maw of machine guns yawned in their faces. Local peasants who had spotted the group of Jews brought the Germans to their hiding-place. A cruel and hopeless battle broke out between the uneven forces. Of this whole group, only one young woman remained alive. She hid among the thick bushes and survived the battle. She described the events of that terrible day: ''One by one the comrades fell. Everyone knew that the battle was lost and that there was no hope of getting out of the trap. They angrily stormed the enemy but the latter's forces were much greater. . . . The Germans advanced, hoping to capture several of the Jews alive. Finally there remained only three who continued to fight. . . . The three fought to the bitter end, and when their ammunition was just about gone, they turned their guns on themselves and killed themselves with their last bullets. The pride of victory was on their faces when they returned their souls to their Maker, for they had thwarted the German plans to take them alive.''

On Yom Kippur 1943, the Day of Judgement for all mortals, the Judge of the Universe behaved with extreme severity towards these fighters, just as He behaved towards the thousands of Jews who were taken from the Vilna Ghetto to be slaughtered two years before, on Yom Kippur 1941. Thirty-four pure souls went to Heaven before the Gates of Mercy shut. In a common grave near the town of Vidzy, seven Betarists, each of whom set an example of heroism and bravery, found their final rest: Josef Glazman, Miriam Bernstein, Lyova Ziskovich, Moshe Brause and his wife, Chaim Luski, and Shimon Brant. May their blood be avenged.

An underground shelter
(Zemlyanka) in Rudnik Forest.

Rudnik Forest

The Rudnik Forest, one of the biggest forests in Poland, begins fifteen kilometers from Vilna. The length of forested area is 60 kilometers and the width 40 kilometers. The Vilna–Grodno highway crosses the forest and there are hundreds of paths connecting the dozens of villages in and around the forest. A central path crossing its length is called "The French Way," a reminder of the days when Napoleon and his troops crossed this path on their way to Moscow. One of the most scenic routes is the "Kopana." Large trees tower on both sides and a fresh spring gushes. Pilsudski and the Polish President Moscicki used to go on hunting trips in Rudnik Forest. Further along the French Way, in the direction of the town of Rudnik, stands the grand Pilsudski–Santkova summer palace. Nearby on an exposed hill is a monument to the Russian soldiers and officers who fell in the area in battle against the Polish rebels in 1863.

Those traveling the French Way can get the impression that they are in a sparse wood. But if you stray from the path several meters in either direction, the forest begins to grow thicker. Your feet sink in muddy swamps, full of rotting leaves and tree trunks, and inhabited by a whole kingdom of insects and mosquitoes. Here you can find places where even in broad daylight no sun rays penetrate the thick branches. Every so often, you can see a small island within the swamps. Most of these islands can be reached by narrow rickety bridges, which were laid for the hunters. It is never silent. The twittering of birds blends into an endless symphony. The wild and uncorrupted nature takes your breath away.

This was the site of our new base.

After parting with our comrades in Narocz Forest, we set out at night on a 200-kilometer trek to Rudnik Forest. According to the instruction we received, we were to avoid clashes with the enemy and reach our target safely with our transmitters. The danger was greatest when we had to cross rivers, railways, or main highways. In those places we always feared meeting up with enemy guards.

The next day we rested among the bushes on our way and reached the Viliya River that night. All the bridges had long ago been burned by the partisans, so the local people used boats to cross the river. All these boats were concentrated in one place, but for security reasons we did not want to use them.

The night was dark and a heavy rain fell. The river was stormy and turbulent. Such weather was ideal for us. The Germans would not venture out on such a night. We walked along the shore and looked for a boat. From time to time solitary shots split the air. Apparently the German guards were amusing themselves by firing rounds. We finally found a small dinghy without oars which could carry only two people. After a long search we found the owner of the dinghy who was fast asleep in his hut. He reluctantly agreed to carry us across. The dinghy crossed the river nine times back and forth, and each time the old peasant crossed himself and said: "For dozens of years I earned a living by fishing in this river, but I never dared to set out in such weather." We believed him. Sometimes it seemed that the current and the wind would capsize the small boat. But the old man's experience stood him well and we safely reached the other shore.

On the fifth night of our journey, we reached the Vilna environs. We circumvented the city in an arc of several kilometers. When we heard wagon wheels we hid until we discovered that they were the wagons of peasants. We jumped out of our hiding-places to hear from them what had happened in the city. They complained about the hard times, the oppression and terror of the Nazis which was growing ever harsher. Without any sympathy they told us that the Germans were slaughtering the Jews again. This time, they said, the Jews were not brought to Ponar. They were shot at work in the airfield in Porubanek and other places.

For over a month we had not received any news from the ghetto. Under the conditions in the ghetto, a month was an eternity. Our hearts pounded with fear over the fate of our comrades in the city. Who knew how many Jews had died and how many of our friends were no longer alive? The peasants gave no details.

In the swamps of Rudnik Forest, near the village of Zagorany, a channel spills into the swift-moving Merichanka stream. This was the place where we had to meet Petras, a Russian who before the war had been secretary of the Communist Party in Trakai Province and was now living underground in the villages and the forest. His liaison, who had visited Narocz Forest, had told us then that a large partisan movement could be set up in this area. A meeting had been arranged to discuss the matter. Special signs were to be made in the sand to mark the place. Every five days Petras would come to the meeting place and wait for our arrival.

At dawn our commander went with one of the partisans to the appointed place and returned an hour later, announcing that he found the date of the previous day marked in the sand, which meant that we had to wait four more days for Petras to come.

Our situation was not good at all. First of all, we lacked food and did not know how to go about getting it. We were unfamiliar with the forest and the surroundings, but we did know that it was full of German guards. The German soldiers often entered the forests to gather wood or to look for eggs in the nearby village. However, we had strict orders not to go far from the meeting place.

The next day our radio operator succeeded in contacting Moscow. Our mood improved. We were no longer alone. They already knew about us in Moscow and one could suppose that they would not abandon us. . . . There was a state of readiness in the forest and we heard the din of many vehicles. From early morning, shots rang out almost without interruption. We knew the reason: the previous day at dusk, three of us had gone to Zagorany to look for food. The local people had apparently reported the fact to the Germans and they began a hunt for us. We went deeper into the swamps and reached places which seemed never to have been touched by humans. For two days we heard the noise and roar of bullets at a short distance. But the Germans could not imagine that we would hide among the swamps only several dozen meters away from them. They went deep into the forest but found nothing. This same tactic was to save us in the future.

Four days later the commander went out for the second time to the meeting place. We waited anxiously for his return. If Petras did not come that day as well, we would be helpless. It would be too dangerous to remain a few more days in the same spot. The local peasants were gifted with a special sense. From the flight of the bird, from the song of the nightingale and from the blowing of the wind, they knew that something unusual was happening in the forest. Sooner or later they would bring the Germans to us.

Around noon the commander returned with two strangers. One of them was dressed in civilian clothes and introduced himself as Petras. The second, dressed in the uniform of a Russian officer, was Grisha. Some time ago he and several comrades had escaped German captivity and they were now living on the other side of the forest, 30 kilometers away. Petras and Grisha said that the Germans were still looking for us and that we must not remain in the same place. We set off immediately, and after several hours of exhausting marches among the swamps, under the thick branches of the trees, we reached a shelter, about which we had been told by Petras and Grisha. This place was a *zemlyanka* (a bunker) in which Petras and his comrades had lived up to several months ago. We planned to stay there, for it was the safest place in the whole area. We were about to enter the cabin but suddenly a shock went through us. We saw before us a seated human corpse. His eye sockets were black and seemed to glare at us in anger for disturbing his rest. The skull was already rotted, the stomach was decomposing, and only the clothes were intact. A stench pervaded the hut.

Petras thought hard and finally said: "Some months ago one of our boys disappeared. We thought that he had gotten tired of the hard life in the forest and had returned to his village, as many do. But, apparently, he fell into the hands of the police and they forced him to show them our hiding place. I suppose they killed him after they did not find us here. This means that the police know about this place. If so, you must not tarry even a minute longer." We found a suitable place to set up camp, and during the first days, we were busy mainly procuring arms, mobilizing people, and organizing a food supply from the neighboring villages.

Once at nightfall we reached the village of Darguzi, near the town of Olkieniki. This was the largest and wealthiest village in the area, with hundreds of households. We set up guards on all sides of the village and went from house to house in search of arms and food. In one of the houses our boys found a Lithuanian policeman from Olkieniki who had come to visit his relatives. We took him with us to our camp. In the darkness of night, he did not notice Jews among the partisans who took him captive. To find favor among the partisans, he began to boast about his "heroism" in murdering Jews in various villages of Lithuania. He hoped in this way to gain the sympathy of the Lithuanians. But even the fellows who were not known for their great sympathy for the Jews were shocked by his accounts. After many interrogations, he was shot.

The sentence was carried out by a Jew. It is interesting to note that those same heroes who maltreated Jewish children and women, and killed them in all kinds of bestial ways, did not show any courage whatsoever when their turn came to leave this world. For hours the policeman wept bitterly, prostrated himself on the ground in front of the Lithuanian partisans, and begged them to have pity on him, his wife, and his children.

Our camp grew quickly. We were joined by a group which had come from Russia more than a year before, and had not yet succeeded in organizing partisan bases. We were also joined by young people from the neighboring villages. Two more companies came from Narocz Forest. We already numbered about 60, mostly Lithuanians. The number of Jews was about ten.

At that same time a second group of members of the Second Fighting Organization left the ghetto directly for Rudnik Forest. The first group, which had left in April 1943, under the command of Betarist Dov (Borka) Friedman, dispersed after four of its eight members, including the commander, Dov, and Betarist Shmuel Levin, fell in battle against the Germans. The second group numbered 25 fighters. It set up camp a few kilometers from our camp. The news they brought from the ghetto was very disturbing. During our free time we would visit our Jewish comrades and make plans together how to bring more Jews out of the ghetto to the forest.

A huge psychological gap divided the Jewish partisans and our Lithuanian comrades. Once, at dusk, we sat down to eat around the campfire and discussed the question of what had prompted the village youths to leave their homes and families and come to the forest. One said: "I raped a girl and her parents pressed me to marry her. As I did not want her, I left my village and came here." A second said that he had had a quarrel with his neighbor, set fire to his neighbor's barn one night, and ran away from the village fearing retribution. A third said: "At a party in the village, a fistfight broke out between me and a policeman over a girl. The girl detested the policeman and followed me, and I got scared and came here." Another said that he was sick of the life in his parents' home and the hard work in the fields.

Did they dream of revenge like we did? One cannot really say so. They thought about robbery and pillage and all kinds of adventures. No, there was nothing in common between what had brought us to the forest and what had motivated them to leave their villages.

Blood for Blood

On the eve of Rosh Hashanah, the commander announced that the next day we were to go into battle. Though our arms were not the best, they were good enough to set a trap for the enemy. All that night the non-Jewish partisans sat and divided among themselves the booty that would fall in their hands from the action: one said he would wear a German officer's uniform the next day, the second would have a new pair of boots, a third wanted a watch. . . .

The commander chose nine men, three of them Jews. They received one machine-gun, a Tommy-gun, and three rifles. "Long Jonas" was appointed commander of the operation.

We had to leave for the main Grodno–Vilna highway, which crossed the forest 10 kilometers from our camp. Up to that day there had been uninterrupted movement along the highway. No German vehicles had ever been attacked. A string of army positions lined the highway. According to the plan, we had to shoot the drivers to stop the cars and afterwards take advantage of the confusion to storm the other Germans and kill them.

Before dawn, final instructions were given and the weapons distributed. I received the heavy machine-gun and Shlomo was chosen as my helper. Tevke, the third Jew in our party, was "number two" for the light machine gun.

Some time later, the unit was lying in ambush among the bushes and waiting for a round of shots from the commander as a sign to go into action. A quarter of an hour passed and we heard the noise of vehicles coming from Grodno. A gunshot resounded. That was the signal. But it was followed by only solitary rifle shots and the rattle of the heavy machine-gun. Some of the arms did not work and several fighters were so frightened by the noise of the machine-gun that they could not fire their weapons. This was their first time in battle. Horrible shouts were heard from the three vehicles, full of German soldiers. But they continued to move and stopped only several hundred meters from our place of ambush.

The non-Jewish partisans were ashamed to return to camp empty-handed after all their bragging the evening before. The commander decided to prepare a new ambush some distance away from the first. He lacked experience and did not understand that we could not stay in the same area, because the Germans who were attacked would call for reinforcements and we were unable to enter battle with such a small unit.

About an hour later, cars approached from Vilna. The signal was given to begin the attack. The Germans, who apparently had heard about the previous attack, were not surprised this time. They returned heavy fire. Suddenly Shlomo and I felt ourselves alone in the fray. We looked around and saw that our comrades were running for their lives towards the forest. We were angry at our comrades who had abandoned us, and increased our fire. Fierce fighting broke out between the Germans and our sole machine-gun. The Germans began to approach under cover of heavy fire. We had no choice but to retreat. We ran towards our comrades, who had already entered deep into the forest. Shlomo, who was not weighed down because we did not have much ammunition left, caught up with the rest of the unit.

I remained alone with the heavy machine-gun and the German fire was growing stronger and nearer. I suddenly noticed Tevke, who lagged behind because he was burdened with the bullets for the light machine-gun. We realized that we could not run much longer. Not wanting to leave the weapons behind, we decided to hide. We crawled under the bushes and hid in a swamp until we got our wind back. The machine-gun was ready to greet the Germans, should they discover our hiding-place.

Shots rang out on all sides. Apparently, the Germans had penetrated the forest and wanted to surround us. Several hours later, just before sunset, the shooting stopped. The Germans had obviously despaired of capturing the partisans.

We were famished. Since the morning, we had not eaten anything. We were dying for a cigarette but the tobacco in our pockets was wet because of the swamps. We decided to wait until dark before leaving our hiding-places, because the Germans might have set an ambush for us.

There was great turmoil in the camp. By afternoon five of the people had returned and at dusk the commander of the operation and one of his men returned. They had lost their way in the forest and barely managed to find it. While running they threw away their ammunition and some of their clothes. They did not know the fate of the two missing fighters but they thought they had fallen in battle. There was sorrow in the camp over the two Jews, but there was more grief over the lost machine-gun, for it was the only one of its kind in the whole forest.

Late that night the camp guard had noticed two people approaching and notified the command. An order was given to be on the alert. Scouts were sent to find out the identity of the two strangers, and they were amazed to recognize Tevke and me.

With cheers of joy, all the fighters came to greet us. The commander lined up all the partisans, placed us in front of them, and began criticizing the commander of the operation and those who had fled. Afterwards he praised Tevke and me and advised everyone to learn a lesson from the two Jews who kept their heads and did not panic. "They, too, could have thought only of saving their skins and arrived in camp with you,'' he said, ''but they chose to risk their lives rather than leave their weapons behind.''

From that day on the status of the Jews rose in the camp. The next day, intelligence brought news that in our attack of the previous day 3 German officers were killed, and 15 German soldiers, including two officers and three sergeants, were seriously wounded. It was the first time since the outbreak of the war that Germans had been killed in this area and the bullets which struck them down were fired by Jews.

Forays

Even though the Headquarters of the Second Fighting Organization in the Vilna Ghetto received no news from the first company which set off for the forests, it remained firmly convinced that more people had to be sent there. In the beginning of September 1943, following the Estonia actions, when the F.P.O. Headquarters sent companies into the Narocz Forest, the Second Organization began dispatching units again to Rudnik Forest.

On September 11, after several unsuccessful attempts, they succeeded in letting out a group numbering 22 people. That evening, the police officer Natan Ring, who was also a member of the Headquarters of the Second Organization, went to the ghetto gate and, under his supervision, the people left the ghetto.

A wagon loaded with garbage left at the same time. The wagoneer was a Tatar, Romka Kuzminski, and hidden under the garbage were the company's arms. (Romka Kuzminski helped the Jews and was one of the most trusted liaisons of the partisans. He was killed by the Germans in his village Sorok-Tatar, when they learned of his relations with the partisans.) The fighters went out, two by two, gathered at the edge of the city, removed the arms from beneath the garbage, and continued on their way. Their guide was Chaim Soltz, a middle-aged Jew and a native of Olkieniki, who had spent his life transporting trees from the forest and smuggling goods between Poland and Lithuania via Rudnik Forest. He knew every forest trail.

By midnight they arrived at the outskirts of the village, Sorok-Tatar, on the edge of the forest, and decided to take a shortcut through the village, despite the fact that a mixed German and Dutch garrison was stationed there. While passing the guards, they made a lot of noise, and the Germans, afraid that large forces of partisans were moving through, did not dare go after them or even shoot at them. During the day they camped in the forest and the next evening they continued along their way in search of the partisan bases.

Several kilometers from the base was the village of Marcelin. Chaim Soltz, who had many acquaintances among the villagers, hoped to hear where the partisans were camping, but was unable to get any information. Early the next morning the company met up with two partisans, one of them a Jew named Zaitsev. These two told the headquarters about the arrival of a Jewish company from Vilna. Some time later, three non-Jewish partisans set out to meet them and greeted them with insults: "Why didn't you come until now? So long as the Germans did not harm you, you served them faithfully. And only now, when they have begun to annihilate you, you come to hide with us." And they ordered them to return to the place from where they had come, and if not, they would feel the might of the partisans.

The Jewish fighters were filled with fear. Had they traded one disaster for another? Apparently, Jews were not wanted anywhere. However, Chaim Soltz quickly regained his self-confidence and told them: "We did not come to you and we are not asking for your protection. We were called here by Batya and we will speak only to him." The magic word had its effect.

"Batya" was a legendary figure among the partisans and especially among the local peasants. During the days of Soviet rule, he was the police chief in the town of Olkieniki. When the war broke out, some of his friends retreated with the Red Army and some went to serve the Germans. But Batya went to the forest. Despite his advanced age—he was over 60—he was full of energy and courage. Many legends spread in the area about the heroism of the "white old man," as he was called. Once, during the first winter after the outbreak of the war, while he was still alone in the forest, he set out in the dead of night for Olkieniki, came across the Lithuanian police chief, and asked for 300 spoons, forks, and knives, saying that it was for a celebration among the partisans. "And if you even dare to imagine imprisoning or killing me," he told the Lithuanian, "you will regret it, for the whole town is surrounded by my boys and the proof is that I have come to you alone and without arms." About an hour later the Lithuanian police chief brought him all the utensils he had requested.

Batya was a friend of the Jews, and Chaim Soltz had known him before the war. The next day he appeared, arranged a place for the Jewish fighters to set up their camp, and spent the night with them over a glass of whiskey telling stories about life in the forest.

On September 12 a second company of 25 people left the ghetto, and the following day, a third company departed. The leaders of these companies were Shlomo Brand and Natan Ring. The last company left the city in a car rented from the Lithuanian police. Fifteen kilometers from Vilna, the two companies met and together they entered the forest. They numbered more than 70, all of them young people experienced in the use of arms and eager for battle. Right away they exchanged their guns, the only weapons they had, for rifles of the Russian partisans. Two weeks later they already had seventeen rifles.

In the forest they found the Lithuanian camp to which I belonged and which numbered several dozen people. This camp was headed by Gavris, the leader of the Lithuanian partisans in thc Vilna District, who had recently arrived from Moscow. There was also a camp of experienced partisans, armed with modern automatic weapons, and led by a young Russian, famous for his bravery, named "Mishka Capitan."

The first permanent camp of the Jews in the forest was set up about two kilometers from the Lithuanian camp. Stakes were driven into the moist earth and were covered with branches. These "tents" did not give protection from the rain and any reasonably strong wind could topple them. But the people had no working utensils, so the job was done with bare hands. Several large tents were set up to house the people and one tent was designated as a food storage, though for the time being there was not even a semblance of a food stockpile.

Every night several fellows went to the nearby village of Marcelin to buy food from the peasants or to dig up a few potatoes and vegetables from the fields. However, this was not enough to feed seventy people and the money would not last long. The people were in a state of semistarvation. Sometimes the Jewish lads from the Lithuanian camp succeeded in taking out a little food from the storehouse and bringing it to the Jewish camp. Once they even brought a live lamb and a feast was held that night in the Jewish camp. It was the first time since their arrival in the forest that they satisfied their hunger.

Little by little, they adjusted to living conditions in the forest and decided to go out on a foray, like all the partisans. One evening three lads, led by Shlomo Brand, went to the village of Solcza, near Olkieniki, and despite the strong resistance of the peasants, took several wagonloads of food from the village, returning to the forest under a torrent of bullets. This is how a foray was carried out: first, guards were set up on both sides of the village and then the fighters were divided up into smaller groups of three to four people. Each group entered a house and asked the peasant to prepare a quantity of food. While the peasant and his family were preparing the food, the partisans searched for arms and confiscated everything that could help the camp, including clothes and utensils. When everything was ready, the peasant was told to hitch up a wagon, load it with his goods, and remain in his home for a time if he valued his life. At the edge of the village, at a predesignated spot, all the wagons would gather and together they would leave for the forest. The whole operation was carried out in great haste, for they wanted to reach safety before dawn. The horses and wagons were later returned to the peasants, several of whom would sometimes wait on the edge of the forest.

In the beginning both the partisans and the peasants lacked experience. However, in the course of time, both sides learned their roles. The peasants learned how to hide their food and belongings, claiming that the Germans took everything away from them, while the partisans learned how to locate the hidden food supplies, either by stripping the peasants or threatening them. Naturally, the peasants reported the thefts to the Germans. It occasionally happened that a caravan of loaded wagons making its way to the forest suddenly came under heavy fire from a German ambush along the road. Sometimes partisans were killed and wounded in forays. Generally, they had to abandon the wagons to fight the Germans, and they returned to camp empty-handed.

The partisans finally started using trickery: they would take several peasants with them as wagoneers, and so as not to risk an ambush attack, would send the peasants ahead with the wagons. Only after the peasants passed safely through the dangerous area would the partisans follow. At the edge of the forest they would free the peasants and send them home. Not wanting to risk their own lives, the peasants finally stopped asking for help from the Germans.

If it was hard for the Russian partisans to get food, it was much harder for the Jews. The peasants regarded the Russian partisans as a force backed up by a large and powerful country which, even if it was not always victorious on the battlefield, was, nevertheless, a power to be reckoned with. But who stood behind the Jews? The peasants were not interested in saving Jews. On the contrary, even the non-Jewish partisans were grateful to them when they killed Jews or refused to give them food. Thus, the peasants treated the Jews with contempt and arrogantly refused their demands. But they soon learned that they were dealing with proud and embittered Jews, and that a bullet shot by a Jew strikes just as hard as one fired by a Russian. Yet, since they did not want to admit that the Jews were also fighters, they called them "bandits." In their complaints to the German authorities they reported that "Jewish bandits" robbed them of their possessions and gave them no rest. They asked for German protection against this lawlessness. German help was not late in coming. The Germans began distributing arms among the villagers. They also hired agents among the peasants and spread antipartisan propaganda. In most of the villages, the peasants began stationing guards at night, and when the guards detected partisans approaching, they alerted the villagers, who opened up fire. The result was that only rarely were forays carried out without clashes and casualties.

The partisans were generally disdainful of these missions, for, after all, they were not battles and did not directly harm the enemy. But, in fact, these actions were more dangerous than sabotage or attacks on the Germans, since in battle one generally knows the strength of the enemy and attacks from advantageous positions. And when setting off on a sabotage mission, the fighters advance carefully and try to make their way without attracting attention. Sabotage is carried out in a place where the enemy forces do not expect it. On the other hand, in forays, the fighters expect an attack, an attack not on their own conditions and terrain. And after the operation, they must spend several hours returning to base with loaded wagons; they never know where the enemy is lying in ambush and from where the bullets will come.

Despite all the difficulties, the fighters tried to prepare a stock of food for the people in the camp.

Left to right: Doba Debeltov, partisan liaison; Chaya Shapiro (Lazar), member of the Second Organization, expert in explosives; Dina Grinwald, partisan liaison.

The Three Jewish Camps

On September 21, a group of fighters went out on a reconnaissance mission, myself at their head. From the morning, frequent shots were heard and we went out to discover the reason. On our way we saw a man hiding among the trees. He turned out to be a Lithuanian Jew from the Vilna Ghetto, named Paul Bagriansky. Three days before, he had left the ghetto together with a young girl named Taibel Gelblum. They were out on a mission for the F.P.O. to scout the roads. They were told that they would meet partisans in the village of Marcelin who would update them on the situation. During the day they hid in the forest and the next night they returned to the vicinity of the village. At midnight they felt hungry and entered the home of the forest guard to ask for food. He claimed that he had none in the house but was willing to go to the village to get some. Not having eaten a bite for two days, they had no alternative but to trust him.

More than an hour passed and he did not return. This aroused their suspicion and they decided to leave the house and wait among the trees nearby. The moment they opened the door, they were met with a shower of bullets shot at close range. The house was surrounded by German soldiers. Taibel Gelblum was killed on the spot, and Bagriansky took out his gun, shot his way out, and escaped to the forest. The whole thing lasted only a few minutes and he did not understand how he succeeded in remaining alive. The Germans, who were taken aback at first, came to their senses and began to shoot after him, but he found refuge in the swamps. He hid there all night and we found him in the morning. Bagriansky's story was confirmed the next day. The partisans heard that his shots killed three people, including the forest guard, and wounded several others.

Four days after our meeting with Bagriansky, two girls arrived from the Vilna Ghetto: Doba Debeltov and Fania Yocheles. They had left the ghetto before its liquidation. Two hours after their arrival came Chaya Shapiro. She said that she had been taken out of the ghetto by the Germans and the Ukrainians with the last

Shmuel Kaplinski, commander of the partisan brigade, husband of Hienna Borowska.

Itzhak Chuzhoi.

Jewish group, but escaped on the way to Rossa, despite the many guards who watched over the Jews. She told us that the ghetto had been totally liquidated.

Several days later two groups came to the forest, each numbering 50 people. One of them was headed by Abba Kovner, Hienna Borowska, and Shmuel Kaplinski, and consisted of the fighters who had left the ghetto through the sewers. The second group came from the Keilis block and was led by Aron Aronovich. The Jewish camp received the two groups with open arms, fed them, and assigned them areas to set up camp.

At about the same time, the commander of the Lithuanian Partisan Brigade, Yurgis, reached Rudnik Forest, together with more than 40 people. Among these were Isser Schmidt, a Lithuanian Jew who had recently arrived from Moscow and, as was customary among partisans, did not use his real name but rather a pseudonym, Didialis. He was to assume an important position in the Jewish partisan camps.

The newcomers found a more or less organized camp. The people were divided into companies, each headed by a commander. There was also a food stock and an arms stockpile of seventeen rifles. In ghetto terms, these were good arms, particularly since the new arrivals from Vilna brought nothing but pistols and one faulty automatic. The camp consisted of strong young men who had already acquired some experience in forest life. On the other hand, half of the new arrivals were young women and forest life was a closed book to them. One might have imagined that the newcomers would accept the authority of the veterans, but they could not come to terms with this. Borowska, a veteran Communist who had had an important position in the ghetto, certainly did not intend to accept a minor position in the forest, controlled by Red Soviet partisans. And in no way could she agree that the Jewish camp be under the command of people whose political past was, in her opinion, ''dubious.''

Borowska turned to the commander of the partisan movement in the Vilna District, Gavris, an old acquaintance of hers. While living under the Soviets, they worked together in the Vilna Municipality and the two were happy to meet again in the forest. Kovner had a reputation as head of the Fighting Organization in the ghetto, while the names of the people heading the Jewish camp meant nothing to Gavris.

Gavris was told that before the exit from the ghetto, the headquarters of the Second Organization had asked for money from its members, and only those who could pay the requested sum were allowed to leave for the forest. Gavris and his entourage interrogated those in the Jewish camp to find out whether it was true that F.P.O. members were asked to pay money to leave for the forest. Some of the people denied this, but other confirmed that they had paid money, although not to their Organization's leaders but rather to the Lithuanian police, in whose cars they left Vilna. As the first slander did not produce the desired results, Gavris was told that among the veterans of the Jewish camp were former ghetto policemen who had had ties with the Germans. To make matters worse, there was not one Communist among them.

Gavris was willing to accept these pretexts. He decided to divide the Jews into three camps and he appointed Abba Kovner, Shmuel Kaplinski (Borowska's husband), and Yaakov Prenner as their commanders. Natan Ring and Itzhak Chuzhoi, the former commanders, were appointed as their seconds-in-command. Hienna Borowska was made political commissar of one of the camps. Gavris also chose names for the camps: "Avenger," "To Victory," and "Death to the Fascists." A short time later two other commissars were chosen for the Jewish camps: Didialis and Berl Sherezhnevski, one of the Communist activists in the ghetto, who previously had been in the Lithuanian camp.

The Jewish camps were included within the Lithuanian Brigade and were subject to the Brigade Headquarters. The Headquarters assigned a new location to the Jews because the former site could not accommodate so many people. To get to the new place one had to walk along rickety bridges for several kilometers and over deep, reed-covered swamps protruding with rotting trees. In terms of security, the place was better, but it was impossible to dig bunkers and trenches in the marshy soil.

The food supply was also very difficult. The area between the new camp and the location accessible to wagons was several kilometers long and had to be covered by foot; this, while carrying a load on our shoulders, our feet sunk in waist-high mud.

During these days two women fighters were sent to Vilna to establish contact with the Communist Party in the city and to form ties with the Jews in the Keilis

Paul Bagriansky, member of the F.P.O., liaison with "Mishka Capitan."

Yaakov Prenner, one of the leaders of the three Jewish camps in Rudnik Forest, member of Betar.

and H.K.P. blocks. Doba Debeltov and Dina Grinwald were equipped with Aryan papers and set off for the city. But they lost their way in the forest and at dusk fell into an ambush of Latvian soldiers who hid behind the bushes. They were arrested and the soldiers accused them of being Jews and of having ties with the partisans. Doba and Dina denied the charges vehemently. They claimed that they were Poles who left Vilna to get food from the villages. Their Aryan papers did not help them. They were led to the village of Marcelin, where a guard of Lithuanian soldiers was stationed. After heavy interrogation the soldiers decided to take the two prisoners the next day to the town of Rudnik, the location of the police center for the whole area.

At midnight the guard was changed in the room where the two girls slept, and the new policeman who enter the room was drunk and soon fell asleep. Doba decided to risk her life and escape. She got out of bed, went into the kitchen, opened the window, and jumped out. The next day she arrived at camp and related what had happened.

The Lithuanians took Dina to Rudnik, and after lengthy interrogation, she succeeded in persuading the police commander that she was, indeed, a Pole. She asked to be escorted to Vilna by a policeman and arrived safely in the city the next day.

Doba Debeltov was sent to Vilna a second time and this time she arrived safely; together with Dina, she carried out the assigned tasks. They took out forty people from the Keilis outside the city. Doba returned to Vilna and Dina brought them to the forest.

The fighter Lena Zatz was sent out several days later to get various documents. She carried out the mission and returned safely to camp. A week later Dina Grinwald took out another forty people from the Keilis and brought them to the forest quickly and safely.

*Shmuel Shapiro, member
of the Second Organization,
killed by Russian partisans.*

The First Grave in the Forest

There were about 20 rifles among the 250 people in all the Jewish camps. It was impossible to think about fighting actions with so few weapons, especially as there were only two or three bullets for each rifle. Besides the rifles, there were three automatics, several dozen pistols, and a small number of grenades. The Brigade Headquarters, which was in constant radio contact with Moscow, promised that arms and equipment would soon be sent from Moscow and parachuted down to them. In the meantime, there was no alternative but to make do with sabotage acts. On October 7, 1943 at dusk, 35 fighters, headed by Itzhak Chuzhoi and Aron Aronovich, set out on the first operation. On part of the Vilna–Grodno road which lay between the two villages of Pirciupie and Ziemnica, they cut down 50 telegraph poles, chopped the wires into pieces, and destroyed the transformers. At dawn they returned to camp, pleased that they had succeeded in carrying out their mission despite the many guards and garrisons in the villages. Four days later, 25 fighters went out on another mission. They cut down 70 telegraph poles along the highway near the village of Kripsovka. Natan Ring headed this action.

One day orders were received from Brigade Headquarters to set up road-blocks along the routes leading from the city to the town of Rudnik, since information had been received about enemy concentrations in this town. Fifty-five men and women fighters—three companies headed by Natan Ring, A. Aronovich, and myself—went out at dusk with part of the arms (a part always remained in the camp in the event of unexpected danger). We took axes and saws with us. We walked together for some kilometers and then split up into separate companies and each went to the assigned site. For hours on end the fighters cut down trees to lay across the roads. The barking of dogs in Rudnik, the howling of the wolves, the sound of the saws, the boom of falling trees, and the reports of shots on all sides—all of these blended in a wild and moving symphony.

At the end of the operation we put up a sign on the roadblock, warning against mines. A meeting place was fixed for the three companies. However, as I was walking back with my company, we saw from afar a flicker of a campfire among the trees. We knew that there were no partisan bases in that direction and, furthermore, we partisans would never make a fire in a place that could be seen from afar. We decided to move closer to the campfire to find out to whom it belonged. For over an hour we moved towards the glow. We tried to go in a straight line, mindless of paths. In many places we made our way among the trees only with great difficulty and occasionally came across swamps which had to be circumvented. We covered a long distance and the fire did not grow any closer. It seemed that the more we walked the further the fire got. The people were dead tired and the fire was still far away. Suddenly an unusual sight met our eyes: the "campfire" grew larger. A full moon rose on the horizon.

The more people we had in the partisan camps, the more pressing the matter of a food supply. Despite the many efforts made to solve this problem, it was impossible to feed the hundreds of people. Every night groups of fighters went out on food forays, and though they never returned empty-handed, there was still not enough food. The food was concentrated in a central storage area and the portions were divided according to the number of eaters. Bread was divided into small pieces and given only to the sick and weak, upon the doctor's recommendation. Potatoes were also considered a luxury. The main food was *balanda*—black flour cooked in water, without oil or salt. The lack of salt was sorely felt, but it was very expensive both in the cities and the villages, and only rarely could a small quantity be obtained.

Not only did we get sick of *balanda* quickly, but it had a bad effect on the health of the partisans. Stomach disorders were rife. There were fighters who, during forays, pocketed various food items for themselves and afterwards ate them secretly in the forest. But when this became known, they shamefacedly had to promise that they would never do so again.

One day a company went on a food foray to a Lithuanian village across the highway. On the way the Jewish fighters encountered the Russian partisans of Mishka Capitan, who were also going to one of the villages on a similar mission. The two companies decided to carry out the mission together, because they knew that the village which they intended to infiltrate was well armed and that it was dangerous to enter with small forces.

The two companies decided upon a password so that the partisans could recognize one another in the dark. Though the people were fired upon from all sides, they succeeded in carrying out the operation without a hitch. But just as they were about to leave the village, the Russian partisans began shooting left and right. Shmuel Shapiro was leaving the home of one of the peasants, carrying a sack of potatoes over his shoulder. Seeing the partisans shooting, he shouted out the password but the Russians did not answer him. They pointed their guns at the Jew and wounded him mortally.

Shmuel Shapiro was a strong fellow who was feared by non-Jews. He was a native of Lipowka, a Vilna suburb, and all his life he had dealt in cattle and meat. The Jewish camp pinned much hope on him. He was very well acquainted with the way of life in the villages and the areas in which the partisans were active, and his courage was as great as his strength, though he was already middle-aged. Now he was struggling with death. He asked to be shot and put out of his misery, but no one could bring himself to oblige. He died a few days later, after requesting to be buried according to Jewish law and to have *kaddish* said over him.

On Yom Kippur Eve 1943, the first grave was dug near the Jewish camp. During the burial, mention was made that Shapiro fell not from enemy bullets but from the bullets of ''brothers-in-arms.'' We were sad and embittered.

At that time, Mishka Capitan sent a request to the command of the Jewish camp. He had a lot of arms and a lack of people and wanted some Jewish boys to join his fighting companies and two girls to work in the kitchen. The leaders knew very well the fate of Jewish boys alone among dozens of non-Jews who, no matter how good they were as fighters, were ruffians whose main concerns were pillage, murder, drink, and women. But the Jewish Command did not have the courage to refuse the request. They did not even pity the honor of Jewish women.

Two emissaries came to the forest: Chaim Yellin, a Communist activist from the Kovno Ghetto, and Albina, who came from Vilna. They came to give Yurgis a report on party activity and to receive instructions. Chaim Yellin spoke about the organized youth in the Kovno Ghetto who wished to leave for the forest. With Yurgis's permission, groups of Jewish youths were leaving the Kovno Ghetto and arriving in the forest. A few kilometers from the Vilna camp was a new camp of Kovno Jews. Most of them were armed with good weapons. Yurgis appointed Kostya, a parachutist from Moscow, to be camp commander.

Already in the first days, the youths from Kovno felt that in leaving the ghetto they had gone from bad to worse. The Lithuanian commander treated the Jews with open hostility, and dozens became hapless victims of this commander, who lost no opportunity to embitter the lives of the Jews. Excellent lads were tortured and maltreated by Lithuanian thugs and had no one to protect them.

The Brigade had a "Special Affairs Division" (N.K.V.D.), headed by the Lithuanian Stankevich, sent from Moscow. After the arrival of Didialis and Sherezhnevski to the Jewish camps, they, together with Borowska, began to organize the Komsomol and to set up a "Special Affairs Division" among the Jews as well. Thus began a period of internal espionage in the camp. Division agents reported to Headquarters about everything that happened among the partisans, even the content of every idle conversation among them. Their ears strained to catch every sound and their eyes searched every corner. No one could express his opinion freely anymore.

As there were many Jews in the camp who had not yet accepted the new situation, including those who were the first to arrive in the forest, it is no wonder that the agents had their hands full. In this way the Headquarters heard about the plans of the former commanders to gather their people (about 70 in all), leave the camp, and set up a new camp which would not be subject to the present command. The Headquarters people began to fear that they would be left without arms and their best fighters would leave them. They plotted ways of thwarting the plans and a short time later found a way to consolidate their power and strike fear into the hearts of the fighters.

One day it became known that Lutek Zeltwasser and B. Zaltshtein, who had been policemen in the Vilna Ghetto and had arrived in the forest with one of the Keilis groups, had disappeared from the camp. Later Lutek's boots were seen on the feet of one of the agents. It turned out that the two fellows were shot by order of the Headquarters after they were sentenced to death for having served as policemen in the Vilna Ghetto.

The division worked without let-up. They gathered incriminating material against anyone disliked by the command or who could pose as rivals. All of this went on secretly, but eventually came to light. People began to feel that something was not right in the camp.

The rainy season began. The tents, which were in poor shape to begin with, provided no shelter against the rain and constant dampness. At midnight a mass emigration began: people left their tents and looked for shelter among the branches. Sometimes a fighter would wake up in the morning to find himself lying in a big puddle. No one undressed even during sleep, and the wet clothes clung to their shivering bodies and encumbered movement. The only shelter was near the campfire. It became a vital need and the center of life in the camp. There the food was prepared and the arms were cleaned. There the partisans ate, talked, made plans, sang, and boasted. In the free evenings they would sit for hours around the fire and their dreamy eyes following the dancing flames. During these hours, romances were born between young people who had never known pleasure in their lives.

Two boys reached the Jewish camp. One of them was a Jew from Ejszyszki (Eišiskis) named Pochter. He said that he, his mother, and his brother had hidden with a peasant near their town, and when he heard that Jews had come to the forest, he decided to go see them. He was ready to do anything to be of help to us. The next few days he came to us every so often bringing important news or arms. The second was a Russian officer in the Russian Army, who had escaped from German captivity and was now wandering around the local villages, waiting for the war to end. He also promised to visit us from time to time.

On the eve of Yom Kippur two companies left the camp on fighting missions. One numbered 20 people and went to an area along the enemy's communication lines near Vilna. The second consisted of only four people: Witka Kempner and Chaya Shapiro were sent to Vilna to sabotage the city's electric system and Mattityahu Levin and Israel Rozov went to destroy the city's water station. They arrived in Vilna two days later in the evening, laden with explosives. They spent the next day in the Keilis, where they found a 60-member organized group ready to leave for the forest. That evening they went into action.

Some distance from the Keilis, two Poles, members of the Communist Party, were waiting for the two girls to bring them to the place of action. Chaya Shapiro blew up a transformer on Subocz Street and Witka Kempner blew up another on Orzeszkowa Street.

That same evening the fellows blew up the water plant. As a result of these actions, there was a blackout in a large part of the city and some quarters suffered from a lack of water.

After the mission, the girls met in the woods outside the city with the Keilis people and they all went to Rudnik Forest. The partisans received the girls and the newcomers with great enthusiasm. The addition of fresh forces brought relief to the monotony of daily life, even though most of the newcomers were without weapons. Only the commanders were not pleased by the arrival of the new group. They ordered that no more units be brought from the city.

At this time Natan Ring learned that his mother was in danger in Vilna because she lacked a *Schein*. He decided to go to the city to take her out of the Keilis and to arrange a bunker for her. Mitya Lipenholtz, later to become one of the best commanders in the Jewish camp, went with him. He hoped that he might still find somone from his family to bring back to the forest or for whom to arrange a safe place.

Peneusov Family, active in repairing weapons in the forest.

Dr. Sola Gorfinkel, a physician who treated partisans in the Nacza Forest.

Hienna Borowska

During the first few weeks, there was much discussion in the ranks of the Jewish Communists as to the nature of the Jewish camps. Many believed that there was no place for separate national camps. This internationalist position was held by Berl Sherezhnevski. He and his supporters felt that the Jewish camps should be dismantled and merged with the Gentile battalions. This would give the Jews an opportunity to become familiar with their duties and become good fighters. The Communists made themselves oblivious to the fact that there existed separate camps of Lithuanians, Poles, White Russians and so forth; they insisted that isolation was not the way—the Jews had to demonstrate their loyalty to the Revolution and be the first to do away with boundaries and bring down the partitions.

Hienna Borowska and her faction did not go along with this philosophy. Their argument was that the existence of separate Jewish camps increased the prospect for drawing the Jewish masses to Communism. In the camps, commanded by the Gentiles, who were anti-Semites to boot, there were factors which would drive Jews away from the Movement. Such factors did not exist where Jews filled the posts.

Borowska did not base her stand on nationalistic sentiments, nor did it stem from love for the Jewish people. She had reasons of her own. She knew, for example, that although hers was a high position in the Jewish camps, there was no scarcity of experienced and valorous fighters among the Gentiles ahead of her, since they had served in the vanguard of combat action. Jews did not have much of a chance to attain key posts in the non-Jewish partisan camps. On the other hand, the Jewish camps could be managed on ideological merits, without any need for military proficiency.

For these reasons, Borowska put up an uncompromising fight for the maintenance of the Jewish camps, and she was able to convince the Brigade staff. From the historical perspective, her reasons did not hold up. What is important is that she must be credited with the fact that, prior to the Liberation, there were, in the Rudnik Forest, purely Jewish camps—a very rare phenomenon in the Russian partisan movement during the Second World War. Maintenance of the separate camps was not only of immense value; it also saved the Jews much suffering and needless sacrifice.

Several kilometers from the Jewish Vilna camp, a dozen armed Jews from Grodno set themselves up in one of the Batya shacks, scattered throughout the forest. The Grodno group befriended the Vilna camp and told them much about their life in the forests. Among others, they told them of the Nacza Forest in the vicinity of Radun, famed in the Jewish world as a center of Torah learning, the residence of a renowned scholar, the Chafetz Chaim. The Grodno group was intending to return to the Nacza Forest, with its many Russian partisans and Jewish units. This forest bordered on the Russka Forest, located in the extensive General Province.

According to the Grodno people, they left the Nacza Forest a number of months previously because they were given several important missions to perform, and they had no reason to think that the situation had worsened. On the contrary, they were sure that thousands of other partisans had entered the forest, to the point that the place had become a partisan enclave. The farmers in the villages of the area openly showed their support for the partisans and extended to them all the help they could. They even helped Jews who had escaped the massacre, hiding the survivors in their homes.

In one of the groups reaching the forest was a young couple: Sola and Emma Gorfinkel. She was a chemistry student, while he was a graduate physician, but with little practice. Upon his arrival, Sola Gorfinkel at once set about organizing medical services in the camp. He put up a tent, built some shelves, and lined them with vials and instruments he had brought along. On the tent, he hung out his shingle: "Ambulatoria." Despite his meagre means, he set up an exemplary clinic, aided by his wife and Hannah Azgut, a Vilna nurse.

There was no dearth of patients. Ailments were widespread. The faulty nutrition and constant humidity, along with the poor sanitary conditions, weakened the powers of resistance and opened the door to disease. There were many cases of vitamin insufficiency, evident mostly in ulcerated jaws. Feet were greatly affected by ill-fitting shoes; the leather had rotted back in the ghetto. Many people faced the prospect of a shoeless winter. Only once in a while did a villager provide a pair of fitting shoes.

In time, word of Dr. Gorfinkel's skill spread throughout the forest, and many came to ask for his help. Few physicians get to serve their "internship" under such conditions. Gorfinkel was privileged to reach the Land of Israel and work with the same intense loyalty that marked his personality, at Hadassah Hospital, Jerusalem. He was killed by an exploding Arab shell during the siege of the city.

The Peneusov family was expert in metalworking, back in the ghetto. In their small dwelling they set up a repair workshop for the weapons of their group. They set up a similar workshop in the forest. All the weapons brought from the ghetto were in poor shape. The father and his two sons were kept busy. The Russian and the Lithuanian camps heard about metalworkers in the Jewish camp, and work kept streaming their way.

The three smiths contributed a great deal to the improvement of the relations between the Jewish camp and the others. Most importantly, the Peneusovs took every opportunity to increase the Jewish arsenal. As remuneration for work they did for the other camps, they asked payment in the form of damaged, out-of-use weapons. The Gentiles gladly gave them the junk they had, which was soon rendered operative.

During the first months of the Jewish camps, the smithy was in the Peneusov tent. The partisans knew that if their weapons were repaired in the smithy, they would be dependable.

Soon the metalworkers began producing important parts as replacements. On one occasion a partisan, out on a foray, lost the bolt of his automatic in the darkness. Since there were only three such automatics in use, everyone in the camp literally held his breath until it was announced that another bolt had been success-fully fashioned. Later, a woodworker was added to the shop, and soon the wooden stocks and other wooden parts were being fashioned.

On a certain occasion, Moscow sent a dozen wireless operators, with special equipment, to pick up the information issued by the clandestine broadcasts of the German Army. The twelve did their work in an atmosphere shrouded in secrecy and apart from the others. Only a few among the partisans knew about the existence of this unit and the role assigned to it.

Once, a vital instrument of the wireless crew went awry. The experts spent days trying to repair it, in vain. Having no alternative, they came to the Peneusov family. The brothers, Borya and Avraham, toiled at it the whole night through. By dawn, the instrument was operational. In their message to Moscow, the Russians mentioned the metalcraft family by name, emphasizing the fact that it was thanks to the Peneusovs that the unit was able to continue its important work.

One day, Soviet planes dropped weapons for the partisans. Several para-chutes did not open, and some of the weapons were smashed upon landing. The next day, the Peneusov workshop was crammed with broken automatic rifles, pistols, and cartridge belts. It seemed that none of these could be salvaged, but the father and his sons managed to repair the lot.

On another occasion, heavy stuff was parachuted down: anti-tank machine-guns, except that the barrels did not fit the carriages. The error had been commit-ted, apparently, while the material was being packed. The partisans were dis-mayed; there was no heavy armor in partisan hands anywhere in the forest. After much hard work, the metalworkers put the guns into working order.

An exemplary indication of their expertise: they put together landmines which the Germans found impossible to dismantle.

The Peneusov family reached Israel in the stream of "illegal immigrants," but the younger son, Borya, who had fought death a thousand times, fell ill and died at the age of twenty-five.

Israel Shmarkovich, from Ejszyszki, who served as a guide in the forest.

Time to Depart

The Command saw that the time was ripe to carry out plans to rid itself of rivals. It was learned in the camp that orders had arrived from the Brigade's Headquarters that some of the people had to leave the present bases and move to the Nacza Forest, about 100 kilometers from the Rudnik Forest.

The people were amazed by this strange order. All the information so far about the Nacza Forest had come from the stories of the Grodno people, who were not the most reliable sources since they had left the place several months before, and it was impossible to know to what extent the situation had changed in the meantime.

If the Command really wanted to set up bases in a new place, it first had to scout the area. And how was it possible to set out on such a dangerous course without arms?

There were now more than 300 people in the Jewish camps, but they had only thirty rifles, several automatic weapons, a few dozen pistols, and very little ammunition. It was clear that those leaving would receive only part of the arms.

Moreover, the experience of the Jewish fighters was not very reassuring. Many had been in the forest for only one month and they already had to set out on a dangerous course. Obviously, if these people encountered Germans, they would all be killed. But the order did not take these factors into account. It simply said: Make preparations to leave.

It turned out that the High Command had thought for some time that the number of people in the Jewish camps should be reduced. There were various reasons for this. Fist of all, it was difficult to feed such a large number of people, and a situation of semistarvation could develop in the camps which would endanger everyone. It was also understandable that the Command did not look kindly on many people who, owing to the shortage of arms, could not be regarded as fighters, and in the event of danger, would only be an encumbrance. Moreover, there was a need to get rid of nonconforming, undesirable elements who, nonetheless, had no political disqualifications which would justify action on the part of the Special Affairs Division.

It was, therefore, the Command of the Jewish camps which proposed to the Brigade Headquarters to send part of its people to establish bases elsewhere. The Command promised that it had accurate and detailed information on the situation in the Nacza wilderness.

The Brigade Headquarters did not delve into the matter, but was ready to consider any proposal aimed at reducing the number of Jews under its command, particularly as no aid or equipment was requested.

When the camp heard about the plans, many jumped at the opportunity to leave. Though there was fear of the unknown, many were willing to take the risk, if only to get out from under the control of the Command.

The Headquarters circulated rumors that Nacza Forest was a land overflowing with milk and honey and promised those leaving that they would find a wonderful life there. Moreover, reports had come to Vilna that the Germans had begun assembling a large military force to surround the Rudnik Forest and burn out all the partisans. The reports also had it that fierce arguments were going on in the Headquarters itself, because everyone wanted to be among the fortunate contingent scheduled to leave.

In the camp, preparations were made for the departure. A list was drawn up of the departees, including 111 names: 35 women and 76 men.

The people were divided into two companies. The commander of the first was Shlomo Brand, one of the bravest fighters and a thorn in the side of the Headquarters people, who on several occasions looked for a pretext to begin an investigation against him. However, there was nothing to grab onto. He had not been a policeman in the ghetto, nor had he cooperated with the police or the

Judenrat. The only stigma which could be attributed to him was his nationalistic views and the fact that he was one of the founders of the Second Fighting Organization in the ghetto.

Though this was no reason to begin an investigation against him, it was sufficient reason to add him to the departure list. The fellow was too proud and too much of a truth seeker. He would not conform.

The commander of the second group was Aron Aronovich, a Bundist. Though he was unrivaled as a fighter, he was a "petit-bourgeois" and it was unbefitting the dignity of the "progressive" Headquarters people to be seated with him at one table.

Berl Sherezhnevski, one of the Communist leaders, was selected as chief commander and political commissioner. Not so long ago he had had a falling-out with Hienna Borowska at the Party and Headquarters meetings. They had had strong differences of opinion which had developed into open hostility. Borowska wanted to get rid of him and asked the High Command to appoint him to this position. And Sherezhnevski was willing to go. He did not want to stay under the same umbrella with Borowska.

I was appointed commander of the reconnaissance unit which had to go ahead of the camp and see to it that it would not fall into an ambush or meet up with large enemy forces.

Within a few days everything was ready for the departure. Shoes were repaired, packages were wrapped, and weapons were distributed. The departees received eleven rifles, each with two or three bullets, several guns, and two automatic rifles (belonging to Berl and me). These were the weapons we had brought with us from the Narocz Forest.

It was decided to maintain constant contact between the departees and the camps through messengers. The Brigade Headquarters and the Jewish Command promised that all weapons received in the future would be equally divided among the departees and those remaining, and that we would receive our share at the new bases.

Selected as guide was the Russian lieutenant Kolya, who had already made a number of visits to our camp. Kolya, according to the Headquarters, knew the way very well and could be relied upon to bring us safely to our destination. (A few months later Kolya was caught by the partisans and executed on the charge of having ties with the Germans.)

The day we were to leave, the partisan Doba Debeltov returned from Vilna after completing her fourth mission to the city, bringing with her five young men from the Keilis, carrying two automatics and three rifles. Borowska ordered them to stay outside the camp until we left, so as not to have to give us our share of the weapons they had brought.

At midday of November 3, 1943, a call-up of the whole camp took place. Brigade Commander Gavris addressed the assembled people and waxed eloquent about the important responsibilities of the mission: the war to the bitter end against the Nazi enemy and the liberation of the homeland from foreign yoke. He repeated the promise that arms would be sent. The camp commanders who remained also spoke about the tasks of the departees and wished us success.

The time for parting had come. Everyone was moved. Friends who had dreamt together in the ghetto of the happy moment when they would be able to fight shoulder-to-shoulder in the war of revenge against the enemy and go to the forest together to realize their dream were now parted, not knowing if they would ever meet again.

We moved off at dusk, full of hope. One hundred eleven people left to greet the new day, unaware that within days they would experience endless hardship.

Before we left Rudnik Forest, we met several of the Grodno people, who joined the departees. Were it not for these people and were it not for Israelik, it is very doubtful that even one of the 111 people would have remained alive.

Israel Shmarkovich was a boy of about 17 years. Together with his father, he has escaped from Ejszyszki at the outbreak of the war and for many months the two had wandered among the villages, in the woods, and in the forest. All the roads and byways within an area of dozens of square kilometers were as familiar to them as the paths of their native city. They also knew the peasants of the area and their knowledge served them well in times of great danger.

Israelik became attached to the camp of departees with all the fervor of youth. With his great devotion, he was able to save the camp of departees on a number of occasions. In moments of extreme danger, when the Grodno people left the camp and dispersed, Israelik remained with his new friends to serve them and show them the way. Despite his young age, he had an out-standingly developed sense of responsibility. He knew that it was his sacred duty to try to save the lives of the camp Jews as much as was in his power to do so.

He also possessed other valuable traits. He was courageous and fearless, yet modest and diffident. He was as learned in war strategy as the most veteran fighters. Everyone knew that when he fired a rifle, an automatic, or machine-gun, he would never miss the mark. And if he went out on a reconnaissance mission, he would bring back the most detailed and most reliable information. If he marched at the head of the camp, one could follow him blindly.

If after weeks of hunger and frost, under the constant attack of the enemy and the "White" roving bands, our people remained alive, it was thanks to Israelik.

"Ruvka Di Hatuna"

It was a rainy night. The rain fell without respite. We were soaked through and through and our clothes were heavy on us. Our feet sank in the mire of the fields and a thick layer of mud clung to our shoes.

Our feet, too, felt as heavy as lead and we had to walk many kilometers that night. From time to time we sat down to rest. The guide knocked at the window of a peasant's house on the side of the road to ask whether we were going in the right direction and whether the area was quiet. The people were hoping that they would be able to rest for a while, but the commanders urged them on. By dawn, we had to reach a place where we could stay all day without attracting attention in the area.

By midnight there were already many stragglers, men as well as women, but it was impossible to make allowances for them. All efforts had to be made to reach the next station by the designated time.

The next day was spent in a woods of young birch trees. On one side of the copse was a stream which ambled among the pastured fields. Beyond the woods was a large expanse fading into the horizon. It was feared that herdsmen, searching for a lost young lamb or an errant cow, might find the people hiding in the woods or that that peasants' dogs might detect us.

Therefore, the silence of the grave pervaded the encampment. It was impossible even to light a fire because the smoke might give us away. The people shivered with cold in their drenched clothes and huddled together. This one busied himself cleaning his weapon, that one, repairing his clothes, and another, extracting from his sack the portion of food he had received before setting off. However, we could not satisfy our appetite. The portions were enough for only two days and it was impossible to know what the next day would bring.

The sky was gray and our hearts were heavy.

The next morning at roll call it was discovered that Aronovich, the commander of one of the companies, was missing. No one knew what had happened to him. He had not been seen for hours. There was speculation that he had fallen asleep at one of the stations along the way and had not been aware that the others had continued the journey. It was hoped that he would return to Rudnik Forest since he did not know the way. With this thought, the people comforted his wife, who was also among the departees.

By the second night, we had reached a river at the edge of the Nacza Forest. Two poles served as a bridge. The river was not deep, but because of the rains it had overflowed its banks. A long time passed until all the people reached the other side. Most of them did not succeed in crossing without falling into the water and drenching themselves.

We entered the thick of the forest. Even on clear nights it was difficult to find the way, let alone on such an overcast night. The guides were at their wit's end. That night we had to reach the partisan bases on the other side of the forest. It was impossible to tarry there and to continue by day, since no one knew the security situation in the area.

The deeper we entered the forest, the thicker it became and the larger the swamps. No one could see his neighbor in front of him.

The situation was saved by a boy from Ejszyszki, whom we called "Ruvka Di Hatuna." He felt the way with his hands. He moved along like a hunting dog smelling the tracks of wild animals and told us if we were going in the right direction or not.

The people followed him in a rear line which became ever longer until, after some time, communication was broken. We began to call out and to light fires, but the stragglers did not see the tiny lights enveloped by the darkness. The voices and the shouts were growing louder by the minute and their frightening echoes reverberated throughout the forest. All of this in an unknown territory, infested perhaps by enemy troops.

Ruvka did not let us down. He guided the people along the right route and, with the remainder of our strength, we scurried after him. The partisan base was a few kilometers away, and dawn would soon break. Everyone prayed silently that the night of horrors would soon end.

To reach the partisan base, we had to pass through swampy land. However, since we had already strayed from the high road and were again in the forest thicket, it seemed that we had nothing to fear. Israelik, another partisan, and I went to search for the home of the keeper of the forest, known for his sympathy to the partisans, to hear about the situation in the area. His home was at the edge of the forest, in a place bordering the Third Reich.

He was shocked and fear-stricken by the unexpected visit. Some days before, he said, thousands of German, Lithuanian, and Ukrainian soldiers had arrived and, with the aid of tanks and planes, had begun ridding the forest of partisans. All the camps that were in the forest, including the Russian camp, which was well armed and headed by the famous brigade commander Stankevitz, were defeated in battle. The remnants of the camps broke through the enemy ring and escaped towards Russka Forest. Enemy patrols were still in the forest and were continuing to search for solitary partisans who had managed to hide. Ukrainian guards were occupying abandoned partisan bases.

There was no time to lose. Our people were approaching the enemy-occupied bases and any minute they would fall into enemy hands. To make matters worse, dawn was breaking and we would not have time to retreat to the depths of the forest.

The situation was beyond despair. After a short consultation it was decided to spend the day in the nearby woods beyond the road, in the hope that the Germans would not think of searching such a tiny copse.

Utterly exhausted, hungry and shivering with cold, the people lay on the wet ground among the young trees. Despite the great fear we felt on hearing shots starting at dawn, one by one we fell asleep.

In the afternoon when we awoke from our sleep, we were surprised to find ourselves covered with a layer of snow. We got up and shook off the first snow of winter, which melted away after a short time.

From afar, the echoes of explosions were heard. The Germans were bombing Russka Forest and the villages suspected of sympathy towards the partisans. We eagerly awaited the coming of night. Though we knew that the night would not bring a solution to our problem, at least at night the partisans felt better. The darkness protected us from strangers, and allowed us to spring into action from our hiding-place. A partisan lived and operated by night. It seemed as if night were created expressly for him.

The commanders decided on retreat. At dark we left along the same route by which we had come. Once again we were in the thicket of the trees and the swamps. But this time we were not in such a hurry to leave.

By dawn we reached Mizantsa Forest, four kilometers from the Radun Forest. There, in hiding, we found about 150 Jews from the nearby town who had managed to escape during the last slaughter. They were living in tents and they included people of all ages.

They included gray-haired old men, children, babies, and sucklings. Entire families had succeeded in saving themselves from extermination. There was a father and three nubile daughters. In normal times he had been known to invite to his home students from the Chafetz Chaim Yeshiva, in the hope of marrying off his daughters. Now his main concern was just to guard the honor of his daughters.

Here was a family blessed with many children. The elderly grandmother could not forget the good days when schoolchildren would recite the Torah and the house was full of the sound of merriment. Now the children's faces were serious and sad. With fear in their eyes, they shrank from every shadow and shook with terror at every sound of rustling leaves.

Sadness and depression filled the camps. In the evening, the women gathered around the fire and talked in whispers while gloomily preparing the small food portions. The children huddled together to warm their thin bodies, chilled by the evening. Some of the men prepared to leave for the villages to search for food, while others stood under the trees murmuring praise and thanks to the Creator of the Universe, who had given them one more day without misfortune. So they had done the day before and so they would do the next day, thus fulfilling the prayer, "Blessed be the Lord each day."

These Jews were making plans. They were preparing bunkers in safe places where they would spend the coming winter. They were also preparing a food stockpile. Several of them were armed and most of them knew the surroundings and had acquaintences among the peasants. The unfortunate souls! How could they know that in a few months' time the "White" roving bands would gain control of the area and slaughter them, with the help of the same peasants they had trusted.

Our commanders decided to send messengers to the Rudnik Forest to report to the Brigade Headquarters on the situation and to request permission to return, for each day we spent in that area increased our danger. Towards evening three people set out, including the guide, Kolya. The remaining people anxiously awaited their return and the news that they could go back to the camp.

Natan Ring.

Executions

Commander Aronovich, who lost his way on the first night after we left Rudnik Forest, suddenly reappeared. He said that that same night he had fallen asleep at one of the stations where we had camped, and when he awoke, he no longer saw anyone around. For over an hour he went ahead in search of the caravan, but in vain. He finally decided to return to Rudnik Forest and then rejoin us as soon as possible. Arriving in the Rudnik camp, he learned that a group of people had recently come from Vilna, carrying arms. He asked the Headquarters people to give him part of the arms for those who had left, but his request was denied. He was regarded with suspicion, as if he had purposely left the caravan.

That same evening, a special call-up of all the people was held. No one knew the purpose of this call-up but it was regarded as a bad omen, especially when it was learned that the commander would personally direct it. At the appointed time, Didialis, the political commissar, appeared and read out the order of the day: after a thorough and prolonged investigation, the Special Affairs Division had sentenced to death four partisans: Natan Ring, Schwartzbard, Itzkovich, and Keves. The death sentence had been carried out at noon.

After reading out the order, Didialis gave a speech, in which he said: "Had Natan Ring's guilt been only that of having ties with the Gestapo while he was a police officer, we might have overlooked it. Yet, we have learned from reliable sources that he maintained these ties and went to the city some time ago to give information to the Germans about the partisans. We had no choice but to save our honor and destroy the evil in our midst. The same applies to the other three. There is substantial evidence that while they were ghetto police, they cooperated with the Gestapo, and only death can exonerate them.'' After Didialis had finished, Kovner rose to speak. He spoke with great pathos, calling those who were executed ''traitors'' and justifying the severe sentence imposed on them. In the end, he waxed eloquent and said: ''If Gens were here himself, I would gut him like a fish and put an end to his life.''

The effect on the camp, Aronovich told us, was terrible. One of Ring's friends fainted. Many people's eyes were filled with tears. Depression and mourning filled the camp. Everyone knew that Natan Ring was one of the most courageous fighters in the forest and that the charges against him were baseless. Ring had gone to Vilna to arrange a hiding-place for his mother. Mitya Lipenholtz, one of the superior commanders, who accompanied Ring to the city and returned with him to the forest, testified to this.

As for the other three, there was hostility towards the policeman Schwartzbard, whose attitude towards the Jews in the ghetto had been very harsh, but Keves served as a policeman for only a short time after the ghetto was set up. As for Itzkovich, it is true that he served in the police all the time, but he was one of those who did not know how to ''get along,'' and despite his service, suffered hunger.

It was also known that in the Russian and Lithuanian camps, there were people who had worked for the Gestapo, who had served in the police under German command, and had even taken an active role in killing the Jews; nevertheless, they were not tried and their qualifications were not questioned. Did the Jews, of all people, have to be so zealous? It was also known in the camp that none of the other commanders would have dared to appear before the Jewish partisans to try to justify the sentence. But Kovner was ready to carry out this task. (Incidentally, after the liberation of Vilna, several Communists, including Berl Sherezhnevski, admitted to me that Natan Ring and his comrades should not have been executed, as there was no evidence against them.)

The next day, related Aronovich, details were learned about the execution of the four. In the morning they had been told by the Headquarters people to prepare to go on a mission. Natan Ring understood that something was amiss. He asked one of his friends for a gun, went to the repair shop, and asked that it be fixed. When his friends asked him where he was going, he said: ''I think that this will be my last journey.'' He hid the gun in his sleeve and joined the other three who left, accompanied by Didialis and a member of the Komsomol, Danke Lubotski. They passed the former base which had been abandoned some time before, and met up with the Lithuanian Stankevich, the head of the Special Affairs Division of the Brigade Headquarters, and some of his aides. Ring and his comrades were immediately surrounded and Stankevich's men began to read the charges and the sentence. They went on reading and suddenly Natan Ring pulled out his gun, shot at Didialis, and shouted "Let's escape!" The four began to run, Ring all the while shooting at his captors. But, in his excitement, he missed his target. Meanwhile, the four were showered with bullets and three of them were killed.

Keves, injured in the leg, was caught alive. He said that if his guilt were proven, he would accept his sentence. Danke Lubotski went up to him with the charge sheet in his hand, and said to him in a friendly manner: "Let's sit down and I will explain to you what is written here." They sat down, and while Lubotski explained the charges, someone came up from the rear and fired a round of bullets into Keves's head.

The next day Didialis and several Komsomol members went to the place of execution and distributed among themselves the clothes of the dead men. Didialis took Natan Ring's watch and boots for himself and told his comrades not to appear in the men's clothes for the time being so as not to cause anger. The bodies were left unburied.

Aronovich's sad account put an end to the partisans' last hopes of returning to Rudnik Forest. Had they come to the forest to engage in mutual killing? All of them, the commanders and the fighters, decided that they would not return to Rudnik Forest, despite their unbearable situation. They preferred to remain in a place where danger lay in wait at every step, rather than return to the oppressive regime in the Jewish camp.

We remained in the Mizantsa Forest for three days, and then went to the Stuyar Forest, near Nacza Forest. Israelik was once again our guide. He knew a place where Jews once hid. After a night of hard and tiring walking, we arrived at our destination. The road was fraught with obstacles: large swamps and huge trees which had fallen by themselves or were uprooted by the wind. But these obstacles also protected us somewhat from unexpected attack.

On a small hill overlooking the swamps stood a number of empty tents. Nearby we found decaying corpses and human bones. The local peasants told us that one day Polish bands had attacked the forest and killed close to 100 Jews who were hiding there. Despite the tragic fate of our predecessors, we began to organize our life in that place. The most pressing matter was that of food. For a week we had hardly eaten anything.

That evening a unit went out on a foray, though the people were utterly exhausted. But the next day we refreshed ourselves with soup. The three plates which the unit brought back from its mission were passed from hand to hand.

Life began to return to normal. The people were recovering from the walk and were mending their shoes and clothes. More tents were set up and it seemed that we were finally going to have some rest. People were already thinking about actions and sabotage against the enemy.

One day there appeared in our new camp two partisans from Russka Forest who had been sent by their commander to scout the area and see if the enemy attacks had stopped and whether it was possible to return to their former bases. The Russian partisans were amazed to see in that dangerous area such a large camp with almost no arms. The well-armed Russian brigade had not yet dared to return. When we told them that we had come there to set up new bases, they could not believe it. They said that the commanders in Rudnik Forest apparently wanted to get rid of superfluous people and, therefore, had sent us to an enemy-ridden area, knowing full well that we would never return.

Our commanders said that they had an announcement to give to the commander of their brigade but the two partisans laughed at them and said that their leader would not want to talk with "superfluous partisans." We implored them to agree, at least, to take back two people from the camp to establish contact with their commander. They remained adamant in their refusal and finally left to report that it was still not possible to come back, as strong Polish bands were in control of the area.

We had pinned so many hopes on establishing contact with the local brigade commander. Now these hopes had gone up in smoke.

Aronovich and I went to Mizantsa to wait there for the return of our messengers from Rudnik Forest, but the messengers did not come. While we were returning to camp, a fierce storm arose. Hundreds of trees were uprooted and carried away like chaff by the wind. The tents in the camp collapsed and all our meagre possessions were blown away. Only by miracle was disaster averted, though we heard that there were many victims from the storm in the area.

It was two days later when the storm finally died down and the clouds dispersed. A unit went out to bring back food and, meanwhile, the tents were set up again. Now, we thought, surely we must have experienced the worst. Little did we know.

A group of partisans.

The "White" Roving Bands

The next morning the unit which had set out in a foray had not yet returned. It was headed by Shlomo Brand and consisted of the best fighters. It had to return before daybreak, since it was unthinkable to be in enemy-controlled territory in the daytime. In general, a partisan did not leave the depths of the forest in broad daylight, even with the best of weapons.

The young men in the camp had forgotten the hunger which had plagued them since the night before. Now they were afraid for their lives, though no one dared voice his terrifying thoughts. Scouts were sent to the edge of the forest but there was no sign of life from the missing group.

They had taken almost all the arms the camp had, and if a calamity befell them, the camp would be helpless.

The worst was already expected, when suddenly Shlomo and his friends came running and said that on their way they had met up with a Polish roving band and only by a miracle did they manage to escape. They had succeeded in collecting several wagons laden with food, but they had to leave them at the edge of the forest among the bushes, a few kilometers from the camp. Had they tried to bring the food to the camp, none of them would have remained alive. Only in the evening would it be possible to go and get the wagons. However, if the Poles would find the wagons during the day, they would realize that there were partisans in the forest, and that would be the end for the camp.

The camp was put in a state of alert. Plans were made on how to retreat in the event of attack. Guards were sent to scout the area. After some time, two young men returned and announced that they had succeeded in reaching the place where the wagons were hidden but did not find them there. The disappearance of the wagons presaged disaster. We could expect an attack any minute.

Guards were maintained and scouts were stationed along the way up to the main road so that they could give warning of danger.

In the afternoon there was a sudden burst of gunfire into the forest. The shots were getting closer and there was no escape. In front of us were the bloodthirsty Poles and behind us were the swamps.

An order was given to retreat into the heart of the swampy area. The women went ahead, followed by the unarmed men. The armed group remained in place to cover the retreat.

The retreaters' feet sank in the mud and it was impossible to go on. The mud was waist-high, and all the while bullets were buzzing overhead.

There were, all in all, only about 30 bullets among us. The Poles, on the other hand, were as well armed as a regular army. Each of their squadrons numbered 50 men, headed by a professional officer. Each 10-man detachment had a heavy machine-gun and several automatics, as well as rifles and hand grenades. One Polish detachment could destroy our whole camp within minutes.

By evening the shooting ceased and only occasionally did a solitary shot split the air. The Poles had not yet determined the nature of their enemy and they had apparently decided to postpone the attack until the next day. Perhaps, seeing that their shots had not provoked a response, they had drawn the conclusion that there were no partisans in the area.

Whatever the reason, we had to take advantage of the darkness and disappear. But how could we leave the swamps, when the only way out was in the hands of the enemy?

At midnight, scouts went out to reconnoitre the area. After some time they returned and informed us that they had seen green spots of light among the trees. At first they had thought that they were wolves' eyes, but after an investigation they discovered that the lights were signals of the Poles. The situation was hopeless. The road was blocked before us.

Once again Israelik saved the day. Of all the Grodno people, he was the only one who remained with us. All the others had scattered upon hearing the first shots.

Israelik promised that he would take the people out of the swamp area. By a side-path circumventing the Polish position, the people made their way out. Israelik marched in front and warned those behind him to move in absolute silence.

By daybreak we had arrived at the edge of Nacza Forest. Nearby was an underground shelter where Jews had once hidden. Now we found only their rotting corpses; they had been murdered by the Poles.

Despite the fact that the shelter was narrow, most of our people entered it. All of them were dead-tired and soaked to the bone. Outside it was snowing. The crowding in the shelter was awful. Even with everyone standing, it was too narrow to hold all of them. The air was suffocating and the people were dizzy from hunger and weakness.

Sentries were posted at the edge of the forest. We hoped that another day would pass peacefully and that we would be able to continue to move at night. No one knew any longer where we were going.

At midday the sun's rays broke through the leaden clouds. The snowflakes on the treetops glittered like thousands of scattered pearls. The people began to go out, exercise, and breath the pure air. But suddenly the roar of bullets shook the forest.

The people ran out of the shelter and hurried after Israelik, who led us into the thick of the forest. Sentries were left behind to cover the retreat. The armed group which constituted the rear returned fire and succeeded in slowing down the progress of the enemy.

Many of the people were barefoot, for in the confusion of the escape they had not had the time to gather their shoes which were still stuck in the mud. For a minute it seemed as if the enemy would catch up with us, but Israelik, who led the procession, and the armed group at the rear thwarted the murderers' plans.

After hours of running, it seemed that the immediate danger had passed and it was possible to sit down and rest. We decided that we would wait until evening and then make tracks towards Rudnik Forest.

The barefooted ones, who trampled in the snow without protection against the cold and dampness, tied rags around their feet. They did not want to lag behind their comrades.

In the evening we crossed the river near the forest and found ourselves in open country. We stopped near one of the villages. Some members of our group entered a peasant's house to find out the situation and to request a little food to revive the weakest women. However, the peasant said that only a few minutes before, "White" vigilantes had visited his home and had asked for food. They might return any minute. This was the third day, said the peasant, that Polish bands were camping throughout the area.

The caravan continued on its way. It was now passing through desolate fields, far from any settlement, and the way was difficult and tiring. Suddenly the group halted: a woman had fainted from exhaustion and hunger. Several other women said that they were unable to go on. One young man became ill and had to be supported as he walked. The next station was far away.

The five sentries who watched over the hut were not with us, and with them we had lost five rifles, almost half the arms of the whole caravan.

With superhuman strength the caravan succeeded in covering a distance of many kilometers that terrible night, and by dawn it had arrived at a solitary peasant's house near a woods. It was decided to camp. We entered the large threshing-room, which was full of fodder, and the peasant's family was forbidden to leave the house that whole day.

At noon there appeared two Jews from Ejszyszki, the brothers Zalman and Akiva. They said that they were hiding in the woods, amidst the swamps. They had set up a tent and there were other Jews with them. The area was quiet and the peasants were helping them with information and food. They also said that they had a Christian acquaintance who often traveled to the other side of the Niemen (Nemunas) River and returned with wondrous stories about the partisans living there. The area was vast and included dozens of villages under partisan supervision. The Germans did not dare enter these areas. There were also hundreds of Jews there who were not partisans and they were living in peace in the forests. Some of them had already succeeded in crossing the front lines and reaching Russia. In short: Paradise on Earth.

Berl Sherezhnevski, our political commissar, was very excited by this account. After all, he was a veteran Communist. For many years he had sat in prison for his beliefs. Throughout all his years of political activity, he had never failed to carry out a task assigned to him. Now, too, despite our desperate situation, he was not particularly anxious to return and confess our failure before the Brigade Headquarters. He also remembered the enmity between Borowska and himself, and knew that she would exploit his failure to denigrate and shame him.

He believed that we should make one more attempt. However, as the experience of the last few days had proven that one should not set out on an unknown route with a large number of people, he decided to send most of the people back to Rudnik Forest, there to wait for further notice. In the meantime, he and several others would continue to scout the area.

Before sunset, Berl convened the fighters and selected 18 of them, including the company commanders. All the others were ordered to leave. The people bitterly accused Berl of betraying them, of leaving them to be destroyed while he saved his own life. Two young couples announced that they would not obey him and left the camp. (Some time later we learned that they had been murdered by the Poles.)

After tempers cooled somewhat, the people realized that if they did not waste any more time and if they made great effort, they could reach Rudnik Forest by dawn. Eighty men and women, tired and embittered and possessing four rifles, disappeared into the night.

Berl Sherezhnevski and his people settled in the tents of the Ejszyszki people amidst the swamps. For ten days they reconnoitered the area to find a place suitable for the establishment of bases. However, they discovered that the whole area was under the control of the ''White'' bands which roamed around unchecked, wreaking havoc.

Various rumors were circulating concerning the relations between these Poles and the Germans. It was said that the Germans themselves were organizing the bands and arming them so that they could fight against the ''Red'' partisans and annihilate the last of the Jews who were still in hiding.

The rank and file in the bands knew nothing about the agreement with the Germans. They thought that they were fighting to free Poland. However, their leaders had accepted the authority of the enemy and were collaborating with it. They carried out their task faithfully, at least concerning the annihilation of the Jews. Thirsting for blood, they were hunting down the last remnants of Jews in the forests and destroying them.

One day Shlomo Brand and two other fellows went out to search for the five partisans who remained as sentries during the attack of the Poles on Nacza Forest. After many mishaps they succeeded in crossing the enemy territory and reaching the Mizantsa forests.

There they found four of the five. One of them, Moshe Sarakhan, was killed while carrying out his duties. He was a young fellow, from a family of porters, who had been nicknamed the ''Strongman'' in Vilna because of his physical prowess. Even the Germans enjoyed seeing displays of his strength. He would take four sacks of flour, each weighing 100 kilos, and would place his father, himself a powerful man, on top of them, and would then lift the whole load on his broad shoulders without showing strain.

He was of great benefit to the partisan camp. Once, at the end of a foray, when the partisans were hurrying back to camp, dawn having broken, one captured cow had refused to budge. It would have been a pity to leave it, as its acquisition had involved effort and risk. Moreover, it had been a very long time since the people in the camp had tasted meat. The partisans were at a loss. But Moshe went up to the cow, raised it on his shoulders, and put it on the wagon.

Now Brand and his comrades heard that Sarakhan was no longer alive. A murderer's bullet had pierced his heart.

Berl saw that no good would come from a prolonged stay in that remote place and decided to return to Rudnik Forest with his fighters.

After hours of walking, they came upon a Polish band, and a fight ensued. The enemy advanced on them from three sides and forced them to retreat. When the shooting stopped, it was discovered that half of the people were missing. Following a long search, they were found hiding in the woods several kilometers away.

Meanwhile, dawn had broken and it was impossible to continue moving. But it was unthinkable to stay put for two whole days. The people hid in an abandoned village bathhouse in the middle of a field. The shots in the area did not stop and the situation was becoming steadily worse. For three days the people had not eaten. A little longer and they would not have the strength to break the siege. When they finally managed to leave and arrived in Rudnik Forest, they were tired and exhausted and their clothing was in tatters.

The reception they got was not particularly cordial. After the 80 returned, Didialis, Borowska and Kovner criticized Berl and his people *in abstentia* and accused them before the Brigade Headquarters of abandoning 80 people to save themselves. When the "traitors" appeared, they were ordered to surrender their arms and leave the camp.

However, Berl and his people announced that if an attempt was made to take their arms, they would open fire. Berl also announced that he was unwilling to be judged by the commanders of the Jewish camps. He would present his case only before Yurgis and Gavris, the Brigade commanders.

The tension was mounting from minute to minute. There was danger of a fraternal war. In the end the Command backed down and gave up their demand that the returnees surrender their arms. However, Berl and his group were not to be fed or given shelter from the rain and cold until the completion of the investigation.

The Brigade Headquarters decided to remove Berl and his accompanying commanders from their posts and to disperse the people among the existing Jewish camps.

Mitya Lipenholtz.

The Agent Učkuronis

During our absence, changes had taken place in the life of the camp. The people had grown more accustomed to life in the woods and had become experts in the partisan "profession." The number of arms had also increased.

The camp was now in a new and more convenient location on top of a hill among the swamps, close to the French Way. Most of the people were busy digging underground shelters under the supervision of Mitya Lipenholtz, a building technician.

The shelters were built in this manner: a pit was dug in the shape of a rectangle, measuring 50 meters in length, and 4 or 5 meters in width. Along the center, a kind of deep canal was dug about a half meter deeper than the pit itself. This was for passing among the sleeping areas. The walls were supported by poles and the sleeping areas were also buttressed by poles.

The pit was covered with a roof reaching the surface of the ground, and branches and leaves were used to camouflage it. On both ends of the passage were doors; an aperture in the roof allowed for ventilation. Whoever succeeded in finding a nail struck it in the wood overhead and hung his possessions and weapons on it.

Even in the daytime it was as dark in the shelter as at dusk. It was always suffocating and crowded there. Sand seeped in from the walls and the ceiling. And as we always slept in our clothes, it was no wonder that the lice and fleas multiplied. It was as vulnerable to the rain and wind as our former tents.

The two shelters were inhabited by close to 250 people. Other shelters were being dug: smaller ones for the command, a clinic, an arms workshop, food warehouse, and so forth.

We heard of several unfortunate incidents which occurred the previous month. During a big storm, several people had been injured. Thanks to the tireless efforts of the doctor, Gorfinkel, all of them recovered, except one. Senja Rindzunski remained a cripple all his life.

One of the young people who had moved from the command of our camp to the Russian camp, Zalman Toker, was caught napping while on guard. Such cases were not rare in the forest and the guilty parties were punished. However, this time the guilty one was a Jew, and, therefore, his sentence had to be stiffer. At the order of Mishka Capitan, Toker was executed.

Some time after this case a company of Russian partisans left on an operation. It fell into a German ambush and came under heavy fire. During the retreat, a bullet hit the rifle of a Jewish lad named Moshe Epstein, knocking it out of his hands. In the general confusion he ran with everyone else and only later did he realize that his rifle was missing. But it was impossible to return, since the area was already in German hands. Shamefacedly, he returned to the camp without his weapon.

Mishka gave him a choice either to obtain a rifle or be executed. Epstein went to his former commanders—Borowska, Didialis, and Kovner, and begged them to lend him a rifle to save his life. He promised in the name of all that was dear to him that he would bring them another rifle as soon as possible. But the commanders hardened their hearts and made him return empty-handed. Mishka Capitan knew no pity; he gave the order to have Moshe executed.

Since life in the camp had entered a routine, more operations were undertaken. The first concern was the supply of arms. One night a 40-member company set out, under the command of Kaplinski, to confiscate the weapons from the inhabitants of the village Posol.

While the men were busy searching the houses of the village, the peasants called for reinforcements from the nearby villages and from the nearby garrisons. A fierce battle broke out which lasted two hours. Despite the fact that the enemy suffered losses in dead and wounded, it succeeded in surrounding the few partisans, owing to its greater number of weapons. It seemed that the end was near. But at the last minute, the men broke their way through to the river near the village and crossed it. At daybreak they returned to the camp.

A second company, headed by Yaakov Prenner, penetrated the town of Olkicniki, though a garrison numbering more than 200 men was stationed there. The company succeeded in getting its hands on a few hundred kilos of petrol. But just when the men were leaving the town, a German guard spotted them and opened fire. The squadron was already in the forest near Olkieniki but the shots were getting closer.

Such was the way of the Germans: when they heard shots, they did not even bother to find out from where they came. They opened fire from all positions in the area.

It was New Year's Eve, 1944. All the villagers in the area were out in full force celebrating the Christian New Year. When the peasants heard the shots they joined in the merriment.

Though the situation of the Jewish fighters was not very good, they could not help but marvel at the fantastic beauty of the night. Red, pink, and blue firecrackers illuminated the snowflakes, which glimmered in rainbow colors against a background of green trees, and the symphony of gunshots seemed to be an accompaniment to a dance of forest demons, about to begin.

For some hours the men wandered along the forest paths, their feet sinking in the soft snow. In the morning they brought their cargo to the camp, happy that they had returned safely from the party which the enemy had held for them on the occasion of the New Year.

Several days later 40 people set out, under the command of Kovner and Elchanan Megid, to blow up a bridge on the Vilna–Orany road. From the day we blew up the bridges on the Vilna–Grodno road and rendered it useless, the Vilna–Orany road had served as an important artery of transport for the German forces.

From the beginning of the operation, our people came under heavy fire from the direction of Olkieniki and the neighboring village of Derguski. The fighters returned fire and completed the mission while exchanging shots with the enemy.

The mood in the camp was improving. The dream of a war of revenge against the enemy was being realized.

One evening at the end of December, the unit left our camp on a foray in the village of Dajnowa. As was customary, guards were posted and the men divided into groups and entered the peasants' homes to look for food.

At midnight shots were heard at the end of the village. The partisans and the loaded wagons were immediately concentrated in one place and some people went to find out the reason for the shots. Two men came running and said that while they were in the home of one of the peasants, the house was surrounded by the enemy, who opened the door suddenly and fired shots inside. Their comrade Danke Lubotski was killed on the spot, while they succeeded in jumping through the window and escaping, with the enemy shooting after them and throwing grenades.

Lipenholtz, the commander of the operation, sent some of his people with the wagons into the forest, and he and several men waited there to see what would happen. The shooting did not resume, and when the silence had continued for some time, Lipenholtz and his companions approached the house in which the three partisans were attacked.

The house was empty and only Danke's body lay on the floor. He no longer had a weapon. It was clear that this was not the work of the Germans. Lipenholtz went to wake up the head of the village. He took all the men he found in the latter's home and told them that they were being held responsible for Danke's death.

The village leader, who wanted to save his life, said that that night a Polish guest named Andreuszkewicz had come to the village and it was rumored that he had ties with the Gestapo. Perhaps, said the village leader, he was the one who caused Danke's death.

After a search the Polish agent was found. His weapon was seized and he was led into the forest together with the village leader and his two sons. At the edge of the forest, Lipenholtz told them that if they returned Danke's weapon, he would free them, but if they refused, they would pay with their lives. One of the sons of the village leader went home and a few hours later returned with the gun. The Polish agent was brought to the camp and turned over to the Special Affairs Division. After an investigation he was found guilty and executed.

The next day it was learned that Danke was killed by Lithuanian partisans. The story was as follows: a partisan unit from the Lithuanian camp, headed by Naktis, one of the pillars of the Special Affairs Division, came to the village that night to look for Učkuronis, a dangerous Gestapo agent. For some months, all the camps in the forest had been searching for Učkuronis, and it had already reached the point of a kind of competition as to which camp would capture him.

The Lithuanians had received information that the wanted agent was in that village and went after him. Seeing light in one of the windows they approached and peeked in. They saw people who did not resemble peasants at all. They decided that they were the agent and his aides, and opened fire.

The supply situation was very bad. For almost a month there had been no successful foray. A number of units went out, only to return empty-handed. The peasants were armed and opposed the pillaging by force. Hunger was a constant guest at the camp.

One day a unit went out and succeeded in loading goods onto wagons, but on their way back to camp, the partisans were attacked by strong enemy forces which opened heavy fire on them. Under cover of counterfire, the partisans retreated, leaving the wagons behind. The retreat was difficult. There was no shelter from enemy bullets in the whole area. With great effort, the unit succeeded in disengaging itself from the Germans. However, three remained on the battlefield: Rashka Markovich, Miklishanski, and Shlackman. Afterwards, it was learned that Shlackman was taken alive while seriously injured and died after cruel torture.

A heavy pall fell over the camp. The two young men were excellent fighters. And Rashka—who did not know that dark-haired, bright-eyed girl from the days of the ghetto, where she proved her mettle as chief liaison of the F.P.O.? She was always busy: from early morning to midnight she carried out all the tasks assigned to her promptly, faithfully, and confidently, and in the forest, among the partisans, she did not shame her past.

The partisans could not spend much time mourning their fallen comrades. New tasks awaited them—the war against the enemy, first and foremost.

One day we heard that the Germans were planning to transfer to Germany the factory near Olkieniki. A partisan company set out at night, overcame the guard stationed there, and blew up all the machines.

The Brigade Headquarters gave our camp a quantity of explosives which was soon put to good use. Three military trains full of soldiers, tanks, and ammunition were blown up. Dozens of train cars were wrecked, huge quantities of arms were destroyed, and hundreds of enemy soldiers were killed and wounded.

News reached the camp that peasants, who had pretended for some time to be sympathetic to the partisans, were secretly acquiring arms to fight against us. I was assigned the task of leading a company of partisans to disarm them. For several hours we walked among the neighboring villages and conducted arms searches, but without success. Not wanting to return to camp empty-handed, we decided to make one last attempt. We heard that that same day the Polish agent, Boleslaw Učkuronis, the man wanted for months by all the partisan camps, was visiting the village of Dajnowa. He was the one responsible for arming the peasants and organizing them to fight against the partisans.

When we entered the village, we were told that a big party was being held that night to mark the important turning-point in the peasants' life: from that day on they would not have to fear the "forest bandits" who were impoverishing them. If the partisans continued to disturb them, they could now fight back. Hundreds of young people from the whole area were gathered at the party and the guest of honor was Učkuronis. Our unit numbered only eight but we were undaunted.

The party was still going on. The orchestra was playing and couples were dancing. Others were drinking. Suddenly there was silence. Mouths agape, everyone stood and stared at the uninvited guests who had come to ruin their party.

I told the celebrants that the village was surrounded by hundreds of partisans armed with heavy machine-guns, and that a guard was stationed near every house. If anyone tried to escape, he would pay with his life. Furthermore, I had learned that among them was the wanted agent, Učkuronis. If they would deliver him to us, we would leave them alone and they could resume their celebration; but if they tried to hide him, we would take revenge on the whole crowd.

Despite the threat, no one pointed out Učkuronis. We ordered all the men to stand with their hands raised and their faces to the wall. One by one, we checked them over. Finally, we found the agent in the corner pressed among the women. Before leaving the building, I lectured the peasants, telling them that their alliance with the subjugators would bring them no good, for the Nazis' end was drawing near. I called upon them to rise up against the Germans and ended by warning them not to leave the building until dawn.

Meanwhile, dawn was about to break and it was still a long way to the camp. We drove like mad to the forest on sleds, carrying the valuable booty: the Polish collaborator and three suspect Lithuanian youths. The whole forest was astir. The brigade commander and the head of the Special Affairs Division came to our camp to conduct the inquiry. The three Lithuanian youths were freed for "lack of evidence." Učkuronis was sentenced to death. Many wanted the honor of executing him, for each of us had a long account to settle with the Gestapo and its agents. This was proved by the shouts accompanying each blow on the collaborator's head: "This is for my parents, this is for my wife, and this is for little Ruchele whom you murdered. . . ."

Some of the pain and bitterness which had accumulated over the years found release on that day.

Brothers in the Forests

The roads were fraught with danger. Attacks on partisans increased from day to day. Everyone was against us: Germans, Lithuanians, peasants, "White" bands, and finally, the Cossacks of the renegade Russian general, Vlasov, whose units were camping in the area and who had cavalry, cannons, and tanks. On several occasions the enemy opened cannon fire on the forest, and sometimes the shells fell near our base, wounding partisans.

The situation of the "White" band members had improved. While the Germans stayed within their positions and the night filled them with terror, the "Whites" were not afraid to leave their homes. They were mostly local peasants. During the day they would stay at home and do their work, and no one could prove that the quiet peasant lad who helped his father at work would take up a gun in the evening and join the bands.

The Germans did not dare enter the forests, except with large forces. But a bandsman who lived in the area knew every path in the forest from his early childhood. That was the reason why the bandsmen were so dangerous and why we had to be so careful. Naturally, the partisans could not make war against all the local villages, but it was clear that some action had to be taken which would cast fear over the whole area.

For some time it had been known that the village Koniuchy was a nest of bands and the center of intrigues against the partisans. Its residents, known for their villany, were organizing the people in the area, distributing arms among them which they received from the Germans, and leading every attack on the partisans. The village was well fortified. Every house was a military position and there were defense trenches near every dwelling. There were watchtowers on both sides of the village, so it was not at all easy to penetrate the place. Nevertheless, the partisans chose this very place to carry out an act of vengeance and intimidation. The Brigade Headquarters decided to raze Koniuchy to the ground to set an example to others.

One evening a hundred and twenty of the best partisans from all the camps, armed with the best weapons they had, set out in the direction of the village. There were about 50 Jews among them, headed by Yaakov Prenner. At midnight they came to the vicinity of the village and assumed their proper positions. The order was not to leave any one alive. Even livestock was to be killed and all property was to be destroyed. No one could take booty, for this time the object was to show everyone in the area that the partisans had not come to pillage, but to destroy the evil village altogether.

Up until midnight the villagers would keep a heavy watch. At midnight they would reduce the number of guards, since it was well-known that the partisans would not begin an attack so late, as they would not have enough time to reach the forest before dawn. The villagers certainly could not imagine that the partisans would return to the forest in daylight, victorious.

The signal was given just before dawn. Within minutes the village was surrounded on three sides. On the fourth side was the river and the only bridge over it was in the hands of the partisans. With torches prepared in advance, the partisans burned down the houses, stables, and granaries, while opening heavy fire on the houses. Loud explosions were heard in many houses when the arms caches blew up. Half-naked peasants jumped out of windows and sought escape. But everywhere fatal bullets awaited them. Many jumped into the river and swam towards the other side, but they, too, met the same end. The mission was completed within a short while. Sixty households, numbering about 300 people, were destroyed, with no survivors.

The news spread quickly throughout the area. The peasants exaggerated the incident, speaking of the ''thousands'' of partisans who participated in the punitive action against the village. The next day, the Gestapo heads came from Vilna with large army forces. The Germans photographed the ruins and the charred corpses and publicized the photos accompanied by biting articles on the cruelty of the partisans. However, the operation had results. The area was quiet for a long time.

The problem of a shortage of arms deteriorated steadily. The main headquarters of the Lithuanian partisan movement in Moscow kept promising to send arms, but while planes were often seen bringing arms and equipment for Mishka's Russian camp, the Lithuanian Brigade waited many nights in vain for the promised planes.

One day news came to the Brigade Headquarters that arms had arrived in the Narocz Forests, which were intended for the partisans of Rudnik Forest. The headquarters decided to send people to Narocz Forest to bring the arms. Twenty partisans, including about fifteen Jews, set off. After crossing areas ridden with ''White'' roving bands, they arrived safely to their destination. Several weeks later they returned empty-handed. In Narocz Forest they were told that, meanwhile, other weapons had arrived in Rudnik Forest; hence there was no need to take the arms out of Narocz Forest. They brought back interesting news about life in Narocz Forest and especially about the Jews there.

Hundreds of Jews from Vilna and the surroundings were in Narocz Forest when the Germans launched a major attack on the forests in the autumn of 1943 (that same attack in which Josef Glazman and his comrades fell). After the non-Jewish partisans took away their arms, these Jews remained defenseless. They hid in the swamp area, lay in the mud for days on end, shivering cold, starving, and fearful over the future. About one hundred Jews died in the forests in various ways during the German siege.

When the partisans returned after the siege, the Jews tried hard to be accepted into the partisan ranks, but they were rejected. Without alternative, the Jews set up their own camp and, lacking arms, they could not even contemplate war against the enemy, but instead devoted their thoughts to holding out until better days. They received much help from the Jews in the fighting camps but, despite this aid and the efforts to obtain food, they suffered from starvation.

To ensure their survival, the Jews proposed to Markov that they form a "productive group" which would serve the partisans in various ways. After long consideration, Markov accepted their proposal and the Jewish unit began to work. They set up a bakery, shoe repair shop, locksmith shop, and sausage factory. The partisans from all the surrounding camps were ordering their products. True, it was far from the dreams of revenge that they had in the narrow streets of the ghetto. When the sword of destruction hung over their heads, they had prepared for battle, and when they escaped the Nazi claws, they were sure that the partisans would receive them with open arms and that together they would defeat the enemy. But now they were Gibeonites, the "hewers of wood and drawers of water" for the non-Jews. . . .

One day a new *politruk** arrived from Moscow to Narocz Forest. He assembled all the Jews and promised them that from now on they would be accepted into the fighting units, without discrimination, according to orders from Moscow. This caused great joy among the Jews. Yet, one day followed another and there was no change in their status.Only a select few were accepted into the fighting units.

The Jewish fighters distinguished themselves in heroic acts and their courage became legendary. Had they not been Jews, they most probably would have won the highest distinctions, but because they were Jews they remained anonymous.

Another announcement came that planes from Moscow would arrive at night with arms. The partisans waited all night in vain. After several days they heard that by mistake the Russians had dropped the arms in Naliboki Forest, about 200 kilometers from our base. Twenty-four people, including sixteen Jews, were sent by the Brigade Headquarters to bring the arms. Since the way was difficult and danger lurked at every step in the form of "White" bands, the unit was joined by a 200-strong Russian partisan unit.

On the second day, they met up with strong forces of bandsmen, and only after fierce fighting did they suceed in disengaging themselves. On the third day, when they were camping in one of the villages, a peasant came up to the Russian commander, carrying a letter from the Poles. The latter announced that their forces had surrounded the village and were demanding that the Russians surrender to them and hand over the Jews. If these demands were met, the Poles would accept

---

*A *politruk* is a political officer in charge of ideological discipline—Trans.

into their ranks all those Russians who were willing to fight with them against the Germans. However, if the Russians did not accept these demands, everyone would be killed in battle.

The partisan commander, a Russian major, was not impressed by the threat. He gave an order to prepare to leave. He readied his fighters for battle and placed the Jewish men in the middle to protect them from the murder-lust of the Poles.

They left the village. The battle took place nearby and lasted several hours. Everything seemed hopeless. The Polish stranglehold was tight and there was no way out. But at a certain moment a large number of wagon was seen approaching the site of the fray. They were bringing reinforcements to the Poles. The Russians stormed the wagons and caused heavy losses among the passengers. It turned out that that was the weak point in the enemy encirclement. The Poles in the wagons sought escape and the partisans took advantage of their confusion to break away. The battle ended with many casualties on both sides.

On several occasions, the partisans encountered smaller Polish bands but did not engage them in combat, for the commander knew that he had to reach his destination as soon as possible.

The Naliboki Forest stretched over a huge area in White Russia, almost 60,000 hectares. Roughly 60,000 partisans were concentrated in the forest, headed by the Russian Major-General Platon, who was famous for his bravery in battle against the Germans. This Platon was very sympathetic towards the Jews. Thanks to his favorable attitude, many Jews found shelter in this forest and some of them were accepted into the Russian camps. The number of Jews in the forest grew steadily until it reached 5,000. Platon confirmed that he had received arms that were not intended for him, but having already divided them among his people, he did not want to take them back again. The main thing, he said, was that the arms should serve their purpose, and it was unimportant who held them.

When the group from our camp had spent three weeks in Platon's forest, it encountered a Polish woman who told of the existence of a group of armed Jews in a nearby village. The Jewish partisans hurried off in that direction and, approaching one of the village houses, heard songs within. The melody was very familiar and touching. Were they dreaming? Could it be?

On the soil of White Russia, in an area where the Germans had destroyed almost all the Jews, in a Christian village in the forest, they heard Hebrew songs: "Am Yisrael Chai" and "Anu Olim Artza." It seemed as if these Hebrew melodies were meant to tell the outside world that there were still Jews in Europe, despite the Nazi scourge. The singers were fifteen Jewish partisans who had just returned from a successful operation and were celebrating by singing Hebrew songs and dancing the *hora*. They said that 40 kilometers away was a large Jewish camp numbering more than 1,000 people. They invited the Vilna fighters to join them on a visit to that camp.

The Bielski camp had been in existence since 1942. At first it consisted of only 80 Jews and for a long time they wandered around the town of Novogrudek. The Bielski brothers, who established the camp, and the other commanders set as their main objectives the rescue of more Jews from the ghettos and the concentration of all those who were hiding in various places. For a long time they had maintained contact with the ghettos of Dvorets, Novogrudek, Lida, and the other neighboring towns. When these ghettos were liquidated, hundreds of Jews succeeded in escaping and finding shelter in Bielski's camp.

The camp had endured many hardships. It suffered from a shortage of food and arms; the enemy launched frequent attacks, and the White Russian partisans did not want to recognize it. Sometimes, when the going was hard, the Russians had come and taken the armed men with them for their own purposes, leaving the old men, women, and children to blind fate. Nevertheless, the Jews had succeeded in overcoming these hardships and making a life for themselves in Naliboki Forest.

There were now 1,200 Jews in the camp. Only a third of them were armed and they went out on forays and on military and sabotage operations. There were workshops in the camp handling sixteen different kinds of jobs for the camp itself and for the other partisans in the forest. There was also a kindergarten, a yeshiva, and naturally there were also petty merchants and indigents. In short: a typical Jewish town of Poland or Lithuania. The youth were mainly Zionist, and in the evening and on the Sabbath they would gather and talk about the Chosen Land, evoke past memories, and spin dreams of the future.

One of the pillars of the camp and the chief of headquarters was Eliezer Malbin, a Revisionist and an experienced army man. Many years before he had graduated a military academy and now was successfully carrying out the most difficult tasks, for, besides his military knowledge, he was also gifted as an organizer, planner, and executor of operations.

Not far from Bielski's camp was another Jewish camp named after its founder, Sorin, a Jew from Minsk. In Sorin's camp there were about 600 Jews from Minsk and Smolensk, most of them youths. Until the outbreak of the war they had not known much about Judaism, but Hitler made them aware of their Jewish identity and returned them to their source, and Bielski's Jews were drawing them even closer to Judaism. Two hundred more Jews were in the Yada camp, and in the Lipiczansk Forest near the town of Zhetil there were about 1,000 others.

Our hearts leaped to hear of these brothers in White Russia. Our people were still alive.

Destroying the Evidence

In the summer of 1943, the Germans began to doubt their chances of victory. Himmler ordered that all evidence be destroyed of the genocide in the event of a German defeat. He gave orders to open the mass graves, burn the corpses, and scatter the ashes to the winds. No trace must be left of the murderous deeds.

In Kovno, the local Gestapo authorities vigorously set about carrying out the new order. For this despicable work they employed Jews who had committed various transgressions against German law. One day the Germans caught a group of young Jews in Augustow Forest who had escaped from the Kovno Ghetto. Other Jews were caught while trying to get food from the local peasants. They were sent to work burning the bodies and were joined by Russian prisoners-of-war.

In Kovno, which was once the most important Russian city near the Prussian border, there was a system of fortifications and citadels built by the czars to protect the city. One of these citadels, the Ninth Fort, was chosen by the Germans as the site for the murder of Lithuanian Jews. In the spring of 1943, tens of thousands of Jews were taken from Germany, Austria, and France to "work" in the East. They were taken to the Ninth Fort, where they were all killed.

Eighty people, Jews and Russians, were engaged in removing the dead from the mass graves and burning the corpses. At first the Germans treated the eighty prisoners very harshly, but since, in any case, the Jews had no chance of leaving the Ninth Fort alive, they decided not to suffer the beatings and starvation any longer. They declared a strike until their conditions were improved. At first the Germans tried to put down the strike, but the cruelest means had no effect. In the end, they began to give the Jews luxuries, good food, and wine, and to stop the beatings and the tortures. The Jews returned to work. In the evening, when they returned to their cells, their legs were placed in iron chains. A heavy chain connected one to the next, so that no one could move without moving the whole group.

At night the ghetto residents would see columns of fire and smoke rising from the citadel. The air was full of the suffocating vapors of burning corpses. They knew that these were the bodies of their spouses, children, and parents going up in flames.

From the very first days, the Jewish prisoners thought about escape, but the walls of the fortress, built of stone, cement, and iron, were more than a meter thick and impenetrable. Moreover, the fortress was full of passages, basements, and entrances and no one could find his way. Even if they succeeded in getting out of their cell, they could not find the exit to the yard, and the guard in the fortress was vigilant. The surrounding area was full of spotlights; every two meters, there was a German sentry. The Gestapo watched every movement carefully. Even at night, when the prisoners were sound asleep after an exhausting day and bound in chains, they were still under watch.

Among the Russian prisoners was a Russian captain named Vasilenko. In civilian life he had been an engineer. At the beginning of the war he took part in building the fortifications of Sevastopol and he found that the building system there was similar to that of the Kovno fortificatons. He was the only one who knew his way around the maze of corridors and cellars in the Ninth Fort.

Under his direction the prisoners began to build a tunnel. The work was done with bare hands and lasted several months. Every night of digging brought new obstacles, but the diggers did not give up. Finally the work was near completion. Now the prisoners began to think about removing the shackles. After many efforts they succeeded in forming keys to open the locks. All the preparations were completed. New Year's Eve was chosen as the day of the escape.

It was a clear and silent night. Newly fallen snow covered the ground. The Germans were drinking to welcome in the new year, which was to bring the victory. The sentries were drunk.

The prisoners removed the iron chains from their legs and one by one entered the tunnel. The men at the head broke through the last layer of earth, and cool, refreshing air entered the tunnel. But the escapees still faced danger. The exit of the tunnel was in the yard and they still had to climb the outside wall of the fort. The yard was very large and they had to cross about a hundred meters of snow until they reached the wall. This was a problem they had not foreseen. But there was no turning back. They knew that unless they succeeded in overcoming the last obstacles, they were doomed.

They found three sheets and three people wrapped themselves up in them and crossed the snowy yard. One returned with the sheets. A long time passed before all eighty were near the wall. It was very high and impossible to climb. The escapees stole up to the drunk and dozing entrance guards, found the keys, and left by the main gate. Once outside, they divided up into several groups and went their separate ways.

One group went to the ghetto, and only that one was saved. All the others lost their way or were caught in the big manhunt the Germans conducted when they discovered the escape. For days the escapees hid in the ghetto and then they left for Rudnik Forest and arrived safely to our camp; Vasilenko was among them.

Some time after the arrival of the escapees, Vasilenko was appointed by the

Brigade Headquarters as commander of one of the Jewish camps. Vasilenko was a Jew, but would not admit it. At every opportunity he would declare that he was a true Russian and, to prove that he was not a Jew, he would behave harshly towards the Jews.

One day he sent out partisans to sabotage telephone lines along the Vilna–Lida road. As the partisans were approaching the road, they came under a shower of bullets and had to retreat. But Vasilenko would not admit the necessity for retreat. He chose five Jewish men and sent them on the same operation the next day. He warned them not to show their faces until they had completed their mission. The five lads never returned. While preparing to cut down one of the telephone poles, a mine which the Germans had attached to it exploded, killing all five. The five were Imka Lubotski, Nahum Rudashevski, and Nahum Gelprin from Vilna; Faikovski from Ejszyszki; and Grinberg from Svir. They were not the only victims of the inferiority complex which plagued the Russian officer of Jewish origin.

In the spring of 1944, news came that a group of Jews had escaped from Ponar and were wandering around the forests, looking for partisan bases. A unit of Jewish partisans was sent to scout the area to find them and bring them to the camp. Days later, the unit returned with eleven people, nine Jews and two Russian POWs. The people related that some time after the liquidation of the Vilna ghetto, they were taken from the Lukiszki Prison to Ponar. They were sure that they were going to be killed. But on their arrival they were met by a high-ranking Gestapo officer, who told them: "From this day on you will live here and do very important work for the German Government. The Lithuanian barbarians have murdered more than 100,000 people here and have buried them in the large pits you see before you. This is a serious crime in the eyes of the enlightened world, history, and posterity. To conceal this horrible deed, you must remove the bodies from the pits and burn them, so that after the war, which will end in our victory, the Germans will not be accused of this atrocity. If you carry out your work diligently and faithfully, you will not lack for anything. And when you finish the work you will be taken to Germany to live out your lives there. But if you refuse, you will be shot on the spot."

The people were housed in an underground bunker. The walls were made of large stones; above ground the bunker was surrounded by barbed wire and mines lay all around the area. There were two entrances to the bunker and two ladders leading into it, one for the Jews and one for the Germans. Inside were sheets for sleeping, a food pantry, a kitchen, and a toilet.

The people would walk to work along a narrow path in fields strewn with mines. At the end of their work they were bound with chains and put under heavy guard. Even at night the sentries would go down into the bunker to check if everyone was asleep.

There were various kinds of work: opening the graves and taking out the corpses, transferring them to the site of the pyre, preparing wood, building pyramids of wood and corpses—a layer of wood and a layer of corpses laid crosswise—chopping the bones which remained unburnt, dispersing the ashes, and so forth. About 4,000 corpses would be burnt on each pyre and it would take from seven to ten days until all the bodies would be incinerated.

One can easily imagine the emotions of the prisoners when they recognized among the corpses their wives and children and other relatives and good friends who had been taken from them and killed. One can easily understand how they burned with pain and anger when, with their own hands, they had to destroy evidence of the German crimes and scatter the ashes of their dear ones.

For weeks and months they silently bore their great pain, without any hope of redemption from the hell in which they found themselves. Sometimes the Germans would bring hundreds of people to Ponar to be killed. On those days they would not take the prisoners to work, but in the bunkers the latter could hear the echoes of shots and they knew that the lives of hundreds of new victims had been extinguished.

None of the prisoners believed the German promises that they would be treated well and left alive after the completion of the work, for if the Germans really wanted to destroy the evidence of their crimes, how could one imagine that they would leave alive so many witnesses to their murderous deeds? Hence, from the very first day, they began to plan their escape. After feverish preparation, they started digging an 80-meter-long tunnel.

One spring night the tunnel was completed. The prisoners entered it barefoot, since they had to leave their boots in the chains in the bunker. The night was dark and they left the bunker safely, but some distance away, they stepped on dry branches. Panicking, they began to run and the German sentries opened fire. Of the 80 prisoners, only 40 succeeded in escaping and 11 of these came to Rudnik Forest.

They related that during the months they had worked in Ponar they had burned about 60,000 corpses, but that there were still tens of thousands more in the graves. One of them took out a gold ornament and said that he had bought it as a gift for his fiancée on the day of their engagement. He took it off her neck while her body was burning on the pyre.

For many weeks the Ponar people could not stay inside the camp because of the smell of death and burnt human flesh which clung to them. Changing their clothes and washing themselves did not help. It took some time before they were absorbed in the camp and began to go out on missions. A number of them distinguished themselves in battle, for their hearts burned with revenge after all the horrors they had seen.

Four Cups of German Blood

The winter of 1944 was drawing to a close. The situation in the forest was not very encouraging. The lack of arms was sorely felt and there was growing danger on all sides.

News came that the Germans were concentrating large army forces for an attack on the forest. The situation of the Lithuanian Brigade, including the Jewish camps, was critical. There were hundreds of unarmed men and several dozen women who could become an encumbrance on the camp in the event of an emergency. In such conditions one could not even contemplate self-defense. It was impossible to prepare for battle against the superior forces of the enemy. The only thing to do was to move to other forests for the time being, break up into groups, and wait until the danger passed.

The Brigade Headquarters ordered that the bases be abandoned and that the people gather at the edge of the forest. If the German threat was realized and an attack began, they would move to the Narocz Forest and the survivors would return later to the former bases. There was no other way.

Two sick partisans remained in the camp, who were unable to join the rest. The Command saw no alternative but to leave them behind.

All the camps gathered at the edge of the forest around the Brigade Headquarters and awaited news of the beginning of the German attack. Scouts were sent throughout the area but could not find out anything. It was known that there were large concentrations of enemy forces near the area but the attack was not carried out.

After three days it was learned that the enemy forces had been sent to the front. Apparently, at the last minute the Germans had received disturbing news from the Soviet front and had no choice but to postpone the action against the partisans until a more convenient time.

Spring had come. Once again Nature lifted our spirits and engaged our senses with her beauty. New hope stirred in our hearts. News from the front continued to be encouraging. It told of heavy German losses and the mounting of a large Russian offensive to split the front and deal the Germans a serious blow. Would we be able to hold out until the end to see the defeat of the enemy?

Passover had come, the third since the outbreak of war between Germany and Russia, and the first in the forest. A year ago we were still seated around the *seder* table in the ghetto, where we recalled the Passover nights with our families, together with all the Jews in the cities and towns of Poland and Lithuania. Now these Jews were dead and the small remainder did not dare hope that the next year would find them still alive. Still, we could not help but be moved by the words: "This year we are here; next here in Jerusalem; this year we are slaves; next year, free men." Had the others not put their faith in the deluded and deluding leaders, had they not denied the great truth that there was no hope of survival except through resistance, perhaps they would not have been exterminated. These were our thoughts that Passover in the forest, and our hearts constricted with pain. Hundreds and thousands more could have been together with us had they known how to rebel against the shameful legacy of the accursed Diaspora, the ghetto elders and their blind faith in the honesty of the German murderers.

During this period, we heard that the arms planes from Moscow were finally going to arrive. For nights we waited in vain. Then we went out one more time for a last try. It was the second night of Passover 1944.

The clock showed almost midnight. Many of the partisans had lost hope and had begun to return to the camps. The campfires which were supposed to show our position to the pilots were dying down and no one bothered to add wood to refuel the fire. Even the High Command did not see to this. It, too, was convinced that this time, like all the previous times, we would return to our camps empty-handed.

Suddenly a kind of electric shock passed through everyone. Out of the darkness a thin sound was heard which grew steadily, until we clearly head the roar of plane engines. After recovering from the initial shock, the people were filled with a new spirit. The campfires were rekindled. The tongues of flame reached skyward, as if they knew that our fate depended on their ability to draw the attention of the pilots. Moments later we could see three large planes circling over us at low altitude. They passed over us a few times and then reascended, while bundles detached themselves from the silhouettes of the planes. The parachutes opened and large sacks fell towards us one after another.

When dawn broke, the partisans were still scattered throughout the forest, searching for the parachutes which the wind had carried great distances away from target.

At noon the Brigade Headquarters distributed the arms among all the camps. The joy was unbounded. We had suddenly acquired dozens of rifles, automatic guns, and machine guns. Men who only a short time before were hankering after rifles, now began to disparage them. How disappointed were those who did not receive automatics and had to make do with rifles! Many of us saw as a good omen the fact that the arms had come precisely during Passover. We were already dreaming of the realization of the verse, ''Pour your wrath on the enemy. . . .''

By early morning, we took up positions along the Vilna–Grodno highway, which ran through the forest. For the first time we had antitank weapons which had come to us from the sky. The sun rose and we sat in wait, ready for action. Though there was a lot of traffic on the road in the morning hours, we were not ready to bother ourselves with trifles.

Hours later, the roar of engines was heard from a distance. A convoy of vehicles was rumbling towards us. It seemed we would have a hard battle, but the prize was worth it if we would come out of it alive. Our weapons were cocked and we waited for the signal.

The convoy of armed vehicles was coming towards us. Unknowingly, the drivers were heading straight into the arms of death.

Suddenly the silence was split by the mighty sound of explosions. We opened fire from every weapon. The Germans were surprised at first, but then opened fire.

The battle had its ups and downs. For a moment it seemed that the mission was too hard for us and we would have to retreat empty-handed. But one of the shells of our antitank weapons hit a German armored car and it went up in flames. Our men were encouraged by this success and went onto the road. With a cry of victory, we stormed the German vehicles and killed anyone who crossed our path. A second armored car went up in flames and the Germans began to run in panic. With a song on our lips we returned to camp, laden with captured arms and other materials which the enemy had left behind. We knew that the Germans would not quickly resume traffic on the road. The roadblock of burned vehicles and corpses would serve as a warning to them.

At dusk we gathered around a campfire and expressed our joy through song. Suddenly a hush fell, and the oldest member of the group began to speak: ''It is Passover today. True, we did not sit around the Passover table and we did not eat matzot. But I doubt whether in the whole world there are Jews who observed the mitzvah of the holidays as we did, for today we drank four cups of pure German blood.''

A fiery moon rose on the distant horizon. Silently it surveyed the excited faces, the wild ecstasy, and abandoned dancing around the campfire in the depths of the forest.

Our joy gave way to thought. If Fate smiled on us and we lived to see the Redemption, then we would be obligated to tell the next generation about the terrible events we had witnessed and to dispel the illusion of a Jewish future in the Diaspora.

In my imagination I saw myself journeying through the Jewish Diaspora and telling all the Jewish people what we had undergone. I saw myself convincing them that the time had come to put an end to the accursed Diaspora and warning them that if another Holocaust should befall them, and their enemies should want to subjugate them and put them into ghettos and concentration camps, they would have no chance for survival unless they learned the lessons of the past and took up arms. But this thread of thought broke when I suddenly realized that these plans were superfluous. After all, when the war was over and the evil eradicated, a new world would arise, a world of justice and decency, love and fraternity. The world would be ashamed of the injustice done to us. It would champion us and redress the wrongs.

Yes, we were very naïve.

The desire to live welled up in all of us. If we had come so far already, we wanted with all our heart and soul to hold out until the Redemption. At twilight we gathered around the campfire, eyes shining, and broke out in loud song. Full of longing, we began with Russian songs, and when the heart was warmed, we switched to Yiddish and finally broke out in Hebrew song, which set throbbing the most hidden chords of the heart.

We had decided that if we remained alive, none of us would return to build his life on this contaminated soil, drenched with the blood of our kin and accursed by God. Only a few of us still remained, and no one knew how many of us would live to celebrate the next Festival of Freedom. But we all had one prayer in our hearts: Next year in Jerusalem.

Chaim Lazar (author of this book), commander of the F.P.O., officer of Betar.

Blood and Dynamite

One spring day in 1944 a shudder of joy ran through the camp. News had come that the Brigade Headquarters was giving us a quantity of explosives, enough to blow up four enemy trains.

A shortage of explosives had been one of our weak points. For some time we had been unable to plan serious acts of sabotage because of the scarcity of this valuable commodity. We could not seriously consider combat, be it frontal attacks or ambushes, since this would require many more automatic weapons than we had. We, therefore, put our faith in mines and sabotage operations which caused the enemy very serious damage. For such operations, small groups were sufficient and there was no need for many weapons. They were carried out at night, and in order to reach the target, side roads were used which were usually safe. It was no wonder, then, that we were delighted by the valuable gift from the Brigade Headquarters. We now had the chance of striking heavy blows against the enemy.

The Headquarters people, who were generally not enthusiastic about going to battle, decided this time to enjoy the glory of blowing up trains. For several nights, the political commissar and the company commanders took turns heading sabotage operations and returned to camp victorious.

We had only one more charge left and it was decided that I would have the honor of using it. I received orders to prepare to leave.

The recent sabotage had caused the Germans to become extra vigilant. Armed guards patrolled the railroad around the clock to ensure safe passage for the trains carrying people and equipment to the front. The Headquarters decided that under such circumstances the next operation should be carried out far from the base, between the towns of Olkieniki and Orany.

I was in charge of eight fighters: Chaya Shapiro, Rozka Korczak, Abrasha Chuzhoi, Natan Drotz, Yulik Hermatz, Israelik Shmerkovich, and one Russian. Chaim Soltz was assigned as our guide, as he knew the area and most of the local peasants. Because the place of operation was so far from the camp, we had to walk a whole night, hide the next day somewhere in the forest or in a peasant's home, and carry out the operation the following night.

We left the base before dusk, in high spirits. We crossed fields and walked along paths among the fortified German positions and the armed villages. Before sunrise we reached a village where we were to stay in the furthermost house, which belonged to one of Soltz's acquaintances. To get there, though, we had to pass over the bridge on the Solcha River and cross the whole village. Two of the fighters, Chaya Shapiro and Abraham Chuzhoi, crossed the river on foot and brought us a horse and wagon so that all of us could cross.

The day passed without incident. Our guards took turns on duty, and in the evening we planned to move on. However, Chaim Soltz tried to convince us to return to base. The non-Jew in whose home we were staying had told him all day long about the vigilance of the local villages, the Gestapo agents active in the villages who were distributing arms among the peasants, and the special surveillance of the Germans to protect their transport routes, including ambushes on the sides of the roads. But Soltz did not succeed in breaking our resolve. We continued on our way towards the railroad.

Some time later we sensed that we were not on the right road. It turned out that Soltz was bringing us back to the base by an indirect route. We ordered him to bring us to our destination and he gave in. But meanwhile we had lost valuable time.

It was almost 3:00 A.M. and we were still kilometers away from the railroad. According to partisan practice, we knocked on a peasant's door to ask him about the situation in the area. When the peasant opened his window and saw us, he turned as white as a sheet and whispered: "If you value your lives, leave this area immediately." It seemed that that same night strong German forces were camping in the area and their headquarters were in the very village we were visiting. We heard frequent shots shatter the silence.

Our situation was desperate. It was late and dawn would soon break. Even if we succeeded in reaching the railroad and carrying out the action, the sun would rise, making retreat impossible. Our task was to strike the enemy, not to commit suicide while doing so.

I ordered the fighters to return. By morning we were near Olkieniki and we waited at the home of a peasant, another of Soltz's acquaintances. The house was on the edge of the forest and throughout the day we kept a vigilant lookout. Despite the peasant's constant warnings and advice to return to the base, our minds were made up: that night we would carry out the operation, come what may.

We reached the railroad after midnight. Suddenly we heard the roar of the approaching train and before we could recover from our surprise, it passed in front of us and was swallowed up by the darkness.

Another disappointment! The night would end, and who knew when a second train would pass. Nevertheless, we decided to prepare the mine. The method used to activate the explosion mechanism was quite primitive. A long rope was tied to the detonator, and when the train passed over the mine, the rope was pulled in order to explode the charge.

I had left most of the fighters in the woods about 50 meters from the tracks, and together with two other fighters, I advanced towards the tracks to lay the mine. While we were thus engaged, we detected a German patrol moving in our direction. We crawled away from the tracks so that the patrol would not sense our presence and all the while our hearts jumped with joy. The appearance of the Germans meant that another train would pass that night.

Returning to the tracks to finish our work, we heard the clatter of the approaching train. I took the detonator and moved it closer to the charge. Suddenly the sound of an explosion filled my ears and I felt a sharp pain in my right hand. One of the fighters hidden in the woods had inadvertently pulled the rope, causing a premature explosion. Had this occurred a split second later, the detonator would have been inside the mine and all three of us would have been blown to bits.

Confusion broke out among the fighters but we did not have a moment to waste. We would not have enough time to activate the charge with the reserve detonator. The train was already very near, and the engine's lights were illuminating the area. The German patrol which had passed a short time before might return to find out the cause of the explosion.

Here we were, 70 kilometers from the base, and we had to get back as soon as possible so that I could receive medical treatment.

It was clear that we would have no alternative but to cross enemy territory in broad daylight, a difficult undertaking under normal circumstances, and even more difficult when the commander was injured. I gave orders to remove the mine from under the tracks. My hand was wrapped up in the bandages I always carried with me, and we set off.

We had not even covered 10 kilometers and we saw pink on the horizon. The sun was about to rise. Our situation was precarious. The peasants were beginning to go to the fields, and even though we walked along side paths, someone could sight us and tell the Germans.

In one of the villages, we took wagons and Chaim Soltz led us to the base along a path full of obstacles. We were lucky. We arrived without incident. The sun was already high in the sky.

The news spread quickly throughout the camp. Solka Gorfinkel, our doctor, tried in vain to save my hand. Vaska, a Russian medical student who belonged to the Brigade Headquargers and who served as a doctor, labored alongside Gorfinkel. They both reached the conclusion that my hand had to be amputated.

An operating table was set up in the bunker. The two doctors borrowed a small rusty saw from the arms workshop of the Peneusov family and tried to sterilize it. During the operation, sand from the roof trickled on us constantly. The operation was a success. . . .

Days and Nights of Battle

A rumor reached us that a Jewish army had been set up in Palestine to fight against the Germans. Churchill, it seemed, had declared the establishment of a strong Jewish force to give Jews the opportunity of avenging the deaths of their brethren. All the Jewish soldiers in the Anglo-Saxon armies would be under Jewish command and would be sent to the Western front as a separate Jewish division. Rumor also had it that Churchill had promised to set up a Jewish state in Palestine immediately after the end of the war and that specific names had already been mentioned for Jewish ministers.

This bit of news reached us on the spot from clippings of the illegal press and from the stories of non-Jews who wanted to prove their friendship towards Jews by passing on encouraging news. We did not know the amount of truth in these rumors. For years we had not heard any authorized information about Palestine or the outside Jewish world. We did not know if any efforts were being made on the other side to save us. We hoped and prayed that our Jewish brothers and all of the democratic enlightened world were making all possible efforts to save us and prevent Hitler from continuing his extermination of the Jews.

It is no wonder, therefore, that when the first hazy news came about the establishment of a Jewish army, we walked about drunk with happiness. We were filled with hope that we might still live to meet our Jewish brothers on the battlefield and together we would finish off the evil rule; that emissaries from the Jewish state would come visit the survivors and ships from the Hebrew navy would bring us to the shores of the homeland. There we would march, proud that Hebrew arms had helped free the world from the nightmare of German barbarism and us from the danger of extermination. And we would take extra pride that we, too, carried arms to battle with the enemy, even before the existence of the Jewish army.

We would shed tears over the hundreds of thousands of our brothers who did not live to see this great day because they did not heed the warning of the leader of the generation, Ze'ev Jabotinsky: "Destroy the Diaspora or it will destroy you."

With indescribable enthusiasm, the partisans would now storm the enemy and take revenge. For them, the war had only just begun.

The enemy, repelled at the front, began to feel that even in the rear the ground was quaking beneath their feet. When a convoy set out, it never knew if it would reach its destination, and a train transporting reinforcements of men and ammunition to the collapsing front never knew if it would pass safely through the dangerous areas.

From now on the Germans had to attach a strong guard to each convoy and military train, and even so, they did not dare to set out except in daytime. The Germans had to halt all movement at night across vast areas in the rear, along roads and railways. Nevertheless, the partisans still succeeded in blowing up dozens of military trains on their way to the front. Hundreds of enemy soldiers found their death in the forest areas of Lithuania and White Russia, even before reaching the front and entering battle.

Huge quantities of arms and ammunition were destroyed on the way to the battlefield. Fortified enemy positions were blown up. Factories for the German war effort were destroyed. The roads were sabotaged by the demolition of bridges and highways. The partisans destroyed the foundations of railroads along hundreds of kilometers. On several occasions Vilna was severed from the outside world for days. The partisans cut down hundreds of telegraph poles between Vilna and Grodno, Lida, Orany, and other places. They set up roadblocks on the main highways and set up ambushes near the crossroads. The peasants were persuaded to stop supplying food and paying taxes to the German conqueror.

Operations were varied in scope and nature. Sometimes a whole brigade took part in an attack on the enemy and each camp was responsible for a section of the area of operations. Occasionally the units would stay on the roads for weeks on end. Some of them would reach as far as the German border and execute acts of sabotage there. The German felt the long arm of the forest fighters over hundreds of square kilometers. They had to waste large forces to guard the roads, at a time when every soldier was needed on the front. They had no alternative but to plan how to eliminate the partisan nuisance once and for all.

Our situation grew precarious. The Germans lay siege on the forest, and for weeks only small groups were able to sneak through the enemy guards and go out on actions.

News came that the Germans were concentrating huge forces in our vicinity. Apparently they had decided to finish us off. Even though we were now armed, we still could not contemplate a confrontation with a modern army, equipped with heavy arms, including tanks and planes. The Brigade Headquarters, fearing that the Germans knew our whereabouts, ordered that we evacuate the bases again. We concentrated on the edge of the forest in an attempt to break the strangulating siege.

For several days, the Lithuanian Brigade was concentrated near the village of Selki, on the way to the Narocz Forest. Every battalion camped separately. The retreat plans were ready and the people were divided into fighting units, reconnaissance groups, reserve forces, and so forth. Surveillance was strict and the intelligence service was very active as well, informing us of all the changes taking place in the enemy camp. Every day people were sent to the abandoned bases to see what was happening there. They returned and related that they had seen many local peasants there who had come to take back what the partisans had taken from them.

One spring morning our fate was to be determined. This was the day when the Germans were about to begin their attack. Reliable news had it that we had to prepare for this day. The previous day enemy planes circled over the forest in search of the partisan camps. We waited for this day in fear, since we knew that we had no alternative but to storm the enemy. There was no other way, because even if we did succeed in breaking the siege, we would meet up everywhere with the "White" roving bands which would try to finish the work of the Germans. However, that morning news came that the Germans were suffering great losses in various sections of the front, both in the East and the West, and they had to activate all their forces to stand in the breach. Our hearts beat with both fear and hope.

A miracle happened! The enemy forces were hastily called to the front. Once again we were saved, and we believed that it was due in part to the Jewish army.

Summer came and the news from the fronts continued to be encouraging. Huge acres of Russian land, which had been under Nazi occupation for three years, were liberated by the Red Army. Radio Moscow, which for two years had warned daily of the great danger to the homeland, now changed its tune. The announcer's voice was more aggressive and a tone of confidence in the coming victory could be heard.

We knew that our fate depended on what was happening on the Eastern front, the front closest to us. But, nevertheless, we were tormented by doubt. Precisely along the Minsk–Vitebsk–Smolensk section of the front, closest to us, there was no change. The Germans had repelled all attacks by the Red Army.

One day depressing news came about the death of Batya, the legendary figure of our forest. The man who believed that death had no power over him was felled by bullets from the bands. He had remained alive during the difficult days when he was the only one in the forest. And precisely now, when the forest was full of hundreds of experienced and armed partisans, he was struck down. We fondly remembered Batya as the first non-Jew who supported us when the first Jewish groups came to the forest from the ghetto and the non-Jewish partisans rebuffed them.

Life in the forest was exciting and interesting. The fighters went out on mission after mission, since they saw their *raison d'être* in battle. We feared, though, that if the war continued much longer, we might not be able to hold out. The majority would fall in battle, and who knows whether the Redemption would come too late for us.

Most of the people were hungry for battle. No one wanted to remain in the camp a long time. Even the women working in the kitchen were beginning to rebel. They, too, wanted to leave the vats and the campfires and take part in the fray. Even the children in the camp were no longer satisfied when they were sent with the herd to the pasture, instead of being allowed to go on a mission.

Most of the operations were now carried out in battle. In most cases, the enemy was defeated. Sometimes the Jews rescued non-Jewish partisans in trouble.

Once a reconnaissance unit set off for the village of Skrabochny, near Vilna. The fighters surrounded the enemy in the village and held captive a Dutchman serving the Germans and a young Pole who was also in the employ of the Gestapo. The two prisoners were caught carrying arms. On their return, the partisans met up with two Turkoman POWs of the Russians, who were serving the Germans. The unit returned to camp with the four captives and their booty included a submachine gun, three rifles, grenades, and ammunition. After a thorough enquiry the Pole was executed, while the rest remained in the camp and eventually became loyal fighters.

On another occasion our reconnaissance unit encountered four Russian POWs, accompanied by a German guard unit. After a short battle our scouts overcame the enemy, freed the prisoners, and brought them to camp, where they joined the fighting ranks.

Two scouts who left for the village of Zagariny were attacked in a German ambush. They entered battle with the enemy and defeated them. On the battlefield there lay one dead and one seriously wounded German. Benik Levin, who was only sixteen, received a recognition of distinction for his part in this action.

One day a fighting unit set off for the Lithuanian village of Yurkents near the town of Olkieniki. The village was known for its aggressiveness. The fighters gave the head of the village an ultimatum: either surrender or the village will be set on fire. The villagers surrendered to the Jewish men and handed over their weapons: a heavy machine gun, about twenty rifles, revolvers, grenades, and much ammunition. On the way back they took captive two uniformed and armed officers in the Polish bands. Besides the weapons, the unit brought back to camp a radio receiver, a large quantity of food, and various belongings. The two Polish officers were executed.

One day our unit entered the town of Rudnik, where a German garrison was stationed, and burned the bridge in the town, attacked the police station and jail, and caused the enemy heavy losses. Thus, the fight went on day and night. The enemy was dealt many blows and, without a doubt, the Jewish partisans had a role in hastening the defeat of the Germans.

The Day of Retribution

The first sign of the coming end was the change in attitude of the "White" bands. When the bandsmen saw that the Germans' fate was sealed, they began to give up hope of establishing a "greater, independent Poland." They still remembered the Russian occupation and it was clear to them that Poland could not stand up against mighty Russia. They decided, therefore, to forestall trouble; they began putting out feelers to reach a truce with the partisans.

One day "White" emissaries came to the partisan camp with an invitation for a meeting between representatives of the headquarters of both sides to discuss a truce. A "no-man's land" was decided upon for the meeting, and on the designated day the two sides met there, accompanied by armed forces strong enough to repel a sudden attack, should it occur. The parties met several times but the discussions came to naught.

Meanwhile news continued to pour in concerning the advance of the Red Army. On June 23 news came to us that the Red Army had split the central front near Vitebsk and was making rapid progress in our direction. There was great joy in the camp, but fear as well. Perhaps, we wondered, the retreating Germans would not use the main thoroughfares but would seek refuge in the forests. If so, a confrontation with their superior forces would be unavoidable. Were we fated to be killed on the brink of Redemption?

The front was moving ever closer. There was great preparedness in the forest. All the camps were in a state of alert. We were waiting for orders from Moscow. Perhaps we would have to break through and join up with the advancing Red Army, and perhaps they would also order us to carry out important conquests and pave the way for the Russians. Meanwhile, the Germans were concentrating large forces to halt the Russian advance and to hold their own defense lines. We found ourselves "between the hammer and the anvil."

During the first days of July, we received an order from Moscow to take part in the conquest of Vilna. We prepared for the great day in which we would be allowed to engage the enemy in open battle. And even though it was clear to all that this would be a hard battle, since Vilna and its environs were a well-fortified defense area where the Germans were expected to hold out for a long time, we looked forward to this test. For us it was a battle for vengeance and liberation.

On July 8 all the partisan camps left the forest on the way to Vilna. Well-armed and in united formation, they marched in full daylight, to the amazement of the villagers. Even more amazed were the Polish bands who were astonished to see that even the women were carrying automatic weapons. The closer we approached the city, the clearer we saw the columns of smoke towering over Vilna. The noise of Russian planes filled the air and the Germans themselves were setting afire storehouses, factories, and electric and water plants to prevent them from falling into Russian hands. Chaos reigned. The closer we approached our objective, the greater the tension among the fighters.

We were moving towards the entrances to the city. The steel birds circled in the skies and dropped their lethal cargo on the city's installations. The echo of bombs and the barking of machine guns resounded in our ears. Was it a dream? Had we, indeed, lived to see the Day of Retribution? Was the long nightmare of oppression and murder over, and were the rivers of blood really behind us?

We were excited and also somewhat frightened, for here we were standing on the brink of Revelation. We would soon know the bitter truth. Up until now we could still delude ourselves that someone among our relatives, friends, and acquaintances was still alive. But now all illusions were to be destroyed and we would have to face the truth in all its horror.

After a stormy battle we captured the blazing city.

Memorial service for the dead in Polnar Forest after the Liberation.

After the Liberation

The few Jews who returned to Vilna after its liberation—those from the partisan camps in the forests, those from the far-off Russian plains, and those from the concentration camps—found their mother-city in mourning and ruins.

They walked through the narrow streets of the ghetto, which had formerly buzzed with tens of thousands of oppressed Jews, and found them deserted. Grass was growing in the lanes, as no human had set foot there for ages. Ruins and garbage piles stood like monuments to the dead. Here stood the "kloiz" of the "Gaon," where the sound of Torah was always heard and which smelled of the wax of the hundreds of candles which righteous women would light there. It was all ruins now, and only the chair of the "Gaon" still stood in place. And here was the old synagogue of legend, from which emerged some of the greatest cantors of the Jewish people, who would raise their voices in praise and thanks to the Creator of the Universe and would storm the closed Gates of Heaven on days of trouble and distress. The Divine Presence abandoned it and it was left in ruin. And here was Deutscheshe Street, the heart of Jewish commerce in Vilna. The street which from early dawn until midnight would swarm with merchants, buyers, sellers, middlemen, draymen and porters, waggoners and beggars—Jews who worked hard to earn a living, raised sons and daughters to study Torah, marry, and lead righteous lives. All of this had disappeared forever. The whole street was destroyed from one end to another, like the people who had once lived and breathed there.

One day the hundreds of Jewish survivors from Vilna and the surrounding towns gathered and went outside the city. This time they were not transported by a German or Lithuanian guard. They went to Ponar to pay tribute to the memory of their parents, brothers, and sisters, who were tortured and murdered there and whose ashes had long been carried away by the wind.

One day a funeral took place in the streets of Vilna, attended by all the Jews who were in the city at that time. For some time the market had been flooded with the detached pages of Talmudic tractates, the Pentateuch, prayer books, and other sacred writings, which the Christians had been using for all kinds of purposes. The members of the Jewish religious community decided to collect the "memorials" and to bury them according to Jewish law. The Christians were opposed at first and claimed that the Jews had come to rob them of their property, but with the help of Jewish lads who served in the city police, they succeeded in collecting a large quantity of "memorials"—shreds of prayer shawls from which the Christians had sewn shirts and underwear, strips of phylacteries, etc.

At first the funeral procession went to the "Choir-School" on Zawalna Street. Once again this opulent building, which had been condemned to eternal desolation, accommodated hundreds of Jews. Its recesses echoed with the sounds of eulogies and bitter lamentation.

From there the procession went to the Old Synagogue, whose ruins witnessed for the last time, Jews in supplication and prayer. From there the procession went to the cemetery in Zaretcha.

No Jew had set foot in this cemetery for a long time. The only ones who came there in the days of the Holocaust were a mother and child who, at the outbreak of the war, had escaped there to hide in the shadows of the tombstones. In a place where Death rules supreme, the unfortunate woman hoped to save herself from her pursuers. But the long arm of the murderers found her there. The blood of the mother and child was spilt on the old tombstones. Jewish fighters would come there too, bury their arms in the cemetery and, on leaving for the forests to fight the enemies, would go to the cemetery to remove the arms from the grave.

Now the survivors had come there to bury the ''memorials'' and to weep over the dead. None of the mourners had been able to bring their dear ones for burial there; therefore, all of them looked upon the ragged ''memorials'' as human bodies, the flesh and bones of their relatives which had been collected from all the places of slaughter and brought to a Jewish grave.

The funeral was a pathetic end to what had been a magnificent community. Interred in the grave were not only the relics of myriads of victims, but a whole way of life. Jewish Vilna would never return to life again.

The Gaon Synagogue in ruins.